INSURRECTIONS: CRITICAL STUDIES IN RELIGION, POLITICS, AND CULTURE

RAGE AND TIME

INSURRECTIONS: CRITICAL STUDIES IN RELIGION, POLITICS, AND CULTURE

SLAVOJ ŽIŽEK, CLAYTON CROCKETT, CRESTON DAVIS, JEFFREY W. ROBBINS, EDITORS

The intersection of religion, politics, and culture is one of the most discussed areas in theory today. It also has the deepest and most wide-ranging impact on the world. Insurrections: Critical Studies in Religion, Politics, and Culture will bring the tools of philosophy and critical theory to the political implications of the religious turn. The series will address a range of religious traditions and political viewpoints in the United States, Europe, and other parts of the world. Without advocating any specific religious or theological stance, the series aims nonetheless to be faithful to the radical emancipatory potential of religion.

After the Death of God, John D. Caputo and Gianni Vattimo, edited by Jeffrey W. Robbins

Nietzsche and Levinas: "After the Death of a Certain God," edited by Bettina Bergo and Jill Stauffer

The Politics of Postsecular Religion: Mourning Secular Futures, Ananda Abeysekara

Wondrous Strange: The Closure of Metaphysics and the Opening of Awe, Mary-Jane Rubenstein

Religion and the Specter of the West: Sikhism, India, Postcoloniality, and the Politics of Translation, Arvind Mandair

Plasticity at the Dusk of Writing: Dialectic, Destruction, Deconstruction, Catherine Malabou

Anatheism: Returning to God After God, Richard Kearney

COLUMBIA UNIVERSITY PRESS   NEW YORK

A PSYCHOPOLITICAL INVESTIGATION

PETER SLOTERDIJK

TRANSLATED BY MARIO WENNING

RAGE AND TIME

COLUMBIA UNIVERSITY PRESS

PUBLISHERS SINCE 1893

NEW YORK   CHICHESTER, WEST SUSSEX

The translation of this work was supported by a grant from the Goethe-Institut
which is funded by the German Ministry of Foreign Affairs.

Originally published as *Zorn und Zeit. Politisch-psychologischer Versuch*, © 2006 Suhrkamp Verlag,
Frankfurt-am-Main

Library of Congress Cataloging-in-Publication Data
Sloterdijk, Peter, 1947–
[Zorn und Zeit. English]
Rage and time : a psychopolitical investigation / Peter Sloterdijk.
p. cm. — (Insurrections: critical studies in religion, politics, and culture)
"Originally published as Zorn und Zeit : Politisch-psychologischer Versuch, c2006
Suhrkamp Verlag, Frankfurt-am-Main."
Includes bibliographical references.
ISBN 978-0-231-14522-0 (cloth : alk. paper) — ISBN 978-0-231-51836-9 (e-book)
1. Anger. 2. Anger—Religious aspects—Christianity. 3. Anger—Religious aspects—Judaism.
4. Thymos (The Greek word) 5. Political science—Philosophy. 6. Capitalism—Philosphy.
I. Title. II. Series.

BF575.A5S5613   2010

152.4'2—dc22   2009034870

Columbia University Press books are printed on permanent and durable acid-free paper.
This book is printed on paper with recycled content.
Printed in the United States of America

c 10 9 8 7 6 5 4 3 2 1

CONTENTS

RAGE
AND TIME

INTRODUCTION

Europe's First Word

AT THE BEGINNING OF THE FIRST SENTENCE OF THE EUROPEAN tradition, in the first verse of the *Iliad*, the word "rage" occurs. It appears fatally and solemnly, like a plea, a plea that does not allow for any disagreement. As is fitting for a well-formed propositional object, this noun is in the accusative: "Of the rage of Achilles, son of Peleus, sing Goddess. . . ." That it appears at the very beginning loudly and unequivocally announces its heightened pathos. Which kind of relationship to rage is proposed to the listeners in this magical prelude to this heroic song? How does the singer want to bring to language rage? How does he intend to address the particular kind of rage with which everything began in the old Western world? Will he depict it as a form of violence, a violence that will entrap peaceful human beings in atrocious events? Should one attenuate, curb, and repress this most horrible and most human of affects? Should one quickly avoid it as often as it announces itself, in others or in oneself? Should one always sacrifice it to the neutralized better insight?

1

These are, as one quickly realizes, contemporary questions. They lead far away from the subject matter, the rage of Achilles. The Old World had discovered its own pathways to rage, which can no longer be those of the moderns. Where the moderns consult a therapist or dial the number of the police, those who were knowers back then appealed to the divine world. Homer calls to the goddess in order to let the first word of Europe be heard. He does so in accordance with an old rhapsodic custom: the insight that he who intends something immodest had better start very modestly. Not I, but Homer can secure the success of my song. To sing has meant from time immemorial to open one's mouth so that the higher powers can make themselves heard. If my song is successful and gains authority, the muses will be responsible for it, and beyond the muses perhaps a god, or the goddess herself. If the song disappears without being heard, it means the higher powers were not interested in it. In Homer's case, the divine judgment was clear: In the beginning there was the word "rage," and the word was successful:

Menin aiede, thea, Peleiadeo Achileos
Oulomenen, he myri Achaiois alge eteke . . .

Of the rage of Achilles, son of Peleus, sing Goddess
that murderous rage which condemned Achaeans to countless agonies and
    threw many warrior souls deep into Hades . . .

The verses of appeal in the *Iliad* unequivocally prescribe the way in which the Greeks, the paradigm people of Western civilization, are supposed to confront the entry of rage into the life of mortals: with the kind of amazement that is appropriate for an apparition. The first plea of our cultural tradition—is this "our" still valid?—asks the divine world to support the song of the rage of a unique fighter. What is remarkable is that the singer does not aim for any extenuation. Starting with the first lines, he emphasizes the baleful force of heroic rage: wherever it manifests itself, it unleashes its power on all sides. The Greeks themselves have to suffer even more from it than the Trojans. Already in the very beginning of the unraveling war, Achilles' rage turns against his own people. It is enlisted on the Greek front again only shortly before the decisive battle. The tone of the first verses sets up the program: in contradistinction to their general presentation as mere ghostly shadows, the souls of the beaten heroes, which are mentioned extensively here, descend into Hades. In Hades their lifeless bodies—Homer refers to these bodies as "they"—are devoured by birds and dogs under the open sky.

The voice of the singer passes over the horizon of existence from which he can report such things. It is a euphoric and balanced voice. To be Greek and to listen to this voice mean the same thing in classical antiquity. Whenever one hears it, one immediately knows that war and peace are names for the phases of a life in which the ultimate significance of death is never in question. Death meets the hero early. This, too, belongs to the messages of the hero's song. If the expression "glorification of violence" ever had a meaning, it would be fitting for this entry into the oldest record of European culture. However, this expression would mean almost the opposite of what is implied by its contemporary, inevitably disapproving usage. To sing of rage means to make rage noteworthy, to make it worthy of being thought (*denkwürdig*). However, what is noteworthy is in proximity to what is impressive and permanently praiseworthy—we could almost say: it is close to the Good. These valuations are so thoroughly opposed to modern ways of thinking and feeling that one probably has to admit that an authentic access to the intimate meaning of the Homeric understanding of rage will remain closed off to us.

Only indirect approximations will help us move further. At least we understand that what we are dealing with is not the holy rage of which biblical sources speak. Nor are we confronted with the outrage of the prophet in the face of atrocities against the gods. It is not the rage of Moses, who smashes the tablets while the people bask in front of the golden calf. Nor is it the languishing hatred of the psalmist who cannot wait for the day when the just one will bathe his feet in the blood of the sinners (Psalms 58:10–11). The rage of Achilles also has little in common with the anger of Yahweh, the early and yet rather unsublime God of thunder and deserts, the one who leads the people through their exodus as the "God that bristles with anger" and destroys their persecutors in thunderstorms and floods.[1] However, neither are we confronted by profane fits of human rage, which the later Sophists and philosophical teachers of morals have in mind when they preach the ideal of self-restraint.

The truth is that Homer moves within a world that is characterized by an appreciation of war without limitations. However dark the horizon of this universe of battles and deaths might be, the basic tone of the presentation is determined by the pride of being allowed to be a witness to such spectacles and such fates. The illuminating visibility of these spectacles and fates reconciles with the harshness of reality. This is what Nietzsche referred to as "Apollonian." No modern human being can put himself back into a time where the concepts of war and happiness formed a meaningful constellation. For the first listeners of Homer, however, war and happiness are inseparable. The bond between them is founded upon the ancient cult of heroes. We moderns know this cult only within the square brackets of historical education.

For the ancients this heroism was no subtle attitude but the most vital of all possible responses to the facts of life. A world without heroes would have been worth nothing in their view. Such a world would have meant a state in which human beings would have been exposed to the monarchy of nature without any resistance. In such a world, *physis* would cause everything while human beings would not be capable of anything. The hero, however, is living proof that acts and deeds are also to be done by human beings as long as divine favor allows for them. The early heroes are celebrated solely as doers of deeds and achievers of acts. Their deeds testify to what is most valuable. They testify to what mortals, then and now, are able to experience: that a clearing of impotence and indifference has been brushed into the bush of natural condition. In accounts of actions, the first happy message that shines through is: there is more happening under the sun than what one is indifferent to and what always remains the same. Because true actions have been done the accounts of them answer the question, "Why do human beings do something at all rather than nothing?" Human beings do something so that the world will be expanded through something new and worthy of being praised. Because those that accomplished the new were representatives of humankind, even if extraordinary ones, for the rest as well an access to pride and amazement opens up when they hear about the deeds and sufferings of the heroes.

The new, however, may not appear in the form of the news of the day. In order to be legitimate, it has to disguise itself as the prototypical, oldest, and eternally recurring. It also needs to invoke the long anticipated approval of the gods. If the new presents itself in the form of prehistoric events, myth comes into existence. The epic is the more flexible, broader, and more solemn form of myth, a form that is fitting for presentation in castles, on village squares, and in front of early city audiences.[2]

The demand for the hero is the precondition for everything that follows. Only because the terrifying rage of heroes is indispensable may the singer turn to the goddess in order to engage her for twenty-four songs. If this rage, which the goddess is supposed to help to sing to, were not itself of a higher nature, the thought to appeal to it would already be an act of blasphemy. Only because there is a form of rage that is granted from above is it legitimate to involve the gods in the fierce affairs of human beings. Who sings under such premises about rage celebrates a force that frees human beings from vegetative numbness. This force elevates human beings, who are covered by a high, watchful sky. The inhabitants of the earth draw breath since they can imagine that the gods are viewers, taking delight in the mundane comedy.

Understanding these circumstances, which have become distant to us, can be simplified by indicating that according to the conception of the ancients the hero and his singer correspond with each other in an authentic religious bond. Religiosity is human beings' agreement with their nature as mediums. It is generally known that mediate talents travel separate paths. These ways can, however, intersect at important junctures. "Media" pluralism is thus a fact that reaches back to early conditions of culture. However, at these early times media were not technical instruments but human beings themselves, including their organic and spiritual potential. Just as the singer could be the mouthpiece of a singing force, the hero feels himself the arm of rage, the rage that achieved the noteworthy actions. The larynx of the one and the arm of the other together form a hybrid body. The arm to hold the sword belongs more to the god than to the fighter himself. The god influences the human world through the detour of secondary causes. Of course, the arm to hold the sword also belongs to the singer, to whom the hero, and all his weapons, owe the immortal fame. Hence the connection of god-hero-singer constitutes the first effective media network. In the thousand years after Homer, Achilles is a topic in the Mediterranean time and again. People address Achilles' usefulness for the war-loving muses.

It is not necessary to dwell on the fact that nowadays no one is able to think authentically, perhaps with the exception of some inhabitants of the esoteric highlands where the reenchantment of the world has further progressed. We have not only stopped to judge and feel like the peoples of old, we secretly despise them for remaining "children of their time." We despise them for remaining captivated by a form of heroism that we can only experience as archaic and unfitting. What could one object to Homer from the vantage point of the present and the conventions of the lowlands? Should one accuse him of violating human rights by conceiving individuals all too directly as media of higher commanding beings? Should one accuse him of disregarding the integrity of victims by celebrating the forces that caused them harm? Or should one accuse him of neutralizing the arbitrary violence of war, of transforming its results immediately into divine judgments? Or would one have to soften the allegation to claim that the god has become a victim of impatience. Would we have to claim that he did not possess the patience to wait until the Sermon on the Mount and that he did not read Seneca's *De ira*, the exposition of the stoic control of affects, which served as a model for Christian and humanistic ethics?

Within Homer's horizon there is, of course, no point where objections of this kind could successfully gain hold. The song concerning the heroic energy of a warrior, with which the *epos* of the ancients starts out, elevates rage to the rank of a substance, out of which the world is formed. This requires that we admit that "world" delineates the circle of shapes and scenes of the ancient, Hellenic life of aristocratic warriors during the first millennium before the Christian calendar. One is inclined to think that such a worldview has become obsolete since, at the latest, the time of the Enlightenment. However, to fully reject this image characterized by the priority of struggle will probably be harder for the contemporary realist than the current widespread feeling of pacifism wants to make us believe. Moderns did not fully neglect the task of thinking war. Indeed, this task has for a long time been associated with the male order of cultivation.[3] Students of antiquity have already been measured against the standard of thinking war. This was the case when the upper class of Rome, together with the other Greek models of culture, imported the epic bellicosity of their teachers. The Roman upper class did not at all forget its own rooted militarism. Similarly, since the Renaissance, generation after generation of the youth of Europe learned about this militarism after the exemplary character of the Greeks had again been set up as a guide in the educational system of the newly formed national states. This had far-reaching consequences. Could it be possible that the so-called world wars of the twentieth century also represented, among other things, repetitions of the Trojan War? They were organized by a group of generals, and didn't the leading generals on both sides of the enemy lines understand themselves as virtually the most excellent of the ancients? Didn't these generals understand themselves as the descendents of the raging Achilles and as bearers of an athletic and patriotic vocation to gain victory and enjoy fame by posterity?[4] The immortal hero dies countless times.

The question of whether Homer, just as after him Heraclitus and much later Hegel, believed that war is the father of all things remains open. It is also uncertain—and probably even unlikely—that Homer, the patriarch of the historiography of war and the teacher of Greek to countless generations, possessed a conception of "history" or "civilization." The only thing that is certain is that the universe of the *Iliad* is woven completely out of the deeds and sufferings of rage (*menis*), just as the somewhat younger *Odyssey* is an exercise in listing the deeds and sufferings of cunningness (*metis*). According to the ancient ontology, the world is the sum total of the battles that take place in it. Epic rage appears like a primary energy to its singer, a primary energy that swells by itself, undeducible, like the storm and the sunlight; it is an active force in quintessential shape. Because this energy can rightly claim the predicate first substance "from itself," it precedes all of its local provocations. The hero and his *menis* constitute for Homer an inseparable couple. According to this preestablished union, every deduction of rage from its external provocations becomes superfluous. Achilles is wrathful just as the North Pole is icy, Olympus is shrouded by clouds, and Mont Ventoux circled by roaring winds.

Saying this does not deny that the occasion presents a stage for rage. However, the role of these occasions is limited to literally "conjuring up" (*hervorrufen*) rage without changing its essence. As the force that holds the world together, rage preserves in its essence the unity of substance in the multitude of its eruptions. It exists before all of its manifestations and survives unchangingly its most intensive expenditures. When Achilles perches in his tent and rumbles, when he is hurt, almost paralyzed and angry with his people because the military leader, Agamemnon, has taken from him the beautiful slave, Briseis, a symbolically significant "present of honor," this does not halter his astonishingly raging nature. The capability to suffer from an affront is the mark of a great fighter. Such a fighter does not yet need the virtue of losers, to "let things be." For Achilles it is satisfactory to know that he is in the right and that Agamemnon owes something to him. This guilt is objective according to ancient Greek culture because the honor of the great fighter is itself more objective or of an authentic nature. If he who is first only in rank takes a reward from someone who is first by force, honor is violated at the highest level. The episode of rage shows the force of Achilles in preparatory standstill. Heroes, too, know times of indecision and times of anger, of being turned within oneself. But a sufficiently strong trigger is enough to ignite again the motor of rage, and the consequences are terrifying and yet fascinating enough to qualify for a record of fighting worthy of the title "destroyer of cities" and a battle record of twenty-three destroyed settlements.[5]

The young favorite of Achilles, Patroclos, who had carelessly worn the armor of his friend on the battleground, was slain by Hector, the spearhead of the Trojans. Shortly after the news concerning this ominous event spreads around the Greek camp, Achilles leaves his tent. His rage has once again united itself with him and dictates from this point on—without indeterminacy—the direction of his actions. The hero demands a new armor, and the underworld rushes to fulfill his request. The rage that engulfs him does not limit itself to his body: it sparks across far-reaching network of actions that spans the mortal and immortal worlds. *Menis* takes on the role of an intensely aggressive mediator between immortals and mortals. It compels Hephaestus, the god of forging, to produce the finest of new weapons. It grants Thetis, the mother of the hero, wings in order to speedily transmit information between the forge of the underworld and the camp of the Greeks above. In the inner circle of its potency, *menis* prepares the fighter again against his fateful last enemy. It prepares him for the real presence of the fight. It leads him onto the battlefield, to the place determined by providence. At this place rage will flare up highest and reach the highest degree of fulfilling release. In front of the walls of Troy the consummation of rage is the sign that is necessary to remind every witness of the convergence of explosion and truth.[6] Only the fact that in the last instance it is not the rage of Achilles but the cunning of Odysseus that wins over the besieged city shows that in the fatal plain of Troy there already had to be a second means to success. Did Homer thus not see a future for pure rage?

Such a conclusion would be premature because the Homer of the *Iliad* uses every possible means to extend the dignity of rage. At the decisive moment he emphasizes how explosive the eruption of the wrathful force of Achilles really was. Its suddenness is particularly indispensable as verification of its higher origin. It is part of the virtue of the hero of early Greece to be ready to become a vessel for the abrupt flow of energy from the gods. Still, we find ourselves in a world whose spiritual constitution is clearly characterized by its mediate dimension. Just as the prophet is a medium in the name of the holy word of protest, the warrior becomes a tool for the force, which gathers in him abruptly in order to break through the world of appearances.

A secularization of affects is still unknown in this order of things. Secularization implies the execution of the program that is present in well-formed European propositions. Through them one imitates in the domain of the real what is provided by syntax: subjects act on objects and force their domination on them. It is unnecessary to state that Homer's world of actions remains far away from such circumstances. It is not the human beings who have their passions, but rather it is the passions that have their human beings. The accusative is still untamable. Given these circumstances, the one God remains of course absent. Theoretical monotheism can only gain power once the philosophers seriously postulate the propositional subject as the world principle. Then the subjects are supposed to have their passions as well. Then the subjects are allowed to postulate themselves as the masters and owners of these passions, which now can be controlled. Until then, spontaneous pluralism reigns, a pluralism in which subjects and objects constantly exchange place.

This blurring of subjects and objects shows that one needs to sing about rage in the moment when it is alive and active, when it comes over someone. It is only this that Homer has in mind when he relates the long siege of Troy and the fall of the city, which was almost given up, to the mysterious fighting force of the protagonist. Because of Achilles' rage the Greek course was condemned to failure. Homer uses the moment of truth in which *menis* flows into its bearer; epic memory then only needs to follow the course of events, which is determined by the high and low forces. It is decisive that the warrior himself, as soon as sublime rage begins to become effective, experiences a kind of numinous presence. Only because of this presence can the heroic rage be more than a profane fit when applied to its most gifted tool. To state it with more pathos: through the surge of rage the god of the battlefield speaks to the fighter. One understands right away why we rarely hear two voices in such moments. Forces of this kind are monothematic, at least at the time of their naïve beginnings. They are monothematic because they take hold of the whole man and demand that their one affect occupy the entire stage.[7] In the case of pure rage there is no complex inner life, no hidden psychic world, no private secret through which the hero would become understandable to other human beings. Rather, the basic principle is that the inner life of the actor should become wholly manifest and wholly public. It should become wholly deed and, if possible, wholly song. It is typical of the surging rage that it fully becomes one with its own lavish expression. Under the domination of total expressivity, it is impossible to hold oneself back or worry over self-preservation. Of course there is always "something" for which the fighting takes place. Mainly, however, the struggle serves the goal of revelation: it reveals the fighting energy as such. Strategy, the goal of war, and the rewards surface only later.

9

Wherever rage flames up we are dealing with the complete warrior. As the burning hero enters fully into the fight, the identification of the human being with his driving forces realizes itself. Common people can only dream of this in their best moments. They, too, as far as they are used to postponing things and having to wait, have not completely lost the memory of those moments of their lives in which the élan of acting seemed to flow directly out of the circumstances. To use a phrase of Robert Musil, we could call this becoming one with the pure driving force, the utopia of a life based on motivation.[8]

For people who settle down, such as farmers, craftsmen, day laborers, writers, civil servants, and for later therapists and professors, the virtues of hesitations have become authoritative. He who sits on the bench of virtues usually cannot know what his next task might be. He has to receive council from different perspectives and has to make his decisions based on interpretations of the murmur in which no tenor embodies the main voice. For everyday people the evidence of the moment remains out of reach; at best, the crutches of habit will help them. Habit provides solid surrogates of security, which may be stable but do not allow for the living presence of conviction. He who is driven by rage, however, is past the anemic time. Fog arises, yet shapes become more determinate. Now clear lines lead to the object. The enraged attack knows where it wants to hit. The person who is enraged in the highest form "enters the world like the bullet enters the battle."[9]

The Thymotic World: Pride and War

IT IS BECAUSE OF THE INGENIOUS READING OF HOMER BY THE CLASSICAL philologist Bruno Snell that contemporary reinterpreters of the *Iliad* have become aware of the specific premodern structure of its epic psychology and plot. In the main chapter of his inspiring book *The Discovery of Spirit*, which deals with Homer's conception of the human being, he elucidates an important feature of the text: that the epic characters of the oldest epoch of Western writing still lack, to a large degree, the formative characteristics of the classical conception of subjectivity. In particular, they lack reflective inwardness, intimate conversations with themselves, and the ability to make conscientious attempts to control their affects.[10] Snell discovers in Homer the latent conception of a "composite" or "container" personality, which resembles in some respects the image of the postmodern human being with his chronic "dissociative disorders." Seen from a distance, the early hero indeed puts one in mind of today's "multiple-personality" disorder. For Homer there does not yet seem to be an inner hegemonic principle, a coherent "I" that is responsible for the unity and self-control of the psychic field. Rather the "person" turns out to be a meeting point of affects or partial energies. These energies introduce themselves into their host, the experiencing and acting individual, as visitors from afar. They have come in order to use their host for their own concerns.

The rage of the hero thus may not be understood as an inherent attribute of the structure of his personality. The successful warrior is more than just a character that is exceedingly irritable and aggressive. It does not make much sense to speak of Homeric figures the way school psychologists speak of problematic students. Otherwise Achilles would be presented too quickly as a delegate of extravagant parental ambitions.[11] This would falsely portray him as the precursor of a psychologically deformed tennis prodigy, but because with Achilles we are still in the domain of this container psychology, one needs to pay special attention to the basic rule of this spiritual universe: rage, which blazes up in intervals, is an energetic supplement to the heroic psyche, not a mere personal trait or intimate feature. The Greek catchphrase for the "organ" in the chest of both heroes and regular human beings, the organ from which these great upsurges take their departure, is "thymos." Thymos signifies the impulsive center of the proud self, yet at the same time it also delineates the receptive "sense." Through this sense the commands of the gods reveal themselves to mortals. The supplementary or "joining" quality of impulses connected to thymos explains, by the way, the lack of any control over the affects of Homer's characters. This is particularly strange to us moderns. The hero is a kind of prophet and is assigned the task of actualizing instantaneously the message of his force. The hero accompanies his power in a way similar to how a genius is accompanied by his protégé. When the force becomes actualized the protégée has no choice but to go along with it.[12]

Even though the hero is not the master and owner of his affects, it would be a mistake to think that he is only its blind instrument, without any will of his own. Menis belongs to the group of invasive energies. The poetic as well as the philosophical psychology of the Hellenics included these energies and taught that they were to be considered gifts of grace from the divine world. Just as every gifted person is asked from above to carefully administer the gift that has been entrusted to him, the hero, the guardian of rage, also has to create a conscious relationship to this rage. Heidegger, who we can well imagine to be a thoughtful tourist on the planes of Troy, would probably say: fighting is also thanking.

After the transformation of the Greek psyche from extolling heroic militancy to extolling civic excellence, rage gradually disappears from the list of charismatic affects. Only the more spiritual forms of enthusiasm remain, as in Plato's *Phaedrus*, in which he presents an overview and list of psyche's beneficial obsessions, primarily medicine, the gift of prophesy, and the enthralled song that is granted by the muse. Beyond this, Plato also introduces the novel paradox of enthusiasm, the sober mania of viewing ideas. These ideas are the central reference point of the new science Plato founded, that is, philosophy. Under the influence of this discipline, "manic" psyche, illuminated through logical exercises, once and for all distanced itself from its *"menic"* beginnings. The exorcism of great rage from culture began.

Since then, the rage of citizens is only a guest that one welcomes within a framework of strict regulations; old-style fury does not fit at all into the urban world. Only on the stage of the Athenian theater of Dionysus is it sometimes presented in its old-fashioned, delusional intensity. One may think of Sophocles' *Ajax* or Euripides' *The Bacchae*. However, generally it is presented only to remind mortals of the terrifying freedom of the gods. It serves as a reminder that the gods possess the power to completely destroy whomever they wish. The stoic philosophers, who turn to the civil audience during the following generations, will defend as convincingly as the best Sophists the claim that rage is in the last instance "unnatural" because it objects to the reasonable essence of the human being.[13]

The domestication of rage creates the ancient form of a new masculinity. Indeed, the remaining affects that are useful for the polis are incorporated into the bourgeois *thymos*. *Thymos* survives as "manly courage" (*Mannesmut, andreia*), without which it is impossible for the practitioner of urban life to assert himself. Rage was also allowed to live a second life as useful and "just rage," responsible for protecting its possessors against insults and unwanted impositions. Additionally, it helps citizens to step in for the Good and the Right (or, to put it in a modern idiom, our interests). Without stout-heartedness (*Beherztheit*)—this is how one should better translate the term *thymos* nowadays—bourgeois metropolitan life is unthinkable. (This theme is especially interesting for Germans because they produce a new and special form of stout-heartedness after 1945. I mean the often praised civil courage, the meager level of courage for losers. With this form of courage the joys of democracy were introduced to an otherwise politically timid population). Moreover, the possibility of friendship between adult males in a city still depends on thymotic premises. After all, one can only play one's role as a friend among friends, an equal among equals, if one appreciates in one's fellow citizens the clear presence of universally acknowledged virtues.[14] One does not want only to be proud of oneself but also of the alter ego, the friend, who distinguishes himself in front of the eyes of the community. To be in good reputation among competing men creates the thymotic fluidity of a self-confident community. Individual *thymos* appears now as part of a force-field that provides form to the common will. The first philosophical psychology of Europe unfolds itself as a political thymotic within this horizon.

BEYOND EROTICISM

RECENTLY, THE SUSPICION THAT PSYCHOANALYSIS MUST HAVE BEEN mistaken in an important respect about the nature of its objects has become more concrete. This marks a break with the earlier twentieth-century conception of psychoanalysis as a form of privileged psychological knowledge. Sporadic objections against the teachings of psychoanalysis, which go back to the early days of the discipline, have today turned into a theoretically supported dismissal. The point of origin of this dismissal does not, though, lie in the endless quarrels concerning whether psychoanalytic theses and results are "scientifically" ascertainable. Rather, the origin of the objections to psychoanalysis consists in the increasingly widening gap between psychic phenomena and academically accepted conceptions—a malaise that has already been discussed for a long time by the creative authors and practitioners of the psychoanalytic movement. It is important to note that chronic doubts about its specific efficacy are not the cause of the resistance to psychoanalysis.

The source of the fundamental misunderstanding to which psychoanalysis has succumbed is rooted in its naturalistically concealed cryptophilosophical pretense to explain the human condition in its entirety based on the dynamics of libido, that is, from the standpoint of eroticism. This did not necessarily have to lead to a disaster for psychoanalysis, if the legitimate interest of therapists in the dimension of eros would have been connected with an equally vivid attention to the dimension of thymotic energies. However, psychoanalysis was never willing to turn as much detail and basic interest to dealing with the thymotics of the human being of either sex. It did not sufficiently investigate human pride, courage, stout-hearted-ness, craving for recognition, drive for justice, sense of dignity and honor, indignation, militant and vengeful energies. Psychoanalysis somewhat condescendingly left phenomena of this kind to the followers of Alfred Adler and other allegedly minor interpreters of the so-called inferiority complexes. If at all, it conceded that pride and ambition can take over con-trol whenever sexual wishes do not get realized adequately. With a little irony, psychoanalysis called this transition of the psyche to a second pro-gram "sublimation"—a fabricated elevation for those in need of it.

For the most part, classical psychoanalysis was not interested in con-sidering the possibility that there might be a second basic force operative in the psychic field. This fact changed only marginally through additional conceptual inventions such as the "death drive" or mythic figures with the name of "destrudo," or primary aggression. The psychology of the self that was added later functioned only as compensation. It is understandable that it always remained a thorn in the eye for the classic Freudians, the partisans of the unconscious.

In conformity with its basic erotodynamic approach, psychoanalysis brought much hatred to light, the other side of love. Psychoanalysis man-aged to show that hating means to be bound by similar laws as loving. Both hating and loving are projections that are subject to a repetitive com-pulsion. Psychoanalysis remained for the most part silent when it came to that form of rage that springs from the striving for success, prestige, self-respect, and their backlashes. The most visible symptom of the delib-erate ignorance that resulted from the analytic paradigm is the theory of narcissism, the second offspring of psychoanalytic doctrine, with which the inconsistencies of the oedipal theorem were supposed to be resolved. It is telling that the narcissism thesis focuses on the human forms of self-affirmation. However, it aims to incorporate this thesis against all plau-sibility into the framework of a second erotic model. It thus takes on the futile effort to deduce the peculiar richness of thymotic phenomena from autoeroticism and its pathogenic fragmentations. Although it formulates a respectable educational program for the psyche, a program that aims at the transformation of the so-called narcissistic state into that of the mature love object, psychoanalysis never considered outlining an analogous edu-cational path for the production of the proud adult, of the fighter and bearer of ambitions. The word "pride" is for most psychoanalysts only an empty entry in the dictionary of the neurotic. They have practically lost access to what is designated by the word "pride" because of an exercise in forgetting, an exercise called education.

Narcissus is incapable of helping Oedipus, however. The choice of these mythic models reveals more about the person who made the choice than about the nature of the object. How should it be the case that a young man with a moronic character, someone incapable of differentiating between his mirror image and himself, is supposed to make up for the weaknesses of a man who only gets to know his own father in the moment when he kills him and then, just by accident, bears offspring with his own mother? Both are lovers traveling obscure paths. Both get lost in erotic dependencies to such a degree that it would be difficult to decide which one of them is supposed to be the more miserable creature. One could convincingly start a gallery of prototypes of human misery with Oedipus and Narcissus. One would feel sorry for these creatures but not admire them. Their fates, if we trust the teachings of the psychoanalytic school, are supposed to reveal the most powerful patterns for the dramas of everyone's life. It is not difficult to see which tendency is the basis of these "promotions." Who would make human beings into patients—as people without pride are thus called—can do no better than to elevate such figures as these into emblems of the human condition. In truth their lesson should have consisted of a warning that unadvised and one-sided love easily makes fools out of its subjects. Only when the goal is to portray the human being ab ovo as the "jumping jack" of love is it possible to make the miserable admirer of his own image and the miserable lover of his own mother into paradigms of human existence. One may add, by the way, that the basic contract of psychoanalysis has been undermined by the excessive dispensation of its most successful fictions. From a distance, the cooler youth of our day still knows what was the matter with Narcissus and Oedipus. However, this youth takes only a rather bored interest in their fate. He does not see in them paradigms of human existence, but only sadly trivial losers.

Anyone interested in the human being as a bearer of proud and self-affirmative affections should leave unsevered the knots of this tangled, overextended eroticism. One must probably return to the basic conception of philosophical psychology found in the Greeks, according to which the soul does not only rely on eros and its intentions with regard to the one and the many. Rather, the soul should open itself equally to the impulses of *thymos*. While eroticism points to ways leading to those "objects" that we lack and whose presence or possession makes us feel complete, thymotics discloses ways for human beings to redeem what they possess, to learn what they are able to do, and to see what they want. According to the first psychologists, the human being is quite capable of loving, and this is the case in a twofold sense: he can love according to the high and unifying eros, insofar the soul is marked by the memories of a lost perfection. Second, a human being can love according to the popular and diverting eros, insofar as the soul constantly succumbs to a colorful multitude of "desires" or, we could also say, complexes of appetite-attractions. However, one cannot not surrender oneself exclusively to desiring affects. With equal emphasis it needs to be said that one should watch over the demands of *thymos*, if necessary even at the cost of leaving erotic inclinations unrealized. A person is challenged to preserve dignity and self-respect even while earning the respect of others in the light of their high standards. It is this way and could not be different because life requests every individual to step out onto the external stages of existence and expose his powers to prove himself before his peers. This is necessary for one's own personal benefit as well as for the benefit of the community.

If one wants to replace the second determination of the human being with the first one, one evades the need of having an education in both psychic dimensions. This leads to a reversal of the energies in one's mental household, which results in damage to the housekeeper. In the past it was possible to observe such reversals mainly in religious orders and subcultures that were crazy about humility, subcultures in which beautiful souls sent one another messages of love. In these ethereal circles the whole thymotic field was sealed off by accusations of pride (*superbia*), while one at the same time preferred to indulge in the delights of moderation. Honor, ambition, pride, a heightened sense of self-esteem—all of these were concealed behind a thick wall of moral prescriptions and psychological "insights," which all aimed at fencing off and domesticating so-called egoism. The resentment of the self and its inclination to put itself and what it possesses at center stage instead of being happy with subordination—a resentment that was practiced early on in imperial cultures and their religions—has diverted for more than two thousand years the insight that the often criticized egoism actually presents the best human possibilities. Nietzsche was the first modern thinker to provide convincing ideas about how to address this issue.

It is remarkable that contemporary consumerism achieves the same interruption of pride for the sake of eroticism, an achievement reached without altruistic, holistic, or other noble excuses. Consumerism simply buys the interest of dignified human beings by providing material concessions and discounts. The initially absolutely implausible construct of the *homo oeconomicus* thus reaches its goal in the form of the postmodern consumer. Anyone who does not know of any other desires or is not supposed to know any other desires than those that, to cite Plato, derive from the erotic or desiring "part of the soul," is a mere consumer. It is not an arbitrary fact that the instrumentalization of nudity is the leading symptom of the culture of consumption. Nudity always operates out of an orientation toward desiring. At least the clients who are called to desire do not, for the most part, totally lack forces of resistance. They respond to the pervasive assault on the dignity of their intelligence either with constant irony or with learned indifference.

The costs for a one-sided eroticization are high. In reality, the "darkening" of the thymotic dimension makes human behavior incomprehensible. This is a surprising result, considering this darkening could have only been reached through psychological enlightenment. Once one subscribes to this mistaken view, it becomes impossible to understand human beings in situations of tension and struggle. As usual, this failure to understand supposes the failure everywhere, just not in one's own field of vision. The moment that "symptoms" such as pride, indignation, rage, ambition, overzealous self-assertiveness, and acute readiness to fight occur, the member of the *thymos*-forgetting therapeutic culture retreats into a belief that the aggressive people must be victims of a neurotic complex. Therapists, according to this assumption, stand in the tradition of Christian moralists. These moralists speak of the natural disease of self-love as soon as thymotic energies begin to openly reveal themselves. Had Europeans not heard about pride— or likewise rage—from the days of the church fathers, when such impulses would have been taken as signs pointing to the abyss for those cast away? Indeed, since the time of Gregory I, pride, also known by the name of *superbia*, is at the top of the list of cardinal sins. Almost two centuries earlier St. Augustine had described pride as the matrix for a revolution against the divine. For the church fathers *superbia* signified a conscious state of not wanting as the Lord wants (an impulse whose more frequent appearance in monks or civil servants seems understandable). To claim that pride is the mother of all vices expresses the conviction that human beings have been created to obey, and every inclination that leads out of hierarchical relationships could only mean a step toward corruption.[15]

In Europe one had to wait until the Renaissance and the creation of a new formation of urban and civic pride before the dominant *humilitas* psychology, which was inscribed into the bodies and souls of farmers, clerics, and vassals, was at least partially pushed back by a neo-thymotic conception of the human being. It is easy to see that the rise of the nation-state was a significant cause of reemphasizing and reassigning a leading role to the affects of achievement. It is not by accident that the masterminds who helped to prepare the way for the nation-state, most importantly Machiavelli, Hobbes, Rousseau, Smith, Hamilton, and Hegel, turned their attention again to the human being as the bearer of valuing passions. They were particularly interested in the desire for glory, vanity, amour propre, ambition, and desire for recognition. None of these authors ignored the dangers inherent in these affects, yet most of them made an effort to emphasize their productive aspects for the sake of humanity's being together. Since the bourgeoisie likewise articulates its interest in the inherent value of dignity and, even more, since the entrepreneurial human beings of the bourgeois age developed a neo-aristocratic conception of an earned form of success,[16] traditional training in humility is compensated through an aggressive demand for opportunities to exhibit one's own power, arts, and amenities in front of an audience.

Thymotics receives a second chance in the modern world under the guise of the concept of the sublime. No wonder that the do-gooder of the present instinctively shies away from the sublime as if he sensed the ancient danger in it. The way in which the modern appreciation of effort is enlisted is even more threatening. The partisans of the tearfully communicative eros lament and defy this allegedly inhumane principle not without a sense for the strategic position they are in.[17]

The task is thus to regain a psychology of self-confidence and self-assertion. Such a psychology needs to do more justice to the psychodynamic conditions of our existence. This presupposes a correction to the erotologically partitioned conception of the human being, which characterizes the horizons of the nineteenth and twentieth centuries. At the same time, what is needed is a radical distancing from the ways of conditioning the Western psyche that have deeply engraved us, in the older religious form or in the younger metamorphoses. Most important, we need to distance ourselves from the blatant ideology that results from the Christian anthropology according to which the human being is a sinner, an animal that is sick with pride, one that can only be saved through faithful humility.

Clearly, a movement that would distance itself from these phenomena would not be easy to bring about. Although the phrase "God is dead" is already looked up by journalists on a regular basis, the theistic resources of humility continue to exist in democratic consensualism without being seriously endangered. It is quite possible to let God die and yet continue to have quasi-god-fearing people. Even if it is the case that most contemporary people have been carried off by antiauthoritarian currents, even if they have learned to express their own need for recognition, from a psychological point of view they continue to depend on a relationship of semi-rebellious obedience with regard to the lord who takes care of them. They demand "respect" and do not want to give up on the advantages of dependence. It would be even harder for them to emancipate themselves from the concealed bigotry of psychoanalysis. They continue to believe dogmatically that even the most powerful of human beings cannot be more than a conscious sufferer of his love-sick condition, which goes by the name of neurosis. The future of these illusions is secured by the big coalition: Christianity and psychoanalysis can successfully defend their claim of outlining the horizon of human knowledge so long as they understand this monopoly as providing a definition for the human condition as characterized by a constitutive lack, a lack that used to be known as "sin." Whenever lack is in power, the "ethics of indignity" has the word.

Hence, as long as both of these smart systems of bigotry dominate the scene, our understanding of the thymotic dynamic of human existence remains covered up for both individuals and political groups. Thus access to studying the dynamics of self-assertion and rage in psychic and social systems is practically blocked. In this situation we are constantly forced to grasp thymotic phenomena by way of the inappropriate concepts of eroticism. Under conditions of such a bigoted blockade, the direct intention never really comes to the fore because it is only possible to approach the facts by way of distorted traits. At least the underlying traits are, in spite of the erotic misconception, never fully covered up. Once we have called this dilemma by its name it becomes clear that it can only be overcome through the underlying conceptual apparatus.

THEORY OF THE PRIDE ENSEMBLE

POLITICAL SCIENCE OR, BETTER, THE ART OF THE PSYCHOPOLITICAL steering of the community, has had to suffer most from the thoroughly practiced but mistaken approach of psychological anthropology in the West. This approach misses a whole set of axioms and concepts that would be appropriate for the nature of its object. What from the vantage point of thymotics is seen unmistakably as the primary condition cannot be presented directly through the detour around available erotodynamic concepts. At this point let me mention the six most important principles that can serve as the point of origin for a theory of thymotic unities:

- Political groups are ensembles; they endogenously stand in relationships of thymotic tension
- Political actions are started through a decrease in the tension between centers of ambition
- Political fields are formed through the spontaneous pluralism of auto-affirmative forces; the relationships among these forces change because of interthymotic frictions
- Political opinions are conditioned and steered through symbolic operations that present a sustained relationship to the thymotic emotions of collectives
- Rhetoric, the doctrine of controlling affects in political ensembles, is applied thymotics
- Power struggles within political bodies are always also struggles for priority between thymotically charged, ambitious individuals and their following; the art of the political thus includes the process of compensating losers

If one presupposes a natural pluralism of thymotic power centers, one needs to investigate their relationships according to their specific field regularities. Whenever real force-force relationships are at stake, reference to the self-love of the actors does not help us get further—or if it does, it is only with regard to subordinated aspects. Instead, it needs to be stated first that political units (conventionally understood as peoples and their subgroups) are, from the perspective of systems theory, "metabolic quantities." They continue to exist only as producing and consuming entities that convert stress and fight with enemies and other entropic factors. It is striking that to the present day, thinkers formed by Christianity and psychoanalysis have trouble admitting that freedom is a concept that only makes sense within the framework of a thymotic conception of the human being. Economists zealously recite the doctrines of the latter thinkers, situating the human being as the consuming animal in the center of their appeals—according to which they only want to see human freedom as the choice of feeding dishes.

Through metabolic activities heightened inner achievements in a vital system become stabilized, at the physical as well as at the psychological level. The phenomenon of warm-bloodedness is its most impressive embodiment. With it, the emancipation of the organism from surrounding temperatures was accomplished approximately at the "half-time of evolution"—the biological departure to being able to move freely. Everything depends on one's ability to freely move, an ability that will later be called freedom, with all its different connotations. From a biological perspective, freedom means the ability to actualize the entire potential of the spontaneous movements that are specific to an organism.

The separation of the warm-blooded organism from the primacy of its milieu finds its mental counterpart in the thymotic impulse of the individual as much as it does so in that of groups. As a moral, warm-blooded animal, the human being is dependent on keeping up a certain internal level of self-esteem. This also initiates a tendency toward disassociating the "organism" from the primacy of the milieu. Whenever proud impulses assert themselves, there arises on the psychological plane an inner-outer gradient on which the inner, self-pole naturally has the higher frequency. If one prefers nontechnical parlance, one can contradict the same conception by showing that human beings share an innate sense for the dignity of justice. Every political organization of communal life has to honor this intuition.

Part of the business of morally complex systems—that is, cultures—is the self-stimulation of its actors through an elevation of thymotic resources such as pride, ambition, the need for recognition, indignation, and the sense of justice. Units of this kind cultivate throughout the conduct of their lives locally specific values that can lead to the use of universal dialects. Empirical research can convincingly prove how successful ensembles will keep their form through a higher inner frequency—but what is noteworthy, by the way, is their frequently aggressive or provocative style of relating to the environment. The stabilization of self-confidence in such a group is subject to a body of regulations, which more recent theory of culture has called "decorum."[18] In a victorious culture, decorum is understandably measured according to the polemic values to which it owes its previous successes. This is the reason for the close liaison between pride and victory in societies that have emerged out of successful battles. Groups that are moved by the dynamics of pride often enjoy being disliked by their neighbors and rivals so long as this provides strength for their feeling of sovereignty.

As soon as the stage of initial ignorance among various metabolic collectives has passed, that is, once the mutual unwillingness to recognize one another has lost its innocence, they inevitably enter a situation of being forced to compare themselves and to establish a relationship. This leads to the discovery of a dimension that can be called, in a broad sense, foreign politics. As a consequence of their becoming a reality for one another, the collectives begin to understand one another as coexisting quantities. Through this consciousness of coexistence foreigners are experienced as chronic stress factors, and a society's relationship to them needs to be converted into institutions—usually this takes the form of conflict preparation or diplomatic efforts. From this point onward, each group reflects its own desire for being seen as valuable in the manifest recognition of the others. The poisons of neighborhood slowly seep into these mutually relating ensembles. Hegel discussed this form of moral reflection with the influential concept of recognition. He thus anticipates a powerful source of satisfaction or fantasies of satisfaction. That he at the same time named the origin of countless irritations becomes evident from the nature of the subject matter. On the field of the struggle for recognition, the human being becomes a surreal animal that risks its life for a colored scrap, a flag, a chalice.

Recognition would be better described anew as primarily a matter of interthymotic relationships. What contemporary social philosophy discussed with varying success under the heading "intersubjectivity" often means just the opposition and the interplay of thymotic centers of tension. Where common intersubjectivism is used to present the transactions among actors in psychoanalytic and thus ultimately erotodynamic concepts, from now on it is more advisable to move on to a thymotologic theory of mutual effects and actions of multiple ambition agencies. Although ambitions can be modified by way of erotic affects, taken for themselves they originate in an idiosyncratic center of impulsiveness and can only be understood from the perspective of this center.

GREEK PREMISES, MODERN STRUGGLES: THE THEORY OF *THYMOS*

FOR A BETTER UNDERSTANDING OF SUCH PHENOMENA IT IS USEFUL, as I have already indicated, to go back to the far-sighted formulations in the philosophical psychology of the Greeks. Thanks to the studies of the neoclassical Jewish philosopher Leo Strauss and his school (which have largely and unjustly been claimed by political neoconservatives in the United States), it is again today possible to pay attention to the bipolar dynamics of the human psyche acknowledged and investigated by the great Greek thinkers. Strauss created a situation in which we become aware, apart from Plato the erotologist and author of the *Symposium*, of Plato the psychologist of self-respect.[19]

In book 4 of the *Republic*, Plato presents an outline of a theory of *thymos* of great psychological richness and extensive political importance. The impressive achievement of Plato's interpretation of *thymos* consists in a person's ability to be infuriated. This turn against oneself can come about when a person does not live up to the expectations that would have to be satisfied in order for that person not to lose self-respect. Plato's discovery thus consists in pointing out the moral significance of intense self-disrespect. This manifests itself in a twofold way: First, it expresses itself in shame, an affective, all-encompassing mood that completely fills the subject. Second, this rage-drenched self-reproach takes on the form of an inner appeal to oneself. The act of being dissatisfied with oneself proves to the thinker that the human being has an inert, even if only obscure idea of what is appropriate, of what is just and worthy of praise. When not living up to this idea, a part of the soul, that is, *thymos*, lodges an appeal. With this turn to self-refusal the adventure of independence begins. Only he who is able to disapprove of himself is able to control himself.

The Socratic-Platonic conception of *thymos* presents a milestone on the way to the moral domestication of rage. It is situated halfway between worship of quasi-divine Homeric *menis* and the stoic dismissal of wrathful and intensive impulses. Thanks to Plato's theory of *thymos*, civil and militant impulses receive the right to remain in the philosopher's city. Because the polis that is governed by reason also needs the military, which is introduced here as the group of guardians, civilized *thymos* is allowed to remain within the city walls in the spirit of protection. Plato insists upon the recognition of protective virtues as powers that constitute society in many different ways. Still, in the late dialogue *Politicus*, which deals with the skills required for statesmanship, the well-known allegory of the weavers underlines the necessity of creating the spiritual web of the "state" by interlacing prudent disposition and courageous attitude.

Aristotle also mentions the advantages of rage. His evaluation of this affect is surprisingly positive, at least insofar as it is coupled with courage.

Legitimate rage still has an "ear for reason,"[20] even if it often storms off like an overly hasty servant who does not listen until the end of his orders. It becomes a vice only if it appears together with a lack of abstinence, that is, when it leads to excess. "Rage is necessary. Nothing can be achieved without it. Nothing can be achieved when it does not fulfill the soul and animate courage. One should, to be sure, not make it into a leader. Rather one should only take it to be a comrade-in-arms."[21]

Given that the *thymos* that has been conditioned by civilization is the psychological location of what Hegel depicted as a striving for recognition,[22] it becomes clear why the lack of recognition by relevant others excites rage. If one demands recognition from a specific opponent, one stages a moral test. If the other who is addressed rejects this test, she needs to deal with the rage of the challenger, who feels disrespected. Rage occurs first when the recognition from the other is denied (which leads to extroverted rage). However, rage also flourishes if I deny recognition to myself in light of my value ideas (so that I have reason to be angry with myself). According to Stoic philosophy, which situated the struggle for recognition fully inside the human psyche, the wise person is supposed to be satisfied with self-respect, first, because the individual in no way has control of the judgment of the other and, second, because she who is knowledgeable will strive to keep herself free from all that does not depend on herself.

Usually the thymotic impulse is connected to the wish to find one's self-worth resonating in the other. This desire could easily be an instruction manual for teaching oneself to become unhappy, one with a universal success rate if it were not for those dispersed cases of successful mutual recognition. Lacan probably said what is necessary concerning the profound idea that there is a grounding mirroring process, even though his models, probably unjustly, situate early infantile conditions at the center of investigation. In reality, life in front of the mirror is more of a children's disease. But among adults the striving for reflection in the recognition of others often means the attempt to take possession of a will-o'-the-wisp—in philosophical jargon: to instantiate oneself in what is insubstantial. Lacan's oeuvre moreover expresses the ambition to amalgamate the theory of *thymos* (as it was reformulated by Kojéve) with psychoanalytic eroticism. At the kernel of his project is the freebooting mixture of the Freudian death wish with Hegel's struggle for recognition. Through the introduction of foreign factors Lacan exploded Freud's systematic edifice, but not without claiming that in truth the project meant a "return to Freud."[23]

Without a doubt, the introduction of a thymotic element into psycho-analytic teaching pointed in the right direction. However, the initial consequence was the confusing growth of a performance that popularized the hybrid concept of desire (*désir*). With this concept, Lacan was also able to conceal his strong misjudgment of sexuality. To talk of "desire" was attractive because it covered two phenomena that, although completely different in terms of their origin, could be connected because of their mutual relationality. The confusion was as complete as it was welcome. It is telling that nowadays there are countless confusing "introductions to Lacan"; we are still waiting for a clear summary. As one can see, the reason is easy to point out: Lacan's contributions to the psychological knowledge of the present could only be reformulated by means of a framework in which the relationship of eroticism and thymotics is explained. However, as long as the theory that needs to be framed is intended to be itself the frame and measure, there is no end to the confusion.

Nietzsche's Instant

LOOKING BACK AT THE HISTORY OF THE TWENTIETH CENTURY, AND IN particular its convulsive first half, one gets the impression that it saw the failure of the civilization of thymotic energies on all fronts. This means a failure of the project that Plato demanded, Aristotle praised, and the pedagogues of the bourgeois age attempted to put into practice. If the goal of the political experiment of modernity consisted in translating the thymotic energies of the masses into political forms and in mobilizing these energies for standard "progress," we have to acknowledge a catastrophic failure. This has ultimately led to tearing down the experiments, regardless whether they were conducted under white, red, or brown flags.

To a large extent, this failure was caused by modern radicalisms that attempted, under idealistic as well as materialistic pretenses, to open up untraveled paths for collective rage, paths that were supposed to lead to satisfaction. Leaving modern institutions such as parliaments, courts, and public debates by the wayside, and in contempt of small escapes, these pathways resulted in huge releases of rage, resentment, and fantasies of extermination. They were excesses of previously unknown quantities that should finally be understood as what they were in terms of their psychopolitical quality: a chain of *thymos* catastrophes caused not only by the failure of the traditional religious and civilized management of rage but by the organization of a new politics of rage or, to put it more drastically, the organization of a novel economy of rage. It needs to be insisted on that the violence of the twentieth century did not "erupt" at any point in time. It was planned by its agents according to entrepreneurial criteria and controlled by its managers with long-term oversight for its objects. What at first sight appeared like the highest level of running amok in reality consisted of bureaucracy, party organization, routine, and the effects of organizational reflection.

Before focusing on the new economy of rage, the science of war and resentment, before considering this as the psychopolitical riddle of the twentieth century, Friedrich Nietzsche's unique position in the history of ideas should be pointed out. This author, who is as disturbing today as he ever was, introduced himself to his posterity as the "happy messenger without comparison." At the same time he referred to himself as the "*destroyer par excellence.*"[24] From the "evangelical" perspective he speaks as the teacher of emancipated egoism. From his position as destroyer, he speaks as a warlord who campaigns against morality as a means of domination used by the weak. Nietzsche exposed resentment and its modern repercussions as the fundamental affects of the metaphysical age. His self-consciousness was infused with the certainty that his great deed, exposing resentment as what it is, would divide human history in diametrically opposed periods, just as the Christian calendar divided the entirety of world history into the time before and the time after the birth of Christ. Nietzsche comments on this in his self-portrait, *Ecce Homo*, revealing a deliberate exposition of equanimity: "The concept of politics will have then merged entirely into a war of spirits, all power structures from the old society will have exploded—they are all based on lies: there will be wars such as the earth has never seen."[25]

My goal is not to applaud the prophet Nietzsche for having conceptualized the giant thymotic battles of the twentieth century in advance. Nor do I intend to once again spread out in what sense and based on which teachings Nietzsche was the most inspiring neo-thymotic psychologist of modernity. His fateful interpretation of Christian morality should rather be interpreted within the parameters set by the knowledge of our age as an act of revenge against life. Speaking about "Nietzsche's Philosophy in the Light of Our Experience," as Thomas Mann paradigmatically did in a rich essay in 1947, is not easy. It is not only because of political and technical evolution that the 120 years that separate us from the hysterical-lucid endgame of the author constitute an obstacle for interpretation. Perspectives have shifted significantly; in some cases, even issues of epochal consequence have been clarified.

Today, for example, we can perceive clearly that, in general, Nietzsche's ingenious analysis of resentment and, in particular, of the priestlike type of human being have been burdened by a mistake of address as well as a mistake of dating. The wanderer of Eze and Sils-Maria condemned Christianity by means of a biblical pathos. At the time Christianity had for a long time already not represented an adequate object for such a vehement attack. It had already, particularly in its Protestant wing (which Nietzsche should have known better), mutated into a happy (life-friendly), mild, and humanitarian-supernatural wellness enterprise. The only way it differed from its worldly competitors was in a couple of bizarre suprarational dogmas—complemented by a metaphysically well versed euthanasia, the charms of Church music, and an old-style Sunday collection for the sake of the needy and, lest we forget, a penny for Africa. The fact that Catholicism presented itself after 1870 as being at the peak of its antimodern campaign does not change the general situation. All of its efforts on the theological and political fronts were only the effects of weakness: the flight of the pope into the dogma of infallibility, the mobilization of an external mission, the militant incitement of Marianic fervor, the condemning of liberal and secular books, the founding of ultramontane parties in the parliaments of the secular world. All of these actions revealed the frightful panic of a declining power. The most important symbols for the situation of the Catholic cause remained, despite everything, the expropriation of the church states through the young Italian nation as well as the retreat of the humiliated pope into the walls of the Vatican, where until 1929 he put on the face of a martyr.[26]

At the same time, in the milieu of nationalism and internationalism new and acute breeding grounds for resentment emerged and were supported by an unknown type of clergy, the secular clergy of hate, who stormed against "existing conditions." In defense of Nietzsche's honor, we may say that he was always a strong opponent of both of these tendencies. This does not change the fact that he was wrong about his main enemy and that his main problem consisted in his anachronistic judgment. If it truly was the resistance to resentment that constituted the highest priority of the age, then the "attack" (*Abrechnung*) on Christianity would have had to take a backseat to the struggle against national-revolutionary and world-revolutionary "moodiness" (*Muckertum*), to use Nietzsche's term. In fact, "rage," which is a recurrent point of reference in Nietzsche's deduction of dominating morality from slavish reflexes, can also be applied to the most active movements of resentment of the nineteenth and twentieth centuries. Its timeliness is not exhausted by these considerations. On the basis of everything that we know today about what we might expect, we have to assume that the first half of the twenty-first century will also be characterized by large-scale conflicts. These will be initiated by collectives of rage and by humiliated "civilizations." This is yet one more reason to continue the work that Nietzsche started and to put on the agenda a more fundamental reflection on the causes and effects of rage in modernity.

What primarily needs to be kept in mind against Nietzsche's furious conclusion is that the Christian era, taken as a whole, was not the age of practicing rage. It was an epoch in which an ethics of deferring rage was solemnly implemented. The reason for this is not difficult to identify: it lies in the Christian belief that the justice of God will one day, at the end of all time, ensure that moral actions will be rewarded and immoral actions punished. The prospect of a life after death has always been connected in the Christian sphere of ideas with the expectation of a transhistorical act of balancing pain and suffering. The price for this ethics of abstaining from rage in the present for the sake of retribution in a world beyond was high—Nietzsche's judgment on this point was clear. He insisted on the generalization of a latent resentment that projected the postponed wish for revenge onto its counterpart, the anxiety of being condemned. It was projected into the center of belief, the teaching of last things. The punishment of arrogant people thus became for all eternity the condition for the ambivalent arrangement of men of goodwill with bad circumstances. The side effect of this arrangement was that those people who were good and humble themselves started to be afraid of what they attributed to omniscient evil. I will discuss this issue more extensively in the following chapter, which concerns the wrath of God and the establishment of a transcendent bank of vengeance.

Perfected Capitalism: An Economy of Generosity

IN THE MIDDLE OF THE "AGE OF EXTREMES," AS ERIC HOBSBAWM HAS characterized it,[27] Georges Bataille began to draw from Nietzsche's psychological intuitions their economic consequences. He understood that Nietzsche's attempt to criticize morality, as a last consequence, necessitated a different economy. If one wants to understand morality in terms of thymotic concepts, one needs to reform the economy in a thymotic way. But how could we conceive of an economic life not based on erotic impulses, that is, desire, greed, and impulsive consumption? What would an economy look like were it based on thymotic impulses such as the desire for recognition and self-respect? How would we conceive of the introduction of pride into the capitalist economy, an economy that openly confesses that it abides by the primacy of profit maximization, avarice, an overall unnoble motive that becomes justified even by its defenders only in reference to the claim that the entrepreneurial realist is himself condemned because of the vulgarity of the real. The axiom of everyday business, as is widely known, is that he who wants to come out of a nasty match the winner has to accept the rules of the game. Realism against this background means to be cool with one's cruelty.

The often cited revaluation of values could never approach its goal if it could not manage to show the facts of capitalist economy in a different light. There are two options for the introduction of pride into economy: either one needs to be willing to ruin oneself through ostentatious expenditure for the sake of the prestige of one's name, as did the aristocrats before the French Revolution, or one needs to find a post-aristocratic sovereign use of wealth. The question is thus: Is there an alternative to the blind accumulation of value? Is there an alternative to the chronic trembling in the instant of taking stock? Is there an alternative to the unrelenting compulsion to pay off one's debts?

The search for the answer to these questions leads to a domain in which economic and moral facts are not easy to distinguish. The Nietzsche-inspired critic of the general economy discovers in the heart of common economic life the transformation of moral guilt through monetary debt. It is hardly necessary to state the obvious. The capitalist mode of economy could only have started its victory march because of this pragmatic transformation. The time of guilt is characterized by the pursuit of a criminal by the consequences of his deeds. This time ends consequently with the atonement for the effects of the deeds. To be in debt means thus nothing less than to live through a time of compulsive repayment. However, while guilt makes one depressed, debts make one feel alive, at least as long as they appear together with entrepreneurial energy.[28] Guilt and debt have one decisive connecting trait: both make sure that the lives of those they affect remain bound by a knot created in the past. Jointly they create a retrogressive compulsive union, through which what has been retains its domination over what will be.

To pay off and to pay back are acts that point back to the center of transactions. They are the objective operations that, when translated into subjective feeling, lead to resentment. If one traces the concept of resentment to its material and economic sources, one finds the basic and original conviction that nothing in the world can be gotten for free and that every step must be paid back to the last penny. Here economic thinking passes over into ontology, and ontology, into ethics. Being, which is intended to mean the sum of all transactions, secures a balance between what has been borrowed and what needs to be returned. In the spirit of macroeconomics, which was bewitched at the beginning of the metaphysical era by the idea of reimbursement, one can even interpret death as the repayment of a debt that the recipient of life has borrowed from the giver of life. The highest articulation of this thought appears in an obscure sentence of Anaximander that interprets the basic happening of Being as "reimbursement" (*tisin didonai*).[29] If one wants to understand the degree to which Nietzsche intervenes against the spirit of revenge, one needs to take into account that the author of *Zarathustra* attacks Anaximander himself. Nietzsche aims to efface Anaximander's proposition by stating its opposite: "Observe, there is no retribution."[30]

The other economy is based on the thesis that the worth of paying back is a fiction that is rooted in the compulsive use of the schema of equal value. If one wants to leave the illusion of equivalence one needs to call into question the equals sign between what has been taken and what has been paid back. Moreover, one would have to interrupt the illusion of equal values in order to lend priority to a form of thinking with unequal values. In a transcapitalistic economy, the progressive, creative, giving, and excessive gestures need to become constitutive. Only operations that are engaged for the sake of the future have the power to explode the law of exchanging equivalences, by way of forestalling becoming-guilty and going into debt.

The moral pattern of this new capitalism is the psychologically unlikely but morally indispensable gesture of forgiving someone who is guilty. With this gesture the primacy of the past in a victim-perpetrator relationship is canceled out. The victim supersedes his humanly plausible and psychodynamically legitimate wish for revenge and returns to the perpetrator the freedom to make a new beginning. Wherever this happens, the chain of revenge, the economy of payback, is broken. Through recognizing the inevitable imbalance between guilt and atonement, the person who was harmed once again finds freedom. The time after forgiving can thus gain the quality of an enriching new beginning. With forgiveness, the antigravitational tendency of human coexistence gains the upper hand; antigravitation is movement for the sake of increasing unlikeliness.

In the material sector, the corresponding act is the voluntary offering that is not rooted in having good credit and that does not entail any specific duty on the part of the recipient. The same gesture can manifest itself in the form of debt relief or as the renunciation of the violent collection of an open debt. This also violates the primacy of revenge and the compulsion to pay back. The essence of the gift consists in extending the scope of freedom on the side of the receiver. The gesture is at times augmented to the point of festive generosity, when the giver and the receiver are for a moment connected through joint exaltation, a feeling that can possibly have long-lasting consequences. It stimulates the pride of the recipients to think over what would be an adequate response. It reaches its highest degree in donations to beneficiaries who are not close in time and space to the giver and thus cannot return anything—Nietzsche designed for this form of exaltation the interesting name "love of those most remote" (*Fernstenliebe*). These acts of "giving virtue" leave it up to the future to do with the gift whatever it can and wants. Whereas the common economy that is dictated by the "lower *Eros*" is based on the affects of wanting to have, the thymotic economy is based on the pride of those that are free enough to give.

Bataille traces in Nietzsche's writing the contours of an economy of pride in which the concept of investment is radically modified. While typical investors use their means in order to get back more than they invest, other people invest their resources to satisfy their pride and to attest to their good fortune. Both impulses make it impossible for the providers to expect gains in the same currency, while gains in reputation and pride are completely legitimate and desirable.

However paradoxical this behavior might appear, the economy of pride is founded on the conviction of its participants of their meaningful investments—admittedly only after other dealings have been satisfied. In 1900, the great sponsor Andrew Carnegie expressed this circumstance in a classical expression: "The man who dies thus rich dies disgraced." This is a sentence that the ordinary wealthy person is careful not to cite. From the perspective of experienced givers, holding onto inherited or achieved wealth can only be judged a missed opportunity of expenditure. Whereas the usual types of businessmen can increase, with a bit of luck, their assets or that of their shareholders, this different breed of investor can add new lights to the splendor of the world. Through their dealings, and in how they handle them, they elevate their very existence to splendor. Whoever enjoys this splendor understands that value only comes into being when one, by way of giving everything one has, attests to the existence of things beyond all value; this "constitutes the condition under which alone something can be an end in itself [and] has not merely a relative worth, that is, a price, but an inner worth, that is, *dignity*."[31] The second kind of rich people refrain from the stupidity of accumulation without purpose or goal. They do with their assets things an animal that only wants to have more and more could never achieve. They associate themselves with the power of antigravitation: they change the course of things such that vulgar acts are always more likely to occur.

One has to be careful not to romantically misunderstand Bataille's incitements concerning a universal economy. These ideas do not at all aim at the introduction of a communism for rich people. They also do not point to an aristocratic redistribution of goods in social-democratic or socialist societies. The true significance of these ideas consists in instituting a cleavage within capitalism in order to create its most radical—and only fruitful—opposite. This is different from the traditional conception of the left, a left that has been overpowered by its own depiction of everything as miserable.

If one takes Marx at his word, it becomes clear that the motive for the turn of capitalism against itself was not foreign to him. In contrast, he believed that only the "completion" of the transformation of everything by capitalism could bring about a new form of economy. The possibility of a turn with the name "revolution" is produced by evolution itself. The whole fatal nature of Marxism consists in its undecidability with regard to the question of how much time the capitalist process will in the end need in order to produce the preconditions for a postcapitalist transformation of wealth. Seen from today's perspective, it is self-evident that the big match of capital had, by about 1914, already been played only until about halftime. A long series of intensifications, conflicts, and unraveling still lay ahead. Thus it was still far from being able to transcend itself for the sake of a successive formation. The leaders of the Russian as well as the Chinese revolutions were completely wrong when they claimed Marxist theory for themselves. Both political enterprises created amalgamations of political fundamentalism and aggressive opportunism. Through this combination they lost every sense of economic success, evolution, and necessary temporal order. While the postcapitalistic situation could only be imagined according to Marx's essential writings as the ripe fruit of a capitalism developed "to the end," Lenin and Mao made the principle of the terroristic abuse of unripe conditions into the key to success. Their theories revealed what the term "primacy of politics" implies in its radical interpretation.

One needs to admit that behind the concept of a "perfected capitalism," a long list of unwanted surprises awaits the interpreter, a list no less true today than it was during the time of Marx and Lenin. This concept requires from those who use it a degree of insight into the still unrealized potentials of economic, technical, and cultural evolution, which for understandable reasons the revolutionary leaders could not yet have achieved. At the same time, it demands from those who suffer from the game a degree of patience, a degree that cannot be reasonably expected if one knows where the voyage leads and how long it will last. It is thus not surprising that the idea of "ripe conditions" outgrew the communists, in that this theoretical trope made the revolution necessary where evolution had barely started its work, where productive market economies were to a large degree absent. They tried their best to accomplish the impossible: to transcend capitalism without ever having known it. The flirtations of the Soviets under Stalin and the Chinese in the time of Mao with accelerated industrialization were little more than impotent attempts to keep up an evolutionary appearance. In reality, Lenin's selection of the revolutionary moment was from the beginning purely motivated by opportunism—in accordance with Machiavelli's theory concerning the most favorable opportunity—and Mao Zedong's analogous attacks were to a large degree voluntaristic distortions.

Overhastiness remained the mark of all initiatives in the name of a postcapitalist future from revolutionaries of this kind. It was clear for substantial reasons that the necessary developments would have taken centuries. However, without a sufficient reason—impatience and ambition are never sufficient—the revolutionaries estimated that it would only take a couple of decades; the ultrarevolutionaries even estimated only a few years. The distorted picture with which the revolutionary will justified its plans depicted the chaos of war, post-tsarist Russia, and post-emperor China as "ripe situations." In fact, communism did not produce a postcapitalistic but a postmonetary society. Boris Groys has shown that these societies gave up the steering medium (*Leitmedium*) money in order to replace it with the pure language of command.[32]

The birth defect of the communist idea of economy consisted, however, in more than the magical manipulation of the evolutionary calendar. After all, it cannot be ruled out that revolution comes to the aid of evolution. Its incurable weakness was the furious resentment against property—which expressed itself in the bitter term "private property" (also known as the "private possession of the means of production"), as if everything private could as such be described as something stolen. This affect may claim high moral standards—it is, anyhow, incapable of doing justice to the essence of the modern economy, which is, from the bottom up, based on possession. According to a comparison coined by Gunnar Heinsohn, the communist dismissal of the principle of ownership is akin attempting to accelerate a vehicle by taking out its motor.[33] Moreover, the movements of the left in the Marxist tradition (as well as some of its right-wing fanatic rivals) were never able to get over their mistrust of wealth as such, not even when they proclaimed openly, in close proximity to the government, that they wanted to create wealth more intelligently and distribute it more justly. The left's economic mistake was always at the same time its psychopolitical confessions. To the communists in power, taking satisfaction in the philistine joy of expropriation and longing for revenge against private property was, overall, always more important than any spreading of values. Thus, in the final analysis, not much of the great élan of the egalitarian turn of humanity survived than the blatant self-privileging of functionaries, not to mention the effects of paralysis, resignation, and cynicism.

Nonetheless, at the time of its bloom, the socialist economy also possessed offensive thymotic traits because, as we have seen, all revolutionary projects are borne by and sustained through impulses within the pride-rage-indignation spectrum. Whoever takes the Soviet cult surrounding its "worker heroes" merely as a curiosity in the history of economy needs to consider that left-wing productivism was the attempt to introduce a touch of greatness into a system that suffered from its own vulgar premises.

The thymotic economy latently present in Nietzsche's criticism of morality stimulates an alternative monetary economy in which wealth appears together with pride. Nietzsche's criticism aims to remove the mask of lament from the face of modern prosperity. What is hidden beneath this mask is the self-disdain of mean-spirited owners of large fortunes. They display a form of disdain which is fully legitimate according to Platonic *thymos* theory because the soul of the wealthy rightly attacks itself if it does not find its way out of the circle of insatiability. The pretense of cultivation and interest in culture, which is common in this stratum of society, does not change this fact; interest in fine arts is usually only the Sunday mask of greed. The soul of the wealthy could only be healed through beautiful actions that reclaim the inner approval of the noble part of the soul.

The thymotization of capitalism was not an invention of the twentieth century; it was not necessary to wait for Nietzsche and Bataille to discover its modus operandi. It happens by itself whenever entrepreneurship enters a new territory in order to create the conditions for new revenue and its distributive emission. In regards to creative aggression, capitalism never needed extra help from philosophical mentors. It is not the case that it suffered too much from moral inhibitions. However, also with regard to its generous side, it developed rather uniquely and distinct from philosophy. If at all, it was inspired by Christian motifs, in particular in the Great Britain of the eighteenth and nineteenth centuries. We should not forget that according to Eugen Rosenstock-Huessy's vigilant account, it was in England, even if not often, that a capitalist entrepreneur made four million pounds in earnings in order to give away three million to charity as a Christian gentleman. One of the best known cases of a generous donation from capital gain is connected to the name of Friedrich Engels. For more than thirty years, Engels used the rather modest profits from his factory in Manchester to keep Marx's family in London alive; at the same time, the family head used this money to overthrow an order of things in which a person like Engels was possible and necessary. Be that as it may, the generosity of donators cannot be reduced to a liberalism of "small deeds," typical of bourgeois reform. It would also be inappropriate to dismiss such gestures as paternalism. What becomes visible through them is rather a metacapitalist horizon that becomes clear in the moment capital turns against itself.

"People don't strive for happiness, only the English do."[34] When Nietzsche noted down this bon mot he was probably too heavily influenced by the antiliberal clichés of his time. What makes the aphorism important, nonetheless, is the fact that it reminds us of a time when the resistance to the propaganda of erotization and vulgarization could invoke impulses of pride and honor, impulses that have largely been forgotten today. These impulses established a culture of generosity. This phenomenon increasingly disappears in times of anonymous equity funds. Let us limit ourselves to the assertion that the thymotic use of wealth in the Anglo-American world, above all, in the United States, could become a persistent fact of society. On the European mainland, on the other hand, it could not so far establish itself—largely because of blind trust in the state, subventions, and traditions of celebrating misery.

The Postcommunist Situation

ONE FINAL COMMENT ABOUT THE "SPIRITUAL SITUATION OF OUR TIMES" in order to uncover the strategic perspective of what follows: in the past, one would have called this strategic perspective "engagement." The following considerations are situated within a debate that has moved the intellectual public sphere of the West since the 1990s. To make a long story short, the goal is to take issue with the usual psychopolitical interpretation of the postcommunist situation.

The introduction of this situation was, to a large extent, completely unexpected to people engaging in political debates in 1990. The political interpreters of the postwar era were content with commenting on both the victory of the Allies over the Axis dictatorships and the new world order from the tradition of their discipline. Across the board, there was a large consensus about and commitment to democracy and the free-market economy. Old comrades were granted the meager joy of taking out their antifascist medals from time to time. During this long belle époque (which was only clouded by nuclear threats) there was a consensus that the "working through" of totalitarian excesses in Europe fulfilled the historical obligation of the epoch. Other than that one only needed to sit and watch how liberal civilization with the help of social-democratic correctives made use of the historical demand for a better world. There was hardly anyone who possessed the theoretical means and moral motivation to think beyond the order of the bipolar era. The implosion of the hemisphere of actual socialism did more than condemn its ideologies and institutions to meaninglessness. Most important, it created a situation in which "successful" capitalism had to take on the sole responsibility of the world. But Western thinkers were not provoked into providing exceptionally creative ideas in response to this new order.

It does not require too much concentration to see that some themes and motives of the present book are the product of an imaginary dialogue with Francis Fukuyama's *The End of History and the Last Man*, which originally appeared in 1992. I do not conceal that I am convinced that this publication belongs, in spite of its easily identifiable weak aspects, to the few works of contemporary political philosophy that touch upon the essence of our time. This publication testifies to the fact that academic thinking and presence of mind are not always mutually exclusive. Apart from more recent works by Boris Groys that reveal a new horizon for the diagnosis of our age,[35] Fukuyama's work presents the most thought-through system of analysis

of the postcommunist world situation up until the present day—and the
same can be said about its relationship to political anthropology. In my
opinion, the course of events since 1990 has largely confirmed Fukuyama's
(and implicitly also Alexandre Kojève's) conception, according to which we
can only understand the contemporary global situation if we begin with an
insight into the present state of the struggle for recognition. The fact that
Fukuyama confesses his allegiance to the conservative camp in the United
States does not commit his readers to share the same political affiliation.
The aspects of his work that can be interpreted progressively come to the
fore once one attempts to push the conservative veil to the side. In any case,
the more or less intentionally committed misinterpretations do not deserve
to be taken seriously in a commentary.

Among the interpreters who attribute substantial significance to Fukuyama's attempt to understand the postcommunist situation, Jacques Derrida has, understandably, a special position. In the most insightful of his
political books, *Specters of Marx*, the inventor of "deconstruction" discusses
the theses of *The End of History* in an intensive, if largely skeptical and
sometimes polemical way.[36] Derrida presents a fascinating reconstruction
of Fukuyama's line of argument, not least because Derrida does not argue
in a deconstructive mode—rather he intends to improve the argument.
Derrida is convinced that he is able to prove that Fukuyama's book is in fact
a somewhat hasty application of Hegel to the modern state, a form of Christian eschatology. Such ad hoc narratives, Derrida admits, mainly serve to
satisfy the desire for happy endings to otherwise sad stories. In fact, Fukuyama's book, owing to its evangelic tone, could have only become a media
gadget, more or less misunderstood, as it ran around the world, but without its true problematic having been penetrated. What would be required
for a serious discourse concerning the "end of history" is an illumination
of the obscure relationship between the secular and technological civilizations of the West to the three messianic eschatologies that emerged out of
the religious thinking of the Near East—the Jewish, the Christian, and the
Islamic. It is revealing that in this metaphysical corner of the world, people
still argue about the meaning of the course of the world and the spiritual
orientation of politics at large. "The war for the 'appropriation of Jerusa-
lem' is today the world war. It is happening everywhere, it is the world."[37]
What can be brought to bear against Fukuyama is, according to Derrida, his
hidden, one-sided dependence on the customs of Christian messianology:
it is well known that Christians conceive the Messiah as someone who has

arrived, whereas Derrida emphasizes the Jewish emphasis on waiting for the one who has not yet come. An analogous relation is present in the political narratives concerning the establishment of democracy in bourgeois societies. While the interpreter of successful liberal civilization thinks he is able to assume the actual presence of democracy, his critic firmly defends the view that democracy could only be conceived of as a democracy to come, a future democracy.

As inspiriting as Derrida's commentary on *The End of History* may be, if one compares Fukuyama's book and Derrida's commentary, what comes to mind is that Derrida, without providing any justification, did not adequately discuss the serious part of Fukuyama's attempt to present a contemporary form of thymotology. Derrida justifies this neglect by briefly stating that Fukuyama's conception of *thymos* and *megalothymia* (the human right of pride and greatness) is intended as a counterweight to the one-sidedness of Marxist materialism. To put it mildly, this judgment reveals a rather selective reading of Fukuyama. We thus have to conclude that even such an eminent reader as Derrida missed the point of Fukuyama's book. Following the traces (*Spuren*) of Alexandre Kojève and Leo Strauss, Fukuyama's book intends nothing less than the recovery of an authentic political psychology on the basis of a reestablished polarity of eros and *thymos*. It is obvious that this political psychology, which has hardly anything in common with so-called mass psychology and other applications of psychoanalysis to political issues, moved to the center of the current need for a new theoretical orientation through the course of world-historical events.

No one who understands something about the rules of literary criticism is surprised that, overall, Fukuyama's book received such bad press in European reviews. Its readers wanted to understand it mostly as an extended victory cry of liberalism after the implosion of the Soviet Union and the disappearance of the "socialist alternative." It was presumed that the author, with his thesis concerning the end of history, only provided an updated version of Yankee ideology, according to which the American way of life meant the completion of human evolution from the desert to the shopping mall, from the hand axe to the ballot, from sitting around a bonfire to using the microwave. Since this initial reaction, sneering references to Fukuyama's book became a running gag in the political feuilletons in Europe. Many contributors never tired of repeating that history has, of course, in reality not come to an end and that the victorious West must not sit still after a partial victory in the struggle against ideological specters.

This position is, by the way, fully justified—yet we need to understand it completely differently from the way it is understood by the authors of the abovementioned reviews.

I do not want to ponder for too long the observation that these objections are often presented in a tone of neorealist arrogance, as if the commentators feel superior the moment they uncover a philosophical author as announcing allegedly naïve messages. The anti-intellectual affect of Fukuyama's critics should be mentioned as only an aside. When historians defend themselves against the danger of being fired because of a philosopher, this is not unreasonable. In reality, the author anticipated the most essential concerns and objections of his critics. In the concluding chapter of his book, which carries the ominous title "The Last Men," he pursues with astonishing sensitivity the question of whether the currently successful liberal democracy is actually capable of providing the complete satisfaction of the intellectual and material needs of all of its citizens. His answer is the answer of a skeptical conservative who knows that there are contradictions "at the heart of our liberal order, even after the last fascist dictator, swaggering colonel, or Communist party boss has been driven from the face of the earth."[38]

One can thus not identify the diagnostic lesson that is concealed in *The End of History*. The title only quotes, as we have stated, an original interpretation of Hegel's philosophy by Alexandre Kojève, an interpretation Kojève had already developed in the 1930s. Kojève located the "end of history" in the year of the appearance of the *Phenomenology of Spirit*, 1807. Fukuyama's original insight consists in his attentive observation that wars of prestige and struggles of jealousy between the citizens of the free world moved to center stage just at the moment when the mobilization of civil energies for wars at the outer fronts came to an end. Successful liberal democracies, the author understands, will always be infiltrated by currents of free-floating dissatisfaction. This has to be the case because human beings are condemned to suffer from thymotic unrest, and "last men" even more than everyone else, even though the mass culture we witness in posthistory initially appears in the form of eroticism. The ambitions addressed by mass culture can be as little satisfied as the ambitions of resentments (at least in the case of the greater success of other people).

Once the physical battles have been fought, the metaphysical battles begin. The latter are inevitable because the activity of the liberal world, which consists in the mutual recognition of all by all as equal citizens of society, is in truth far too formal and unspecific to open up individual access to happiness. Especially in a world of universally amended liberties, human beings cannot cease to strive for the specific forms of recognition manifested in prestige, wealth, sexual advantage, and intellectual superiority. Because such goods will always remain scarce, in liberal systems there will always be a large reservoir of distrust and frustration in inferior competitors—not to mention those who are truly worse off and the de facto excluded. The more a "society" is satisfied in its basic features, the more colorfully the jealousy of all against all will flourish. This jealousy entangles candidates vying for better positions in petty wars that permeate all aspects of their lives. At the same time, the system of the "open society" has the advantage of also employing the darker energies. Jealousy constantly generates alternative preferences, in particular in the domain of the ever-increasing and ever-differentiating culture and media business. Sports have become indispensable as an expansive system of winning and becoming famous, of stimulating and channeling postmodern excesses of ambition. Taken as a whole, it can be said that in the insatiable prestige battles of posthistory, elites continuously emerge from nonelites. If a public sphere is dominated by the expressive lives of countless actors who can never really be on top and yet have advanced significantly, then one can be certain that what we are dealing with is a flourishing democracy.

The old world knew slave and serf, the bearers of the unhappy consciousness of their time. Modernity has invented the loser. This figure, which one meets halfway between yesterday's exploited and today's and tomorrow's superfluous, is the misunderstood product of the power games of democracies. Not all losers can be pacified by pointing out that their status corresponds to their poor placement in a contest. Many will object by saying that they have never gotten a chance to participate in order to be positioned according to their merits. Their resentful feelings turn not just against the winners but also against the rules of the game. When the loser who loses too often calls into question the game as such by means of violence, this makes conspicuous the state of emergency (*Ernstfall*) of a politics after the end of history. The new emergency currently presents itself in two forms: in liberal democracy as a postdemocratic politics of order, which expresses itself as the degeneration of politics into policing and in the transformation of politicians into agents of consumer protection; and in frustrated countries torn by civil war, wherein armies of powerful, superfluous people (*Überflüssigen*) continue to annihilate one another.[39]

In the meantime, we have understood that not only the "contradictions" at the heart of our own system but the political culture of the West and its offspring civilizations in the East and in the South have tampered with the postcommunist situation. New movements of militant and energetic, superfluous malcontents, rapidly growing networks that channel the hatred of losers, subterranean proliferations of methods of sabotage and destruction all seem to be responsible for the return of historical terror and the corresponding hopes. It is against the background of such phenomena that we have to understand the countless treatises about the "return" or the "new beginning" of history, which have been flooding the essay market of the West for several years now. The common denominator of such commentaries is the automatic allegation that outbreaks of violence on the global stage would be a new start of a history that had temporarily slowed down. Unmistakably, we are dealing with a simplified version of Hegelianism: if history until now advanced through struggling opposition (as the popularized version of dialectics assumes), we may legitimately conclude that the appearance of new combatants continues the process of history.

It needs to be clarified, against what is proclaimed in the literature, that the occurrence of terrorism in Western civilization's relationship to the outside world, on the one hand, and a new form of the social question in its internal relationships, on the other, should precisely not be understood as a sign of the "return" of history. The modus vivendi of the West and its offspring cultures is indeed posthistorical in essential points. Its form is no longer oriented by *epos* and tragedy; pragmatically, it can no longer be constructed on the successes of a unilateral style of action. At the same time, given the present state of affairs, it is not possible to situate anywhere an alternative to the Western model.[40] So-called global terrorism, especially, is a thoroughly posthistorical phenomenon. Its time starts when the rage of those who have been excluded connects to the infotainment industry of those who have been included, merging into a violent system-theater for "last men." To impute to this business of terror historical meaning would be a macabre abuse of already exhausted language resources. The eternal recurrence of the same, no matter as one-eyed rage or as a form of rage short-sighted in both eyes, does not suffice to speak of a restoration of historical existence. Who wants to attribute clear sight to wearers of black eye patches, to allow them to define the state of evolution?

Concerning the new social question, it is obvious that a return to the mistakes of the past cannot provide a solution. Only a repetition of the posthistorical compromise between capital and labor, that is to say, the future, could provide for a relative appeasement on this front. This would imply a taming of the speculative monetary economy (in recent terms, the capitalism of parasites) and the quick implementation of an economy based on private property in developing countries. To point to the necessity of extending the welfare state to the supranational level describes the horizon for a serious new social politics. The only alternative to such a politics would be the authoritarian turn of world capitalism, in which certain fatal options of the 1920s and 1930s would reappear on the agenda. Indicators pointing in these directions are not at all lacking if one inspects the global situation today.

The second macropolitical task of the future, the integration of non-human actors, forms of life, ecosystems, and "things" in general into the domain of civilization does not have anything in common with traditional questions surrounding history as we have known it. What is sometimes referred to as "ecopolitics" generally rests on the presupposition that problems that have been caused by human beings should be solved by the originators and those affected. This again leads to organizational, administrative, and civilizational tasks, but not to epics and tragedies.[41] Finally, the third major task of the future will be the neutralization of potential genocides in the countries of the Near and Middle East and elsewhere, countries that are populated by angry young men. This task can only be tackled with the help of a politics of posthistorical dedramatization. Time is required for all of these processes. What we do not need is a relapse into "history" as such, but exclusively a time of education (*Lernzeit*) for civilizations.

The reader now only needs to be warned against misunderstanding the indicated recourse to Plato's implicit and secret return to Greek idealism. Plato is appealed to here as the teacher of a more mature view of culturally and politically effective ambition dynamics. We listen to him like we would listen to a guest lecturer visiting us from an eclipsed star. Apart from that, the turn to a higher form of psychological realism has to be carried out using the theoretical means of our time. It will only succeed if one can withstand the temptation to which the European intellectuals in the twentieth century succumbed, willingly and often. These intellectuals have even shown an anticipatory obedience with regard to the suggestive force of realism. They have always showed too much understanding for the all-too-normal actions of human beings who are stimulated by desire and resentment—and justified this understanding in the name of the always one-sided, downcast view of "reality."

Nietzsche's central didactic idea concerning the death of God gains an importance within the context of this introduction. Its psychopolitical implications can be felt with palpable delay. "God is dead" means now that we live in a time in which the old absorption of rage through an austere beyond that demands respect increasingly vanishes. The deferral of human rage in favor of the wrath of God at the end time is no longer an acceptable imposition for countless people, and has not been for quite a while. Such a situation indicates the likelihood of an overthrow. The politics of impatience expands accordingly. It finds adherents not the least among ambitious people who have a talent for expressing their outrage. These actors believe that they should start an assault as soon as nothing can be lost, neither here nor there. Who could deny that the exorbitant terror of the past century—it suffices to refer to the Russian, German, and Chinese exterminations—resulted from the ideological outbreaks of rage through the medium of secular agencies? Who could miss that the stage for the terrors of the twenty-first century has already been set up today?

Thus the way any understanding of both recent catastrophes and those that now announce themselves first needs to recall theology. The alliance between rage and eternity was a Christian axiom. I will have to show how it was possible for the constellation of rage and time—or rage and history—to emerge from this. In our religiously illiterate decades, people have almost completely forgotten that to speak of God in monotheism meant always at once to speak of a wrathful God. A wrathful God is the great impossible variable of our age. But what if, beneath the surface, he is working on becoming our contemporary once again?

Before once again calling attention to this figure that has been covered by the ruins of history, it is useful to look more closely at the business terms of the economy of rage.

RAGE TRANSACTIONS

Rage, oh rage,
is a pleasure that is preserved for the wise.

—DA PONTE AND MOZART,
LE NOZZE DI FIGARO, 1786

THERE IS NO PERSON LIVING TODAY WHO HAS NOT REALIZED that the Western world, and through it also indirectly all other areas of the world, is being irritated by a new theme. With a concern that is half true and half put-on, Westerners raise an alarm: "Hatred, revenge, irreconcilable hostility have suddenly appeared again among us! A mixture of foreign forces, unfathomable as the evil will, has infiltrated the civilized spheres."

Some people, engaged for the sake of morality, make similar observations with a form of realism marked by a tone of reproach. They emphasize that the so-called foreign forces cannot confront us as absolutely foreign. What many people pretend to experience as a terrible surprise is, according to the moralist, only the flipside of the domestic modus vivendi. The end of pretense lies before us. "Citizens, consumers, pedestrians, it is urgent to wake up from lethargy! You do not know that you still have enemies, and you don't want to know because you have chosen harmlessness!" The new appeals to awakening the conscience aim to enforce the idea that the real has not been tamed, not even in the great bubble of irreality that encloses citizens of affluent society like the womb protects a fetus. If what is real is taken to be what could kill, the enemy presents the purest incarnation of the real. With the renaissance of the possibility of hostility, the return of the old-fashioned real lies before us. From this, one can learn that a controversial topic is put on the agenda only when an irritation is transformed into an institution—an institution with visible protagonists and permanent employees, customer service, and its own budget, with professional conferences, public relations, and continuing reports from the problem area. The constant visitor in the West, the spirit of revenge, can profit from all of this. It can say to itself: I irritate, therefore I am.

Who could deny that, as usual, the alarmists are almost right? The inhabitants of affluent nations sleepwalk mostly within illusions of apolitical pacifism. They spend their days in gold-plated unhappiness. At the same time, their molesters, their virtual hangmen, immerse themselves at the margins of happiness zones in the manuals of explosive chemistry. These manuals have been checked out of the public libraries of the host country. Once one has listened to the alarm for some time, one feels like one is viewing the opening credits of a disturbing documentary where the naïve and its opposite are put into a perfidiously astonishing sequence by directors who know how to create effects: new fathers open up cans of food for their children; working mothers put a pizza in the preheated oven; daughters swarm into the city in order to make use of their awakening femininity; pretty salesgirls step outside during a short break to smoke a cigarette while returning the gaze of those passing by. In the suburbs, petrified foreign students put on belts filled with explosives.

THE MONTAGE OF SUCH SCENES FOLLOWS LOGICS THAT CAN EASILY BE understood. Many authors who see their vocation as educating the public in matters of politics—among them neoconservative editorial writers, political antiromantics, wrathful exegetes of the reality principle, converted Catholics, and disgusted critics of consumerism—want to reintroduce into a population of overly relaxed citizens the basic concepts of the real. For this purpose they quote the most recent examples of bloody terror. They show how hatred enters standard civil contexts. They do not tire of claiming that under the well-kept façades, amok has already for a long time been running. They constantly have to scream: this is not a drill! Because for quite some time the public has become used to the routine translation of real violence into mere images, into entertaining and terrifying, pleading and informative images. The public experiences the development of opposition as a tasteless regression into a dialect extinct for many years.

BUT HOW IS IT POSSIBLE TO SERIOUSLY PRESENT RAGE AND ITS EFFECTS, its proclamations and explosions as news? What needed to be intentionally forgotten before the desire could emerge to stare at those who effectively practice revenge against their alleged or real enemies as if they were visitors from distant galaxies? How was it at all possible, after the disappearance of the West-East divide in 1991, for us to come to believe that we had been thrown into a universe in which individuals and collectives could let go of their capacity to have revengeful feelings? Is it not the case that resentment is what is distributed the most around the world, even more so than *bon sens*?

Starting with the mythic era, it has been part of popular wisdom that the human being is that animal unable to cope with too many things. Nietzsche would say that the human being as such has something "German" to it. It is not capable of digesting the poisons of memory and suffers from certain unfriendly impressions. The saying that "sometimes the past does not want to pass" preserves the ordinary version of the sophisticated insight that human existence is initially just the peak of cumulative memory. Memory does not merely mean the spontaneous activity of the internal sense of time. It is not merely the ability to counteract the immediate disappearance of the lived moment by "retention," that is, an inner, automatic function of holding onto temporal consciousness. It is also connected to a saving function that enables the coming back to virtual topics and scenes. Memory is a result of the generation of networks through which the new introduces itself compulsively, and like an addiction, into older episodes of pain. Neuroses and national sensibilities have in common these movements in the domain of trauma. We know about neurotics that they prefer to, again and again, repeat their accident. Nations include the remembrance of their defeats at cult sites to which their citizens periodically go on pilgrimages. Thus it is necessary to put on stage all kinds of cultures of memory both detached from ourselves and with unconditional mistrust, no matter if the memories are dressed in religious, civil, or political garments. Under the pretense of purifying, emancipating, or merely creating identity, memories inevitably support some secret tendency to repeat and reenact.

Even popular victimology more or less understands the reactions of injured people. Through bad experiences they are dislocated from the happy-forgetful center of society to its slippery margins, from which there is no longer any simple return to normal life. One understands this eccentric dynamic right away: to the victims of injustice and defeat, consolation through forgetting often appears unreachable. If it appears unreachable, it also appears unwanted, even unacceptable. This means that the fury of resentment begins at the moment the person who is hurt decides to let herself fall into humiliation as if it were the product of choice. To exaggerate pain in order to make it bearable, to transcend one's depressed suffering, to "sport with his misery"—quoting Thomas Mann's sensitive and humorous coinage about the primal father Jacob[1]—to extend the feeling of suffered injustice to the size of a mountain in order to be able to stand on its peak full of bitter triumph: these escalating and twisting movements are as old as injustice, itself seemingly as old as the world. Isn't "world" the name for the place in which human beings necessarily accumulate unhappy memories of injuries, insults, humiliations, and all kinds of episodes for which one wants revenge? Are not all civilizations, either openly or in secret, always archives of collective trauma? Considerations like these allow us to draw the conclusion that measures taken to extinguish or contain smoldering memories of suffering have to belong to the pragmatic rules of every civilization. How would it be possible for citizens to go to bed peacefully if they had not called a *couvre-feu* for their internal fires?

Because cultures always also have to provide systems for healing wounds, it is plausible to develop concepts that span the entire spectrum of wounds, visible and invisible. This has been done by modern trauma sciences, which started from the insight that for moral facts it is also useful to apply physiological analogies, if only within certain limits. To use a familiar example, in the case of open bodily wounds, blood comes into contact with air, and as a result of biochemical reactions the process of blood clotting starts. Through it, an admirable process of somatic self-healing comes about, a process that belongs to the animal heritage of the human body. In the case of moral injuries we could say that the soul comes into contact with the cruelty of other agents. In such cases subtle mechanisms for the mental healing of wounds are also available—spontaneous protest, the demand to bring the perpetrator immediately to justice, or, if this is not possible, the intention to take matters into one's own hands when the time comes. There is also the retreat into oneself, resignation, the reinterpretation of the crime scene, the rejection of the truth of what happened, and, in the end, when only a drastic psychic treatment seems to work, the internalization of the violation as a subconsciously deserved penalty even to the point of the masochistic worship of the aggressor. In addition to this medicine chest for the injured self, Buddhism, Stoicism, and Christianity developed moral exercises to enable the injured psyche to transcend the circle of injuries and revenge as such.[2] As long as history is an endless pendulum of hit and retaliation, wisdom is required to bring the pendulum to a halt.

It is not only common wisdom and religion that have adopted the moral healing of wounds. Civil society also provides symbolic therapies intended to support the psychic and social reactions to the injuries of individuals and collectives. Since ancient times, conducting trials in front of courts has made certain that the victims of violence and injustice can expect reparation in front of a gathered people. Through such procedures is practiced the always precarious transformation of the desire for revenge into justice. However, just as a festering wound can become both a chronic and general malady, psychic and moral wounds also may not heal, which creates its own corrupt temporality, the infinity of an unanswered complaint. This implies the trial without satisfactory sentence and calls forth the feeling in the prosecutor that the injustice inflicted upon him is rather increased through the trial. What is to be done when the juridical procedure is experienced as an aberration? Can the matter be settled through the sarcastic remark that the world will one day go down because of its official administration—a statement perpetually reinvented as often as citizens experience the indolence of administrative bodies? Isn't it more plausible to assume that rage itself engages in payback? Isn't it more plausible to assume that rage, as a self-proclaimed executor, goes so far as to knock on the door of the offended?

RAGE RECOUNTED

THE EVIDENCE FOR THIS POSSIBILITY EXISTS IN COUNTLESS exemplary case studies, some more recent and some older. The search for justice has always brought about a second, wild form of the judiciary in which the injured person attempts to be both judge and warden at once. What is noteworthy about these documents, given our present perspective, is that only with the beginning of modernity was the romanticism of self-administered justice invented. Whoever speaks of modern times without acknowledging to what extent it is shaped by a cult of excessive rage suffers from an illusion. This is, even to the present day, the blind spot of cultural history—as if the myth of the "process of civilization" did not aim only to make invisible the release of vulgar manners under conditions of modernity but also to inflate revenge phantasms. While the global dimension of Western civilization aims at the neutralization of heroism, the marginalization of military virtue, and the pedagogical enhancement of peaceful social affects, the mass culture of the age of enlightenment reveals a dramatic recess in which the veneration of vengeful virtues, if we may so call them, reaches new, bizarre extremes.

This phenomenon can be traced back centuries before the French Revolution. The Enlightenment not only releases polemics of knowledge against ignorance but also invents a new quality of the guilty verdict by declaring all old conditions unjust before the demands of the new order; hereby the ecosystem of resignation begins to totter. Since time immemorial, human beings learned in this ecosystem to accept the apparent inevitabilities of misery and injustice. The Enlightenment was thus required to allow revenge to be promoted to an epochal motive, as it dominated private as well as political affairs. Since the past is fundamentally always unjust, the inclination increases, not always but with increased regularity, to extol revenge as just.

OF COURSE, ANTIQUITY ALREADY KNEW GREAT ACTS OF REVENGE. From the furies of Orestes to the hysterics of Medea, ancient theater paid tribute to the dramatic potency of revengeful forces. *Mythos* knew as well from early on about the danger that begins with humiliation, a danger almost like a natural disaster. Medea's example shows particularly well the idea that the female psyche passes from pain to insanity with terrific velocity. This is what Seneca wanted to show when he depicts the hysterical heroine as an exemplary deterrent. In modern terminology, one would call attention to the fact that the passive-aggressive character is disposed to enter into states of excess whenever, by way of exception, she decides to become offensive. This is the framing of women on the rage stage, and, often, the privilege of the "great scene" ("*großen Szene*") has always belonged to the "angry sex." The ancients never imagined taking such exempla as anything other than warnings to orient themselves to the middle, away from excesses.

In the *Eumenides*, one of the key plays of Athenian drama, with which the Atride Trilogy of Aeschylus comes to an end, what is at issue is nothing less than the complete break with the older culture of revenge and fate as well as the introduction of a political concern for justice. This form of political justice should be practiced in the future exclusively in civil courts. What is required for the establishment of such courts is the sensible theological-psychosemantic operation in which the old dignified goddesses of vengeance, the Erinnyen, are renamed as the Eumenides, which means "those who want good" or "those caring for what is beautiful." The meaning of the name change is unmistakable: "Where vengeance compulsion was, balanced, prudent justice will be."

Whatever criteria one has in mind when searching the libraries of the Old World, one will come across a large amount of references to the elementary force of rage and the campaigns of vengeful fury. There are traces of a more or less serious game with the romantic fire of rage, though this will become a dominant motive only with the eighteenth century's emerging culture of civil society. Since then, one great revenger hunts another, accompanied by the sympathy of the audience of the modern imaginary. From the noble robber Karl Moor to the angry veteran John Rambo; Edmond Dantes, the mysterious Count of Monte Christo to Harmonica, the hero of *Once Upon a Time in the West*, who has committed his life to a private nemesis; Judah ben Hur, who exacted revenge against the spirit of imperial Rome with his victory in an ominous chariot race, to the Bride, alias Black Mamba, the protagonist of *Kill Bill*, who works through her death list. The time of those who live for the "great scene" has come.[3] When Durrenmatt's old lady comes for a visit, she exactly knows who needs to be liquidated out of the group of friends. Brecht's dreaming Pirate Jenny even knows a better answer to the question "Who is to die?": all.

Stories of this kind seem to be natural ballads. By themselves they appear to aspire to a superior form of recitation and epic detail. By making visible the relationship between suffered injustice and just retribution, more recent acts of rage provide an illustration of the causality of fate. We moderns do not like to dispense with this lesson, however much we agree otherwise with the exercise of enlightenment, that is, the suspension of blind fate. The well-constructed story of rage provides the sublime for the people. It provides the audience with a compact formula for moral if/then relationships even if they pay the price of suspending the slow, formal application of the rule of law in order to practice a quicker form of retaliation. Moreover, rage satisfies the popular interest in acts of which the perpetrator can legitimately be proud: such stories focus on the avengers, who by directly paying back for their humiliation release a part of the discontent with judicial civilization. They provide satisfying proof that the modern person does not always have to travel the windy road of resentment and the steep steps of the judiciary

process in order to articulate thymotic emotions. In the case of injuries leading to chronic illness, rage is still the best therapy. This feeling constitutes
the reason for the pleasure taken in base things.

The dangerous liaisons between the revenge motif and popular narrative
do not need to be unfolded in detail at this point. Apparently these linkages
are so deep that sometimes the return of modern art to its great epic form
is helpful—as in the case of the abovementioned work from the century of
narrative film, *Once Upon a Time in the West*. It has rightly been claimed
that this work provided the art of film with the proof that two formally
impossible things were in fact possible: that serious opera can be appropriated through film and that the lost form of epic can once again be given a
contemporary form.

The affinity between rage and popular narrative forms could be illus-
trated by drawing on a countless number of more recent documents. One
example is particularly illuminating: the picturesque life history of the
Indian rebel Phoolan Devi (1968–2001). From the state of Uttar Pradesh,
Phoolan, when she was still quite a young woman, was the main actress of a
widely watched reality drama that aired across the whole of the Indian sub-
continent. After she had been collectively abused and raped by her husband
and other male inhabitants of her village (including policemen), she fled
and joined a group of bandits with whom she devised a plan to ambush and
liquidate those who were guilty of the crimes against her. The corpse of her
husband is said to have been put onto a donkey and chased through the village. The simple folk celebrated the rebel as an emancipated heroine and saw
her as an avatar of the gruesome-sublime goddess Durga Kali. The photo-
graph that depicts Phoolan Devi's handover of her weapons to Indian law
enforcement officials is one of the archetypical press images of the twentieth
century. One can see in the young fighter all the concentrated anger of being
given over to her undecided fate. After eleven years of prison, without trial,
the "Bandit Queen" was pardoned. Then she was elected into the Indian
parliament, where she served as an inspiring role model for the countless
disenfranchised women of her country. In June 2001, she was shot in broad
daylight in Delhi, probably by a relative of one of her killed rapists. When
she was still alive, Indian folklore took up the story of this charismatic figure, and Phoolan Devi was transformed into the heroine of a popular epic
still sung by Indian villagers.

Rarely do the archaic and the modern interpretations of vengeful rage
come together in one individual action. In what follows I want to follow up

on the assumption that, through the process of modernization, the novel increasingly returns from a literary and ideological mode to the life of individuals and to public perception. A convincing example of this has recently moved the public in Germany, Switzerland, and the former Soviet states. Vitalij K., an engineer from the Caucasus republic of Ossetia, lost his wife and two children in a plane crash caused by human negligence; after a year of mourning, he decided to seek revenge in the name of his family.

On July 1, 2002, a Bashkir passenger airplane from Moscow collided with a DHL freight plane 36,000 feet above Lake Constance. The incident occurred close to the town of Owing, and all seventy-one passengers lost their lives. Among other factors, the accident occurred because of false directions from the control tower in Zurich-Kloten. When the control tower operator in charge realized that both machines were on a collision course, he advised the pilot of the Russian plane orally to immediately start to descend. At the same time, the on-board computer indicated that he should accelerate. The fatal crash happened because the Russian captain gave more credence to the oral instructions, while the DHL place started to decline at the advice of the on-board computer. The ball of fire on the sky above Lake Constance could be seen almost a hundred miles away. In February 2003, the man from Ossetia, who had been born in 1956 and who could be called a winner of the postcommunist situation, appeared at the house of the Danish control tower operator near Zurich. He killed the operator on the terrace of his house by repeatedly stabbing him with a knife.

Before the drama in February 2003, Vitalij K. had attracted attention because he sometimes referred to "Caucasian methods" of conflict resolution. It is clear that the act of Vitalij K. came from a transformation of the work of mourning into a work of rage. Part of this work of rage was the sentence against the controller at the end of a short trial carried out by the court of his own intuition; the sentence was complemented by a penalty phase in which the judge slipped into the role of the hangman. This is a pattern that has increasingly permeated public consciousness since the beginning of modernity. It is not surprising that the Russian public passionately followed the trial in Zurich of Vitalij K. during October 2005 and then protested his eight-year prison sentence. The avenger was promoted to the status of a national hero in his country of origin and across most of the former Soviet Union; for large parts of the population, he served as an object of identification.

FROM CASES SUCH AS THIS, ONE CAN DRAW THE CONCLUSION THAT vengeful impulses do not easily return to reality, at least not as long as cultural codes have failed to establish the conditions for such a return. We can speak of a return, even of a regression, insofar as such acts cannot claim to be justified anymore by official culture. In terms of the history of ideas, the era of the tribal commandment to engage in blood feuds is more than two millennia behind us. Granted, this is not the case everywhere. But the monopoly over violence that the modern state enjoys finds acceptance as a psychopolitical norm from a large majority of citizens and is supported almost without objections by the official pedagogy. Yet it cannot be denied that the imaginary produced by mass media provides an important space for the phantasm of the moral state of exception, including the vengeful attempt to come to terms with rage.

In order to make plausible the return of personal acts of revenge we have to assume that the force of the political and juridical civilization has become discredited. When the public order is accused of malfunctioning or of being a part of the problem (we might think of preferential treatment in court proceedings), individuals can take themselves to be appointed to represent justice as wild judges. In this sense it is possible to take modern revenge romanticism to be a specific part of an all-encompassing return to heroism. According to Hegel's insight, a hero in antiquity was someone who does what is necessary as an individual, someone who accomplishes what could not have been accomplished from the universal at that point in time; the heroism of the moderns lives off the intuition that even after the erection of the rule of law, there can emerge situations in which the universal is no longer operative. That even the nation, or rather the government, can be determined by heroic and revenge-romantic reflexes is suggested by the example of the Israeli president Golda Meir. After Palestinian terrorists attacked the quarters of the Israeli team during the 1972 Olympic Games in Munich, Meir is said to have ordered Mossad, the Israeli secret service, to track the perpetrators and their supporters and kill them without any legitimacy from a court proceeding. This operation (with the code name "The Wrath of God") was less a part of governmental action than a service to the imaginary of mass culture.

The popular and anarchist doubt about the regulatory power of "existing conditions" is connected to the tendency toward the new form of heroic action. Another consequence is the assumption of a permanent state of exception, and thus of the inclination of the actors to claim the right to help themselves in their singular situations. Indeed, some theoreticians of the left such as Walter Benjamin and later Antonio Negri articulated the dangerous suggestion that for the majority of human beings living under conditions of capitalism, the permanent state of exception is normal.[4] Once the "order of things" has become delegitimized, improvisations are needed, including some rough ones. Only a small step is required to go from the political and moral delegitimation of circumstances to their ontological delegitimation, and ontological delegitimations call into question not only the normative foundations of the institutions of the ancien régime but also the authority of the past as such. Once this moment has come, so-called reality becomes an object for revision and, if necessary, is authorized to be torn down. In light of this, the militant slogan of the twentieth century, transformed by Sartre, "*on a raison de se révolter*," would have to be slightly altered. It would need to be translated as: "not he who revolts against what exists is in the right, but he who avenges against it."

The Aggressor as Giver

IN MY ANALYSIS OF RAGE, IT IS NECESSARY TO FIRST TURN TO ITS energetic dimension, and later I will turn to its temporal and pragmatic dimensions. This requires a certain asceticism with regard to reactions and patterns of interpretations. Initially it is necessary to bracket the desire to emphasize the devastating dynamism of rage. The concept of "destruction," at least, needs to be separated from any kind of moral valuation. It has to be understood as a metabolic phenomenon that needs to be investigated beyond either appraisal or criticism. The alleged or real tendency of rage to explode without concern for the future should not be put at center stage prematurely. Finally, it is necessary to leave out the common psychological attributions of motivation, as well as character diagnoses.

This provides a more even-tempered view of the phenomenon of rage, one that acknowledges that we are primarily dealing with an intensive form of energy that is ready to explode or be transferred. If one follows the image of effervescence, which already led the ancient authors to speak of *furor*, of eruption and storming ahead, it becomes apparent how much the expression of rage possesses a giving, even a paradoxically generous trait. As a form of pure extroversion, the uninhibited expression of "foaming" rage adds an especially energetic supplement to the inventory of deeds. Naturally these mostly reveal themselves in a negative light because at first sight they seem only to consist of uproar and suffering. It is easier to become aware of the giving dimension of rage if one regards the object of rage under the aspect of its similarity with the subject.

Whether rage comes on the scene like a sudden explosion or like chronic presentiment (after its hate-inflicted transformation into a project), it draws its force from an excess of energy that longs for release. Rage that manifests itself in punishment or acts of injury is connected to the belief that there is too little suffering in the world on a local or global level. This belief results from the judgment that suffering could be "deserved" in certain situations. The rage bearer sees in those people who are unjustly without suffering his most plausible enemies. He will never be content with the fact that pain is distributed unevenly to the point of intolerability. He wants to return a fair share of the excess of pain that has been stored up inside him to the person who caused it but has not yet been punished. He is infused with the knowledge that those without pain exist in a state of acute deficiency, and what they are missing is suffering. Seeing the deserving go unpunished leads the vengeful individual to the conviction that he owns what others are lacking. He wants to become a donor, a profligate spender, even if he must force his gifts onto their recipients. Their habit of refusing to accept only provides rage and hatred with an additional motive to turn against its addressees.

There cannot be any doubt that there is a link between rage and pride, thanks to which rage provides itself with a moral certainty of its own legitimacy. The higher the factor of pride in rage, the more effectively will the "you may" be transformed into a "you should." The completely motivated vengeful action would be one that takes itself to be the execution of an indispensable, noble necessity. The corresponding empirical models would be revenge murders at the family level and wars of religion and independence on the ethnic and national levels.

As I have already stated, the rage bearer possesses the immediate evidence to assist the object of her rage in overcoming his own lack. Hours not spent in agony, a burning loss that needs to be suffered, a house that still stands in place without having been bombed, a knife that does not stick in the gut of a slanderer: these nuisances need to be overcome. Much more so than in the case of envy, which aims to humiliate and expropriate, rage (and likewise hatred, the conservation of rage) is an intensive turning toward the addressee in the game because it requires an act of authentic expenditure. One thus rightly says that human beings are as a consequence "inflicted with" pain. The vengeful inflictor feels like someone who is rich enough to share something of his richness with his contemporaries.

As a rule, the donation of pain is sent to a precise address; however, the gift usually extends beyond the immediate recipient to affect those near her as well. Often the donator of pain agrees to this excess: if the individual designated as object of rage led a pain-free life, then most likely the people in close proximity also led lives without suffering, defective lives. In this sense it never appears to be completely false for the donator of pain to involve these people. The more desperately the rage bearer's unconditional wish to give expresses itself, the less it is limited by a certain determinate addressee. Just like civil enthusiasm thinks it is embraced by the millions, rage that has been amplified to hatred addresses itself to a universe of unknown people. It is an affect capable of forming obscure general concepts and elevating itself to the level of vague abstractions.

When rage becomes hatred we can witness the basic operations of ideology formation because conceptual fixations are the best preservative for ephemeral responses. He who wants to remember his rage needs to preserve it in hate containers. The advantage of these conceptualizations of rage is that they can be used extensively without ever being used up entirely. Absolute hatred ultimately does not require any determinate object right before its eyes. Its abstractness, which is close to aimlessness, guarantees its spilling over into what is universal. For its bearer, the knowledge that it is turning to the general addressee is sufficient to make sure that he does not waste itself unnecessarily. The condition is reached in which we can speak of expenditure as such, expenditure pure and simple (*sans phrase*).[5] In these divestitures, the rage-filled giver of pain often risks his own life. In these cases, the giver makes himself into a physical addition to the bomb that is supposed to supply the missing suffering.

IT THUS DOES NOT MAKE ANY SENSE TO ESTABLISH A RELATIONSHIP between self-confident hatred and concepts such as nihilism—despite their prevalence as popular explanatory models. In general, the concept of hatred proves analytically unsuitable because it is deduced from the phenomenon of rage and can only be made intelligible as a form of preserving rage. One has to insist that rage, which is a standpoint, even a project, is not at all affiliated with the nothingness we like to claim for hatred. Rage is not merely a militant form of indifference with regard to oneself and others. Even if rage reveals recklessness, it would be a mistake to think that it is indifferent about everything. Rage that has become reified as hatred is resolute goodwill. Initially it appears as a pointed attack that brings about an intense local pain. Then it secures an allegedly necessary increase of pain in the world in order to persist in terrible reports and other media exaggerations. In light of this perspective, it is the subjective and passionate appearance of that which the penalizing judiciary wants to embody objectively and without passion. Both rest on the axiom according to which the balance of the world after its disruption can only be recovered through an increase of pain at the right location.

In the case of individual donations of rage, the person who hates initially draws on her own rage supply, even at the risk of using up her capacity for experiencing rage. Nothing guarantees to the simple vengeful person that his sources are inexhaustible. As long as vengeful energy is not transformed into a project and the individual constantly faces the possibility of returning to peace through satisfaction or exhaustion, the small circle of anger and abreaction belongs to the energetic processes connected to our emotions.

In this sense we can understand the abreactive crime as the manifestation of a power that demands the right to discharge itself even if this puts the actor into a position of moral injustice. This is why crimes from such impulsive sources tend to exhaust themselves when the deed is finished. The moment that the victim is out of sight, the perpetrator is able to forget it. Is it not true, after all, what is said about the brothers of Joseph after they sold him to Egypt, "for their hatred had been taken from them, and in time they were left with only vague recollections of how greatly the ninny had angered them"?[6] Because rage is initially a finite resource, its satisfaction through the deed is often its end, which sometimes compels the actor to surrender deliberately to the forces of law.

An exemplary return of a fatigued vengeful person to endure his sentence is depicted by Friedrich Schiller in his 1792 story "The Criminal from Lost Honor." If Hegel, who read this novella attentively, refers to the sentence as the honor of the crime, we should immediately think of Schiller's poor "sun keeper." This well-known ravager reveals his true identity to a respectful civil servant in a sentimental gesture in order to then surrender himself to the courts. Something similar is done by Kleist in *Michael Kolhaas*, although this German story about the passion of righteousness stands under a darker sign. This story of an overly sensitive person who takes revenge for two horses that were stolen from him embodies the process by which the rage that drives a private person to carry out deeds of revenge becomes a metaphysics of self-administered justice. The fact that the raging citizen who sees his stubbornness fulfilled dies as a satisfied petit-bourgeois is revealing. It expresses nothing less than the anticipation of the reevaluation of all values. The romantics, who opened themselves to the aesthetics of excess, picked up on the feeling that we can no longer depend on God's justice. They reveal a concern for those humiliated on the earth and those who make their contributions to the day of judgment during their lifetimes.

Rage and Time: The Simple Explosion

WHEN THE EXPENDITURE OF RAGE DEVELOPS MORE COMPLEX FORMS, the seeds of rage are consciously dispersed, and the fruits of rage are diligently harvested. Through hate culture, rage is carried out in the form of a project. Wherever revenge intentions ripen, dark energies become stabilized over longer periods. What Nietzsche says about the genesis of conscience, that it is premised on the human who can promise, is even more true for the memory of the one who engages in revenge. This person is an agent who remembers not only the injustice that has been inflicted upon him but also all his plans for paying it back. The person "who may promise" is, according to Nietzsche's complex characterization, the subject with the "lasting will." Once this subject is constituted, revenge intentions can then be sustained over long periods of time—even passed from one generation to the next. Once the stage of transmission has reached the next agent, an authentic economy of rage has come into being. Now the resource of rage is no longer accumulated arbitrarily and occasionally wasted; rather, it is maintained and continually produced as the object of an ongoing project. Once it has reached this stage, rage becomes a treasure trove for its possessor, opening up avenues to transpersonal motives. As soon as collectively administered amounts of rage are stored as treasures or assets, the question becomes pressing as to whether such accumulated assets can be invested like capital. I will answer this later with the support of a new psychopolitical definition for left-wing parties. In reality these parties need to be understood as banks of rage that, if they do their business well, will know how to effect politically and thymotically relevant gains.

If one admits that the banking and saving functions of rage assets are real and efficacious, one also understands how it is possible for rage to develop from its diffused initial stage to higher levels of organization. By passing through this progression, rage travels the road from local and intimate emotion to public and political program. The temporal structure of rage-potentials also undergoes a total transformation. Rage undergoes a metamorphosis from a blind form of expenditure in the here and now to a far-sighted, world-historical project of revolution for the sake of those who have been humiliated and offended.

However, as long as rage remains explosive, it expresses itself by "flaming up": "And the rage of Achilles rose forcefully." The direct thymotic abreaction is a version of fulfilled presence. For the raging person, as for the happy person, time does not exist. The uproar in the here and now neutralizes the retrospective and prospective ecstasies of time so that both disappear in the momentary energy flow. The life of the subject of fury is the sparkles in the chalice of the situation. For the romantics of energy, this acting in anger is a kind of flow. It implies a return to a mystic and animal time that, as its connoisseurs avow, has the quality of the constantly fleeting now.

Rage as Project: Revenge

THE CREATION OF A QUALIFIED OR EXISTENTIAL TIME, THAT IS, A lived time with a retrospective and anticipatory character, occurs through the deferral of discharge. Rage potential is channeled into a vector that creates a tension between then, now, and later. This is why we can say that the raging one who holds herself back preliminarily knows what it means to intend to do something. At the same time, she not only lives in history but also makes history—insofar as making history is the name here for taking motives from the past in order to take care of what comes. In this respect, nothing can be compared to revenge. *Thymos* that has been activated discovers through its desire for gratification the world as the realm of constructing future projections, which gain momentum for the coming attack from what has been. Rage becomes the *momentum* of a movement into the future, which one can understand as the raw material for historical change.

As elementary as these considerations may appear, their implications reach into the innermost motives of twentieth-century philosophy. If they are correct, they necessitate important modifications to one of the most well known theorems of modern philosophy. If they are correct, one should not interpret existential time as the immediate being-toward-death, as Heidegger in *Being and Time* suggests in an interpretation that is as well known as it is rushed. The being-whole-ability of existence (*das Ganz-sein-Können*

60

der Existenz) is what matters to the thinker, an ability that does not depend on the fact of the individual considering his own death in order to ascertain his directedness toward something that is an unconditional future fact. *Dasein* can just as well orient itself because it traverses the distance from humiliation to revenge as a whole. Existential time emerges from such an anxiety (*Hingespanntheit*) toward its decisive moment. Such an act of endowing for one's own being-toward-goals (*Seins-zum-Ziele*) is more powerful than every vague heroic meditation of the end. When *Dasein* is angry it does not have the form of running ahead toward its own death, but of an anticipation of the indispensable day of rage. One would rather have to speak of a running ahead to gratification. If one thinks back to the protagonist of the *Iliad* it becomes clear that a warlike being-toward-destruction has become his second nature. His departure for the last battle in front of the walls of Troy marks the beginning of the sequence of action with which the downfall of the hero became necessary. In this respect, Heidegger's thesis that *Dasein* is being-toward-death belongs to those Europeans who carry on the work of the myth of Achilles throughout the ages.

Revenge emerges out of the project form of rage. This concept initially requires analysis from a neutral and ecological vantage point. One may rightly understand the desire for revenge as one of the most unfriendly desires of humanity. That it belongs to the causes of the greatest miseries is proven by history insofar as it has not yet been classified a "life teacher." Called "*ira*," it is classified among the deadly sins. If anyone could say something positive about it, it is that with it the possibility of unemployment vanishes from the life of avenger. He who has a strong intention to practice a revenge is, for the time being, safe from suffering problems of meaning. A persistent will excludes boredom. The deep simplicity of rage satisfies the all-too-human desire for strong motivations. One motive, one agent, one necessary deed: this is the formula for a complete project. The most important characteristic of a well-organized and well-planned existence manifests itself in the lack of any arbitrariness. The avenger is safe from the "need of needlessness" that Heidegger claimed would be the sign of an existence abandoned by a sense of ne-cessity (*Not-Wenidigkeit*). It is indeed impossible to claim that the avenger would live like a leaf in the wind; chance no longer has any power over her. This way revengeful existence gains a quasi-metaphysical meaning in a postmetaphysical age: thanks to rage the "utopia of motivated life" realizes itself in a domain in which an increasing amount of people feel empty. No one expressed this more clearly than Stalin when he said about

61

his colleagues Kamenew and Dschersinski, "To choose one's victim, to prepare one's plans minutely, to slake an implacable vengeance, and then to go to bed . . . there is nothing sweeter in the world."[7]

RAGE AS BANK: REVOLUTION

THE PROJECT FORM OF RAGE (WHICH ONE WOULD CALL IN POLICE jargon self-administered justice or the mob mentality and in political jargon anarchism or the romanticism of violence) can expand to take on the form of a bank. This elevation (*Aufhebung*) of local anger resources and dispersed projects of hatred into an overarching instance. The task of this storehouse of rage, as for every authentic bank, consists in serving as a collection point and recycling agency for investments. This transition necessarily once again affects the temporal structure of those potentials invested in individual projects. Just as rage in its project form provides for a longer duration and allows for a pragmatic planning process, the bank form of rage requires that individual vengeful plans subject themselves to a superior perspective. This perspective proudly bears the title of "history"—history, of course, in the singular. Through the creation of a bank of rage (understood as a storage place for moral explosives and vengeful projects) individual vectors become part of a single project guided by a single administration, the demands of which do not always coincide with the rhythms of local actors and actions. But now subjection becomes inevitable: countless histories of rage are finally united in one common history.

This transition marks the transformation from the projective to the historical form of rage. As soon as a collective that invests its rage potentials—as well as its hopes and ideals—forms itself into a common, enduring operation, "history" itself takes on the form of an enterprise of the highest ambition. Historical narration takes on the task of accounting for the deeds and sufferings of the significant collective of rage. To say it almost with the words from 1848 of two famous colleagues: all history is the history of rage applications.

Once the rage economy becomes elevated to the level of a bank, anarchistic companies led by small rage owners and locally organized anger groups become the subjects of harsh criticism. At the same time that the level of organization of rage is increased, there is a rationalization of the vengeful energy: it passes from pure impulsivity through a selective attack to a conception of attacks against the state of the world as a whole. From the perspective of the rage bankers, the actions of local anger agencies are blind expenditures that almost never produce any appropriate return because the anarchic acting out of the forces of rage regularly provokes the intervention of security forces, which can easily neutralize individual eruptions of hatred and local revolt.

On this level, vengeful actions are usually persecuted as transgressions or punished as crimes. It is thus not helpful to destroy telephone boxes or to set cars on fire unless the act is meant to integrate the act of vandalism into a "historical" perspective. The anger of destroyers and arsonists consummates itself in its expression, and that it often regenerates itself through the harsh reactions of the police and the judiciary does not change its blindness. It is an attempt to smash fog with a stick. Even a mass movement like that of the slave leader Spartacus in the years 73 through 71 B.C. could not achieve more than a flaring-up of hatred across Italy against the domination of the Roman landowners. Even though the rebellious gladiators of Capua dealt multiple defeats to the Roman army, the final result of this revolt was the horror of 6,000 crucified rebels enduring several days of agony before dying. Its consequences were increased repression and deepened discouragement. The revitalization of the legend of Spartacus and its inclusion in the symbolic arsenal of modern class struggle tells us, however, that in the archives of rage one deals with a "heritage" that is millennia old. Remember: if one wants to cultivate and pass on rage, one needs to make one's offspring into a part of a history of victims who call for revenge.

An analysis of our historical experience shows without a doubt that the small craftsmanship of rage is condemned to exhaust itself in costly botch-ups. So long as the local assets for revolutionary zeal are not pooled at long-term collection points and remain unguided by a visionary leadership, they waste themselves in expressions of their growing unrest. Isolated anger quanta heat up in shabby dishes until they evaporate or leave behind burned sediments that cannot again be reheated. This is unmistakably revealed by the history of smaller protest parties. Only when discrete energies are invested into superior projects and far-sighted, sufficiently calm, diabolic directors take care of administrating collective rage capacities is it possible for multiple, isolated fires to be transformed into one big power plant. This plant could provide the energy for coordinated actions, up to the level of "world politics." Visionary slogans become necessary for this to occur, slogans that do not need merely to address the intense anger of human beings but to reach their inner feelings of bitterness and finally their hope and their pride. The coldest rage writes up its activity reports in the style of hot idealism.

Just like the monetary economy, the rage economy passes a critical marker once rage has advanced from local accumulation and selective explosion to the level of a systematic investment and cyclic increase. In the case of money, one calls this difference the transition from treasure hoarding to capital. For rage, the corresponding transformation is reached once the vengeful infliction of pain is transformed from revenge to revolution. Revolution cannot be a matter of the resentment of an isolated private person, although such affects are also instantiated in its decisive moment. Revolution rather implies the creation of a bank of rage whose investments should be considered in as precise detail as an army operation before a final battle, or actions of a multinational corporation before being taken over by a hostile competitor.

The concept of the coming "revolution," considered in light of the events of 1917, finalizes the transition from the actualism to the futurism of rage. It implies a complete dismissal of the principle of expression. Vengeful acts of expression mean nothing more than a narcissistic expenditure of energy. The professional revolutionary, who is working as an employee of a bank of rage, does not express individual tensions, he follows a plan. This presupposes the complete subordination of revolutionary affects under the commercial strategy. It does not suffice anymore to "embellish the world with horrors," to use the sarcastic-lucid phrase uttered by Schiller's hero in the play *The Robbers*, which Karl Moor proffers to characterize the maxim of his revolt against injustice. Whoever intends to embellish the world in the future needs to go much further in making it ugly than the romanticism of rebels and assassins could ever dream. Individual flowers of evil are no longer sufficient—one needs a whole art of gardening.

The Terrifying Force of the Negative

BY "REVOLUTION," WHICH STILL SOUNDS SOMEWHAT FASCINATING even if it turns out to be increasingly empty, I mean the concept or, better, the phantasm that Lenin and Mao Zedong, the most successful entrepreneurs of rage, had in mind. By "revolutions" they meant that, through disciplined acts of hatred, one day there could be so much additional pain, so much excessive horror, so much numbing self-doubt among the security forces that everything that existed would soon melt down during a day of mass rage. Once what exists has lost its eternal and firm hold, the rotten world can then be created anew through the fire of transformation. But for this to happen, the power of destruction needs to accomplish its work to the very end. Only when what is old is eradicated completely can the reconstruction of the true circumstances can be started on a totally level foundation.

What Hegel referred to as the terrifying force of the negative gains its most distinct contour in this religiously conditioned speculation. Human rage, gathered from all sources and through effective modes of organization, provides for the bizarre calculation of big rage bankers the energy for a new creation. Assuming that the terrible end is sufficiently terrible, it should accordingly pass over into an epochal beginning.

Through deliberations of this kind at the height of unblemished ruthlessness, one can encounter a form of anxiety that would curdle the blood of motley rebels and local hate projects if they were capable of envisioning the great strategic perspectives. The apocalyptic entrepreneur of rage has to prevent the action of local cells from endangering the grand plan with premature activism. This commits him to an extreme ascetics that will also affect his followers. The world revolutionary must unfailingly plan against spontaneous feelings; he must tenaciously dismiss his first reactions. He knows that without the deepest asceticism in the here and now there will never be any reward in the beyond. The more that local outrage is in the right, the more it is wrong when seen from a global perspective. If one aims for the transformation of everything, one needs to curb the impatience of individual vengeful parties. It is much more necessary to commit all factions waiting to explode to staying calm and prepared (*In-Form-Bleiben*) until the day of mature rage arrives.

The temporal structure of revolution thus needs to be conceived of as an all-inclusive advent. Whatever leads to revolution belongs to the meaningful time of real history. The course of this history is analogous to a burning fuse. A great historical experience and a dose of intuition are needed to be able to judge to what extent the fuse of rage has already burned up. If one possesses both, one is qualified to take a leadership role at the top of the rage bank. Such a boss is justified in dictating to his employees from his sovereign position that they should prepare and keep the dynamite dry; the first precondition for collecting rage as part of a political project of global significance is cold-bloodedness. On the one hand, this cold-bloodedness constantly needs to stir hatred and outrage. On the other hand, it is also necessary for securing restraint. This way *Dasein*, in pre-explosive times, is in the mood of waiting while remaining ready for the next fight.

WHERE CAN ONE STUDY THIS HIGHER ECONOMY? NO ONE BELIEVES that studying Heidegger academically will be sufficient for gaining such dangerous knowledge. As much as the affinities with the basic claims of *Being and Time* are obvious, the Master from Messkirch only approached the temporal structure of revolutionary resentment in a formalist way before, for a time, evading it for the black heaven of the "national revolution." Heidegger never fully understood the logical and systematic implications of the concept of revolution. He understood it just as little as he understood the connection between our historicity and *Dasein*'s ability to be resentful. His investigation of the temporal structures of the caring, projecting, and dying *Dasein* does not provide us with an appropriate conception of the deep nexus of rage and time. The birth of history out of the project form of rage and, even more, the totality of processes leading to the capitalization of resentment remain obscure in his work.

APART FROM HEIDEGGER, WE WOULD OF COURSE HAVE TO REFER TO Marx and Lenin as the authorities for the dynamism of prerevolutionary and revolutionary negativity. It is peculiar that studying these authors is currently next to impossible. The reason for this is not that the texts are impenetrable but that the wall of zeitgeist barricades access to them in a way that even the most patient person cannot independently overcome. With the exception of some still citable "passages," the works of the Marxist classics have become practically unreadable for people with contemporary intellectual, moral, and aesthetic reflexes. They seem to be written in an illusionary foreign tongue. Obsolete polemics permeate them to a degree that, for the time being, the deterring effect outweighs even the most motivated investigatory curiosity. Furthermore, they illustrate a fidelity to concepts one usually only finds in fundamentalist sects. Although they appeal to the science of "society" and its "contradictions," many classic leftist texts (with the exception of a few technical primary texts such as *Capital*) can be read only as unintended parodies. Only thanks to a completely untimely ascetics would it be possible to deduce from the writings of Marx and Lenin the building blocks of a theory of the present. (Mao Zedong's works would have to be taken off the list of reasonable literature from the very beginning). Nonetheless, the works of these authors provide a massive compendium of rage insights. Without these, the tragedies of the twentieth century cannot be adequately depicted and explained. I will return to this sunken body of work in chapters 3 and 4 because they indirectly provide information about what lies ahead.

One of the last chances to get to know a little bit more about the unpopular strategies of the major rage economy is to draw on events in the Western world toward the end of the 1960s and beginning of the 1970s. In this morbid but equally glorious epoch, the thousand flowers of radicalism were in bloom as if for the last time. Then, it would have easily been possible to assure oneself of Marx's remark that historical dramas regularly repeat themselves as farces after their first staging as tragedies. In this case, the farce consisted in the attempt to project the circumstances of the 1930s onto those of 1968 and afterward in order to derive the rules for "resistance" against the "ruling system." Back then, one could often hear the doctrine that patience should be the first virtue of the revolutionary. Words of advice like these mirrored a generational conflict in the radical left between the old school and the revolutionary youth. The late-Stalinist intelligentsia advised this youth that, although the revolution had already "begun" and in the future it would be necessary to always count "from now on," the manifest eruption of the revolution should, under no circumstances, be accelerated voluntaristically.

Only today, at the beginning of the twenty-first century, as the peace of real consumerism is threatened through what is in many places proclaimed as "return of history" (part of it being a return of left-fascist whispers at the margins of academia), do we find a new chance to understand what the praise of revolutionary virtues truly meant. Patience designated the attitude of the historical subject of rage. This subject had freed itself from its personal motives through a cold quasi-idealist *ascetics*. Once a private factor becomes part of the inevitable revenge against the status quo (or according to the jargon of the time, praxis), voluntarism and a premature expenditure are unavoidable consequences. They are the "teething troubles" of the growing revolution. Although such eruptive episodes might still seem justified from the perspective of the actors, from the perspective of a leading employee of the world bank of rage they are the worst thing that could happen before the day of decision. The leading functionaries are convinced that a premature eruption will prevent the coming into being of this most intensive tension. Only this tension will allow the collection of globally dispersed assets of rage into one single and final action, which goes by the name of "world revolution." The hostile acquisition of the "world" by those who are worse off presupposes that the various factions among the worse off refrain from wasting their powers in spontaneous and individual ventures.

The most famous examples of an anarchistic waste of rage deposits are the assassins who, on March 1, 1881, killed Czar Alexander II, the famous emancipator of the serfs. The immediate consequences consisted in the intensification of repression and the expansion of an omnipresent police system. Even more devastating was the senseless waste of hatred assets by the imitators of the assassins of 1881. These were a group of students of the University of St. Petersburg who were planning to kill the murdered czar's successor, Alexander III, on March 1, 1886—as is well known, days of political rage follow a special calendar. Among the students was the twenty-one-year-old Alexander Ulyanov. The attempt was uncovered by the police before it could be carried out, and Alexander was imprisoned with fourteen other conspirators. He was sent to court and, in May 1887, hanged with four other insurgents who likewise were unable to feel remorse. The lives of the other ten were spared in line with the manners of a Russian autocracy famous for its acts of pardoning. Vladimir Ulyanov, the "brother of the hanged," subsequently underwent a process of change from which he emerged as "Lenin," the first wholehearted politician of rage in modern times. In this capacity, he came to understand that the way to power can only lead through the conquest of the state apparatus, not through the merely symbolically relevant assassination of its representative.

The often cited phrase of the young Lenin, "we will not go this way," which was probably dated earlier or even invented, is rightly conceived of as the first sentence of the Russian Revolution.[8] With him begins the century of the big business of rage. Who can forgo the killing of the prince, can receive, as a bonus to the conquered power, the dead prince for free.

THE WRATHFUL GOD

THE DISCOVERY OF THE METAPHYSICAL REVENGE BANK

AT THE END OF THE INTRODUCTION I CLAIMED THAT THE psychopolitical constellation of rage and time (or rage and history) is anticipated by the theological constellation of rage and eternity. What this means exactly at this point needs to be developed. Nontrivial insights concerning the function and architecture of monotheistic religions will surface in the course of this investigation.

That theology wants to be a political quantity, that it can, and that it indeed needs to be such follow from a simple diagnosis. The religions that were relevant for the course of occidental European history, that is, the Mesopotamian as well as the Mediterranean religions, have always been political and will remain so as long as they survive. In these religions, gods are the transcendent party supporters of their peoples and protectors of their kingdoms. They exercise this function even at the risk of having to invent a people and a kingdom that suits them. This is especially true for the God of monotheism. This God had to travel a long geopolitical path, from his precarious Egyptian beginnings to his Roman and American triumphs. This is the case despite the assertions of those who worship him: he is not a mere god of empires (since empires are notoriously perishable structures) but the timeless and transpolitical creator and shepherd of all men.[1]

In fact, the one and only God of Israel was initially a god without an empire. As an ally of a small people primarily concerned with their survival chances, he initially did not seem to be anything more than a provincial god. In time, however, he would transform himself into the most politically virulent god in the skies above Mesopotamia and the Mediterranean. Although barely noticeable in the world, he was conscious of his omnipotence. He succeeded in offensively positioning himself against the pompously incarnated imperial gods of the Near East and Rome, at the same time claiming clear superiority. As the claimant of an illustrious monopoly, he invited the ancient people of Israel to live far beyond their political means in matters of religion. He expected that they would trust him and thus hold their heads higher than the most powerful of emperors. He thus revealed himself as the *deus politicus* par excellence, as the party member of all party members, as the anchor of a sacred one-sidedness that manifested itself in the far-reaching concept of the Covenant. As during the blossoming of communism, when the dogma was spread around that Marxist science united in itself objectivity and partisanship, so the Jewish and Christian theologies, which were always blooming plants, have made it clear from the beginning that God's universal justice expresses itself in the preferential treatment of one of the two allied peoples.

We have to assume that there is a constitutive primary phase in the development of the management of rage with a global scope (called, from a modern perspective, the submission of politics to morality, the art of the possible under the art of what can be wished), an initial phase that extends for more than two millennia. In this phase a threatening and sublime conception is shaped, according to which an autonomously steering and judging but also participating and excitable as well as "agitating" (*eifernder*) God constantly intervenes in the course of human conflicts, alias history. Because the history of humanity is to a large extent synonymous with that which upsets God, these interventions mostly happen in the mode of wrath. God rages against his own people no less than against their adversaries. He shows his rage by sending wars, epidemics, famines, and natural catastrophes as servile spirits of punishment (technically speaking, these spirits are secondary causes on behalf of the majesty who is the primary cause). At a later point, it was said about this God that when the day of Last Judgment would come, he would impose eternal bodily and spiritual pain on those who missed the chance to repent during their lives on earth and thus avoided their just sentence.

The motive of the court of judgment originated in the conceptions of the beyond in Ancient Egypt and the Near East. During its culmination in the late Middle Ages and the baroque period, it advanced to become the most astonishing of visual illustrations. If one had to define the, historically speaking, exceptionalism of Christian intelligence, one could put it as follows: Christian thinking is (or was until very recently) that thinking that in its concern for salvation also conceives of its opposite, hell. Even in the twentieth century, the Catholic Irishman James Joyce depicted, with the shiniest and blackest of colors, the metaphysical horror of the experience of suffering for eternity.[2] In light of the influence of this idea, the concept of eternity became associated with a final penal and torture institution, based on a vast divine memory of injustice and corresponding rage competence. With the help of this set of ideas, anxiety became part of the spiritual history of Christianity.[3] It is probably correct to assume that theology secretly dispensed with the unfavorable ballast of dogmatic conceptions of hell during the twentieth century. Insofar as traces of the idea of a wrathful God have seeped into our contemporary memory, it still conjures up the memory of the most Christian of hells.

If the wrath of God is translated back into historical time and taken up by a human, universal direction, "history" comes into being. It enters the scene with a revolutionary climax whose meaning consists in avenging the injustice that provokes rage against those who caused the injustice and, even more so, against its structural conditions. One could define modernity as the epoch in which the motives of rage and immanence become fused. This liaison generates the coming into existence of a globally operative rage agency. In the next chapter, I will describe as the embodiment of such an institution the party that is always in the right. Only a control center of such a scale could realize what Schiller referred to with his dictum that world history is the world's court of justice. But first I want to examine not the translation of Holy Wrath into secular history but its accumulation in eternity.

PRELUDE: THE WRATH OF GOD
AGAINST THE SECULAR WORLD

IF IT IS CORRECT THAT THE GLOBALIZATION OF RAGE HAD TO PASS through an extended theological starting phase before it could be translated into secular control, we are faced with an essential difficulty of understanding.

In the introduction to this work, I attempted to show why it is impossible for modern human beings to understand the rage of Achilles within the parameters of the age of Homer. What follows is an analogous demonstration in regards to the prophetism of rage in the tradition of Judaism documented in the Bible, as well as in the Christian tradition in the Scholastic and Puritan theology of rage. For our contemporaries it is impossible to appreciate the rage of the One God as it has been preached by the interpreters of triumphant monotheism at the highpoints of their self-confidence. It is fundamentally mistaken to believe that it would be possible to do without a reconsideration of the early history of the *horror metaphysicus* because contemporary Islamism provides an example. The wave of violence that is carried out by Islamists at most tells us something about the most recent performances of the well-known tropes of the wrathful God, as well as the agitating God known since the early days of Judaism. It does not help us to diagnose how it was ever possible that God could acquire the attribute of wrathfulness.

To appreciate the authentic teaching concerning God's rage, two concepts are necessary, and their meaning is, if at all, only metaphorically understandable for us: glory and hell. The content of these terms, which formerly depicted the extremes of high and low in a world formed by God's presence, cannot be concretized by contemporaries. We cannot clarify them even given our best efforts. If a modern human being were to be capable of using these concepts according to their metaphysical meaning, he would have to affirm the most horrible sentence of world literature—he would have to agree to the inscription above the gates of Hell in Dante's *Inferno*, where we can read for eternity: "Divine power made me, / highest wisdom, and primal love." The impossibility of deliberately agreeing to these words of terror provides an inkling of the complexity of the task that has to be solved. The solution can no longer be achieved. To see this difficulty means to enter into an investigation concerning the price paid for monotheism. This much needs to be said in advance: the price for monotheism had to be paid by two transactions, of which it is not easy to say which was the more deadly. One was the introduction of resentment into the teaching of last things, the other the internalization of terror into Christian psychagogy.

Before approaching these dangerous domains, we should attempt to ease the censorship of the zeitgeist. Because of this censorship, that theological issues of all kinds are excluded from the domain of topics to be seriously discussed by enlightened human beings. "God talk" has been banned from

European high society for more than 150 years. This is the case in spite of periodically circulating rumors of a return of religion. Flaubert's bon mot in his *Dictionary of Received Ideas* concerning "conversation"—that "politics and religion are to be excluded from it"—is still an apt description of the state of affairs.[4] However often one speaks of a "revitalization" of the religious, the truth remains that simply because there is a widespread dissatisfaction with the disenchanted world, this does not at all lead to a new belief in extra- or superworldly entities. When John Paul II often remarked in a melancholic tone that human beings in Europe live as if God does not exist, he revealed a better understanding of the real conditions than the subversive crypto-Catholics who publish in the culture sections of German newspapers, who would like it the most if they could elect the Lord in Heaven as the Person of the Year.

We can specifically say about the Christian message that it has not been admissible in the secular realm for a long time; it is no longer plausible. The only way to get a hold of its audience is through marginal means of communication, such as TV channels owned by certain sects. This remark will provoke the protest of one or another representative of the church who does not like to admit the possibility that belief in the Redeemer could be a hobby similar to enjoying horror movies or breeding fighting dogs. This reservation can be easily understood, yet it does not change the fact that the Christian cause survives only as a subculture. What is at issue here cannot anyhow be expressed by sociological or statistical data. The alienation of the public from the Gospel goes far beyond Paul's concession that God talk is a nuisance for Jews and a foolishness for Greeks. Apart from nuisance and foolishness, embarrassment is perhaps the best characterization of the contemporary mode of being of the religious. For some time now, religious sensibilities have retreated into the intimate regions of the psyche and are regarded as the true pudenda of the moderns. After the Enlightenment, one has to cross a great threshold of embarrassment to still be touched by the question concerning a praiseworthy Higher Being. Theologians like to react to this situation with the profound remark that modern man still lives in the historical situation of a "distance" to God. However beautiful this phrase is, it is already mistaken. The problem that exists between God and us contemporaries is not that we are too far away from him. Rather, God would get too close if we were to take his offerings seriously. No quality of the God of the theologians reveals this better than the most embarrassing among them: God's wrath.

This said, the following thesis should make sense: what seemed to be the clearest manifestation of a new weight of religion, of a new religiosity as such—the attention that was paid to the dying and death of Pope John Paul II and the choice of his successor, Benedict XVI, in April 2005—actually had little to do with the religious side of the changing of the guard in the Office of the Saint Peter. In fact, the fascination was exerted largely, if not exclusively, by the pompous Roman liturgies based on relics of the imperial Caesarian myth. Without being able to give themselves a clear account of what they were doing, the masses, as well as the media, felt during the course of events how the personal aura of the pope still radiates with the charisma of Caesar. To a diligent observer of the pontificate of John Paul II, it is clear that the papal cult, which the pope cleverly updated, was essentially characterized by a media Caesarism. In spite of all the assertions of the mystic intensity of the event, it was how the Christian message provided a religious form to Caesarian content. Only because of the latter was it possible that *Roma aeterna* could appear as the most successful *content provider* for all secular networks. But what else does this show than that the Church only wins the struggle for attention when it presents a program that can be misinterpreted in a secular, tragic, and spectacular way? Because Catholicism, at least in its Roman form, is in the last instance still more an empire—or, more specifically, a copy of an empire—than it is a church, the embarrassment of religious speech retreats into the background during its main events and completely cedes the floor to the pompous apparatus.

Once again: in a post-Enlightenment atmosphere "God" cannot be a topic under any circumstances, with the exception of special issues of elitist culture journals. A fortiori, a public discourse concerning the "attributes" of the impossible object remains unthinkable. Yet more impossible, if such a comparative form exists, would be the demand to conceive of a wrathful God or a God of rage in a time in which a friendly God is already an implausible hypothesis. But we precisely have to deal with this unpopular entity, which I will refer to from now on in a preliminary fashion as a "thought figure," in order to understand the emergence of the modern economy of rage. We have to trace the preliminary stages of its transformation into a formal banking system.

The most recent opportunity to witness the configuration of the concepts "God" and "rage" was the debate concerning the new forms of religious and political fundamentalism, a debate more than usually visible in the late 1980s. A significant publication from that time was *La revanche de*

Dieu (*The Revenge of God: The Resurgence of Islam, Christianity, and Judaism in the Modern World*), which appeared in French in 1989. The French subtitle did not just mention an advance but, more straightforwardly, a "*reconquête du monde*"—this was of course reminiscent of the historical pattern of the Reconquista. The author of the book, Gilles Kepel, who has been one of the most important voices in matters of culture and politics in the Middle East since this publication, investigates the strategies of the radical monotheist mobilization in various corners of the world. The oriental aspect of the topic seems to be couched in an ecumenical register of old and new fanaticisms.

The ironic tone of the term "*revanche de Dieu*" cannot be missed. The author makes it clear that he discusses his subject matter solely with the means available to a cultural scientist of his time. When he mentions the "vengeful God," he does not affirmatively refer to the theology of the wrathful God. At the center of the investigation is the return of militant religious groups onto the stage of world politics. In the meantime, we have become accustomed to interpreting the resurgence of these groups as "fundamentalist reactions"—they are the expressions of revenge from a heated religious milieu against the dominant secular milieu. Chronologically, the return of fundamentalisms begins with the appearance of evangelical fundamentalists in the United States and their adamant denunciation of the worldview of modern natural science as diabolic. For decades, these groups have been increasing their influence on American society. The trend is continued by the ultraorthodox Jews of Israel, whose agitations can no longer be ignored by any government and who would like to see their secular nation transformed, sooner rather than later, into a rabbi-ocracy; the trend finds its inevitable end in more recent Islamist phenomena. Although the Islamists, just like their Christian counterparts, reveal a tendency toward militant bigotry, particularly unmistakable are the similarities to the years of fighting and defiance of Roman Catholicism during the late nineteenth and early twentieth centuries; however, they add a new element to their political appearances. They draw on historical Islam as a "readymade" in order to arbitrarily instrumentalize it in a terrorist advertising campaign throughout the global public sphere. What Marcel Duchamp achieved for art history during the early twentieth century, Osama Bin Laden repeats with the support of religious technicians for the Islam of the late twentieth century. The significance of the readymade procedure for the modern cultural economy has been laid out in the subtle analyses of Boris Groys, and the effects of his work on contemporary cultural science have barely begun.[5] As a result of the subversive interpretation of the sacred tradition, we see that Islam, and in particular the traditional authority of the *Ulema*, the council of scholars and jurists, is undermined by the rebellious fascination of religious pirates.

This "revenge of God" is launched by the various political surrealists, terrorists, and fanatics through the media of Western entertainment societies, which are always hungry for events. This rage constitutes only a semicomical, semimacabre spectacle compared with to the millennia-old theological traditions, in which mention of the wrath of God and his interventions in human affairs bears a tone of sympathetic seriousness. These interventions were conceived of in both historical and eschatological terms. The memory of this tradition is the first step of the descent into the catacombs of the history of ideas.

THE KING OF RAGE

NATURALLY THE COUNTLESS REFERENCES TO THE FIGURE OF THE wrathful God in the Old Testament interest us here only in a limited manner. The source of the New Testament, as well as sources from later Catholic dogmatism, are only selective and should be consulted from a different point of view. The traces of these traditions in the Koran will be left out here completely because when measured against the bulk of Jewish and Christian remarks they do not provide anything that would be genuinely new. In this chapter we can thus only pursue a few of those theological terms that have been important in the development of the one "God" and the corresponding transformation of God's people into memory devices. The other abundant references to the divine life of affects in the euphoric as well as the dysphoric sense do not concern us in this context.

For professionals as well as amateurs it is a trivial fact that the early depictions of Yahweh, the Lord of Israel, are marked by clear anthropomorphisms (or better, anthropo-psychisms). Every reader of the Bible could make sure that the God of Exodus was still capable of combining the traits of a theatrical weather demon with those of a furious, unrestrained warlord. What is decisive for what follows is, of course, the question of how the first signs of a superior moral view characterize this primitive and energetic, meteorological and military conception of God. Part of this change is the formation of a retention function, which is supposed to prevent the disappearance of the past into what is truly passé and, because of the lack of memory, was never real. Through the divine act of retention, the first project culminating in a "history" means more than the recurrence of the same; it also means more than an expression of megalomania and forgetting, in which empires come and go. The historical progression culminating in the "omniscient God" runs for a long time parallel to the path leading to a god of good memory.[6] The emergence and gaining shape of a retaining, deferring, preserving, and recording activity in God signals the transformation of his exercise of power away from the eruptive style to the habitus of a judge or a king.[7] Rage might have been a plausible but incidental attribute for a God who from time to time slips into the roller of thunders. For a God, however, who is supposed to be a royal judge and demands respect and fear in an aura of numinous majesty, the ability to rage becomes constitutive. About such a God we can say for the first time that sovereignty requires that one is believably threatening.

Through the account concerning the function of God as judge, the temporal profile of his actions change: while he used to be conceived of as a protector of his people, as an impulsive interventionist (one can think of the destruction of the Egyptian army at the Red Sea or the eradication of all of humankind with the exception of Noah during the flood), he initially distinguishes himself through his righteous upsurges—from a psychological perspective, one would speak of momentous decompensations. Between God's aggravation with sinful humanity and the downpour of deadly rain there is but a blink of an eye. The passage concerning the remorse that God felt after having created human beings points to a misunderstanding between expectation and fulfillment insofar as remorse implies a modification to the divine sense of time. The situation drastically changes if one takes into account the final scene of the great flood. Here God raises with the rainbow an important symbol of patience for both sides, a symbol that expresses his intention to never repeat such a destructive action, even though humanity does not significantly differ after the flood, at least in its moral character. Rüdiger Safranski summarizes this fact with the fitting remark, which is respectfully unrespectful: that God transformed himself from a "fundamentalist to a realist." The realist (*der Realo*) is the one who concedes that everything in need of improvement needs time—and which things are not in need of improvement?[8]

As a result of the change of direction toward a conception of God as judge and avenger, the "retentional" qualities of the Lord in heaven increasingly became emphasized. Just as intentions aim at what is present, retentions aim at what is past, and pretentions at what is futural. The royal archival and judicial competences of God from now on become decisive characteristics. They include the abilities to remember what is just and what is unjust and to record violations of the law. But most important, they included the willingness to reserve judgment concerning the just sentence, including the right to pardon or leave the exact moment in which the sentence will be executed undetermined. Such conceptions can only occur in a culture that has for some time possessed two archetypes of "reserving" technologies. On the one hand, it has to possess a granary or, more generally, a stock of supplies. On the other hand, it requires a book or, more generally, written language and the collection of written works in libraries. These need to be complemented through judicial technologies that can determine what is right and what is wrong. The function of the archive is based on these basic patterns. The archive as an institution and in terms of its cultural function unfolds as soon as nervous systems interact with external storage spaces and recording devices, in other words, when it is necessary to organize the cooperation between subjective and objective memories in formal procedures. The judging God is thus naturally the original registrar in the kingdom of ethical life. His office consists in holding on to the memory of controversial events so that they can be taken up again later.[9]

Although the early immanent theology of the Bible tends to posit Yahweh as existing beyond time and, in particular, beyond the fantasies of the permanent persistence and pompous genealogies of surrounding empires, as a judge and chairperson of a court for his own followers, he remains an agent who "breaks in" to the historical destinies of his followers and other peoples. For this reason, the Jewish God of judgment consistently needs to be envisaged as a ruling king, regardless of the empirical nonsense of a kingdom that is, in principal, invisible. Making God into a king introduces a tension to the temporal horizon of his interventions. Divine records of injustice and attempts to preserve rage allow for long distances between the moment of "transgression" and the moment of "revenge." However, they still do not imply that punitive violence is postponed until the end of time or even transposed to eternity.

The Interruption of Revenge

THE BOOK OF GENESIS MENTIONS A BREAK THAT CAUSED LASTING consequences for the organization of the human memory of rage. The report of the first murder, committed by the farmer Cain against his younger brother, Abel, the shepherd who had been favored by God, is also the oldest record on the secrets of injustice. In this history, God appears for the first time openly as the master of facticity: he looks on Abel's sacrifice favorably while ignoring Cain's. For this difference, there is no trace of a motivation. The freedom to discriminate against whomever, wherever he wishes is part of the concept of God. The next, similarly far reaching example of this thesis is provided in the story of Esau and Jacob. Without any documented reason, God loves one and hates the other one, while the created is not allowed to ask his creator: "Why did you create me in such a way that you needed to reject me?" It is expected that the person who is discriminated against needs to master his affects of humiliation: "And the Lord said unto Cain, Why art thou wroth? And why is thy countenance fallen? If thou doest well, shalt thou not be accepted? and if thou doest not well, sin lieth at the door. And unto thee shall be his desire, and thou shalt rule over him" (Genesis 4:6–7). The meaning of this story, which has been inserted at front of the record of action, is obvious: the murder of the brother is not supposed to be misunderstood as a spontaneous impulsive act; it is supposed to count as a result of a suspension of the explicit and clear warning. The deed does not occur in the relative innocence of being overtaken by agitated feelings. In order to commit the deed, the perpetrator has to intentionally transgress a clearly drawn line—only such an act of transgression makes it into a case of true violation in the first place. One can hardly emphasize it enough: Cain does not abide by the law of gravity inhering in a strong affective action; he takes time for his action—he uses a pretense to lure his brother onto an open field in order to strike him dead. From this time on, he lives in the exceptional time of guilt; he is chained to his own dead: "You will be restless and uneasy on this earth," the lord speaks to him. "I will be restless and uneasy on this earth. Whoever finds me will strike me down," the perpetrator responds (Genesis 4:12, 14). Thereupon God leaves Cain with a sign, "so that no one who finds him will strike him down."

Historians of religion associate the sign of Cain with the warning symbol of an ancient oriental tribe in which strict blood feuds were common. It signals that whoever raises the hand against the bearer of the symbol has to be aware that he will suffer from sevenfold revenge. The threat of revenge escalates among Cain's offspring in grotesque quantities. His great-great-grandchild Lamech announces heroically: "I will murder a man for a wound and a young boy for a bruise. If Cain will be avenged seven times, then Lamech will be avenged seven times seventy" (Genesis 4:23–24).

The exploding numbers express an ambivalent situation: although the sign of Cain can be interpreted as the symbol of a universal prohibition against revenge, is this is violated, there exists the threat of excessive revenge. On the one hand, revenge is suspended, but, on the other hand, we can expect an extreme form of revenge if this commandment is not followed. This can only be understood as a symptom for the lack of an effective monopoly over violence. Where there is no central penal authority, the revenge prohibition can only be experimentally instituted through the forceful threat of an excessive reaction. One needs to wait for the introduction of a stable juridical culture with a formal body of law before talionic equations can come into effect: "A life for a life, an eye for an eye, a tooth for a tooth, a hand for a hand, a foot for a foot, burn for a burn, a wound for a wound, a bruise for a bruise" (Exodus 21:23–25). The equality between the sides of these formulas show that justice is to be understood as appropriateness. The measure presupposes someone who enforces it, a role usually fulfilled by early forms of government as the guarantors of the law.

If the degree of the sentence is directly and materially deduced from the suffering of injustice committed, a concept of justice as a simple form of equivalence comes into being. The compulsion to enhance the amount of retribution can thus be dismissed. Instead of the outdated one-to-seven, or even one-to-seventy-seven, from now on the sublime and simple one-to-one will be exercised. To secure retribution, a strong judicial authority is necessary, which initially manifests itself only in the sovereignty of a king. It may be that modern observers will regard such a system as a form of economy of natural goods or, rather, a primitive and inhuman economy of horrors. However, the Mosaic commandments were an important step in the rationalization of strategies of retaliation. Additionally, equality between the value of injustice and that of retribution has an implicit temporal meaning, since order can be reestablished only after the equivalence of the suffering from deeds and the suffering from penalty has been reestablished. This waiting for justice comes to characterize the meaning of time. Through the equation of guilt and penalty, which has been effected by the judicial system, there is a dissolution of local vengeful tensions of the victim or prosecutor, at least as considered from an ideal-typical perspective. When the sun comes up afterward, it still shines on just and unjust people;

at the same time, this sunrise signals the new beginning for the parties who have paid their bills.

The Original Accumulation of Rage

THE SITUATION JUST PRESENTED STARTS TO LOOK VERY DIFFERENT if suffering from injustice is accumulated only on one side, without those sacrificed to the injustice having an effective way to reestablish equality. In such situations, it is likely that strong and chronic tensions of rage will emerge and accumulate into a form of negative capacity. For this possibility we can find at least two significant examples in the Old Testament. The first one is connected to the memories of Israel concerning the Babylonian captivity in the sixth century B.C., to which the word "exile" refers with a richness of subtle connotations. The second example refers to the Jewish conception of apocalypse. Starting with the second century B.C., this conception led to an intensification of propheticism that, through its excessive exaggeration, in turn led to the demand for the destructive rage of God against the incurably corrupt world as a whole.

The mental sediments of Israeli exile and the apocalyptic exaggerations of prophetic anti-imperialism (which initially turned against Hellenic and then Roman foreign rule) have left deep marks in the religious tradition of Western civilization. Both themes remain incomprehensible without assuming the creation of a treasury of rage. Its peculiar dynamic led to a structural transformation of the rage of victims into a lasting resentment. This transformation has a significance for the specific tuning of Western religion, metaphysics, and politics that can hardly be overestimated.

The books of the Old Testament provide ample evidence for the creation of a treasury of rage during the Babylonian captivity and subsequent epochs, in a sometimes sublime, sometimes more direct voice. An example for a sublime articulation of this development written during the age of Babylon and included in the Gospel only later is the narration of Genesis. It is mistaken to assume that Genesis necessarily constituted the beginning of the Jewish canon. In reality it is the result of a relatively late theological attempt to surpass the state of heteronomy. With this attempt the spiritual spokesmen of Israel claimed the cosmic superiority for their God over the gods of the dominant empire during the forced period of exile. What at first seems to be a casual report about last things is in reality the result of an editorial work on matters of competitive theology.

The meaning of this endeavor consists in reinterpreting the God of the political losers as the a priori winner. Even if the heathen kings are able to rule over their territories and slave populations with the support of their polytheistic entourage, none of their decrees will even approximate the domain of the truly divine "It will be." Through Genesis, Jewish theology was able to celebrate its most subtle victory over the teachings of the gods of the Mesopotamian empires.

AN EXAMINATION OF THE LESS SUBLIME BIBLICAL DEPICTIONS OF THE accumulation of rage can be limited to the infamous psalms of lamentation and prayers for the sake of destroying the enemy. These can be found in the Psalms of the Old Testament, a collection of 150 exemplary hymns, praises, and invocations of God that have served the Jews, as well as Christians, for more than a thousand years as the primary source of their practices of prayer. This body of texts presents a spiritual treasury that can easily be compared to the most sublime documents of religious world literature. Although the individual pieces are consistently formulated in the mode of a prayer and thus in the habitus of a nontheoretical relationship to God, they present psychological, theological, and spiritual riches—as is proven by the great history of their reception, reaching from the *Ennarrationes in Psalmos* of Augustine to the studies of Hermann Gunkel and Arnold Stadler. Psalm 139, to take just one example, belongs to the most moving and substantive sources ever recorded. It addresses the being-surrounded of human existence by a creative milieu and the becoming-enveloped of human consciousness by a knowledge of a higher kind. With regards to its latent metaphysical and existential insights, this lyric text is not superior to any spiritual testimony, be it from India or China. Nonetheless, it is precisely this meditation that is torn apart by an appeal to revenge, the force of which is singular in the history of religious literature. Initially the praying person assures himself of his own creation:

> My substance was not hid from thee, when I was made in secret, and curiously wrought in the lowest parts of the earth.
>
> Thine eyes did see my substance, yet being unperfect; and in thy book all my members were written, which in continuance were fashioned, when as yet there was none of them. (Psalms 139:15–16, AV)

IMMEDIATELY AFTER, THE MEDITATION TURNS TO THE ENEMIES OF the praying person. The pious one points his attention to them without interruption. He is subject to a double "compulsory relationship" because, on the one hand, he faces the enemy, the Babylonian oppressor, as an inevitable political opponent. On the other hand, the political enemy also embodies a religious opponent insofar as he enjoys the freedom to hold onto the gods or idols of his own culture and thus despise Jewish monolatry. Both aspects of this front are present when the prayer suddenly passes over into the harshest lamentations:

> Surely thou wilt slay the wicked, O God: depart from me therefore, ye bloody men.
> For they speak against thee wickedly, and thine enemies take thy name in vain.
> Do not I hate them, O Lord, that hate thee? and am not I grieved with those that rise up against thee?
> I hate them with perfect hatred: I count them mine enemies. (19–22)

This poetic description of enemies would be completely misinterpreted as a spontaneous eruption of sentiments against domination. Such feelings are only one of many knots in a network of remembrance that records memories of abuse and humiliation. The same network stabilizes expressive impulses of revenge into repeatable forms. The initial formulation of Psalm 94, "God who is revenge appear" (cited according to the unrevised rendition of Luther) could be used as a leitmotiv and guide to a great part of the Psalms. It returns, in addition to many other places, in Psalm 44. There the following words are addressed to the God of the confederation: "With you we will throw down our oppressors. With your name we smash our opponents" (44:6). Then we read, "Wake up! Why do you sleep, my lord? Awake! Do not condemn us forever!" (24). The most massive intensification of this rhetoric is in Psalm 137, at the end of which we find the following lines:

> O daughter of Babylon, who art to be destroyed; happy shall he be, that rewardeth thee as thou hast served us.
> Happy shall he be, that taketh and dasheth thy little ones against the stones. (8–9)

THIS IS AN ARTIFICIAL FORM OF POLEMIC PRAYER THAT APPEARS foreign to the modern understanding of religion. Nevertheless, it can be understood once such formulations are translated (or better, retranslated) into what, in today's language, would be referred to as "psychological warfare." Because ancient Israel was for long periods in chronic situations of war, its religion was necessarily one at the front. Since warfare always develops a psychosemantic dimension, its development and transcription is to be done by religious leaders, at least insofar as religion and psychosemantics converge. The harsh phrases of the Psalms are intended to compensate for the psychopolitical unlikelihood of the survival of Israel during a time of defeats.

This explains the initially disconcerting observation that prayers can also be polemics. Not less disconcerting, and yet psychodynamically plausible, is the fact that even meditation can be used as a means of propaganda. By turning inside themselves, those praying discover their hatred and thus entrust it to God so that he may draw the right consequences from it. These consequences should have been primarily violent, given the context. The autoplastic function of supplicatory prayer emerges most clearly when the praying group envisions itself in a destructive wish-image in which the oppressor has been overcome. This is revealed particularly well by the problematic meaning of the incomparable psalm of lamentation, Psalm 58:

> Break their teeth, O God, in their mouth: break out the great teeth of the young lions, O LORD.
>
> Let them melt away as waters which run continually: when he bendeth his bow to shoot his arrows, let them be as cut in pieces.
>
> As a snail which melteth, let every one of them pass away: like the untimely birth of a woman, that they may not see the sun.
>
> Before your pots can feel the thorns, he shall take them away as with a whirlwind, both living, and in his wrath.
>
> The righteous shall rejoice when he seeth the vengeance: he shall wash his feet in the blood of the wicked.
>
> So that a man shall say, Verily there is a reward for the righteous: verily he is a God that judgeth in the earth. (6–11)

BECAUSE OF THEIR FUNCTION ONE COULD DESCRIBE SUCH FIGURES as endo-propaganda. Although they seem to present nothing but hate speeches, they only aim indirectly at the real enemy, at least according to their effective dynamics. It is likely that no Babylonian ever took notice of the unfriendly phantasms of the Jewish slaves. It is also rather unlikely that any member of the enemy peoples suffered psychological harm from such prayers of hatred. The meaning of these verbal acts lies almost exclusively in their repercussions for the speaking collective. By participating in the language games of lamentation, the endangered group mobilizes the auto-plastic effects of collective recitation (more specifically, the hearing of the reciter or singer) and thereby reconstitutes itself as the sender/receiver of the message of war and rage.

Genealogy of Militancy

IN THIS CONTEXT, THE RELEVANCE OF THESE OBSERVATIONS ON THE Psalms is the evidence for the primary history of the phenomenon of mili-tancy in the form of the Jewish prayers (in recent times, there have been noteworthy attempts at interpretations devoted to the rescue of these sources).[10] An encompassing genealogy of militancy would first of all have to pay attention to the psychological dynamics of the communication among losers. This dynamics reveals how the inferior transformed their defeats into programs of survival during times of historical confrontation between peoples, empires, or ideological factions. Among these, attitudes of eccentric arrogance recur as regularly as the figure of postponed hope and the dream of a final revenge.

The phenomenon of a loser whose comments are not in line with his defeat is apparently as old as political spirituality itself. In the twentieth cen-tury, this pattern came to be called the "resistance." If one does not know what *résistance* means, one has nothing to do with the spirit of the left. In the context of Western civilization, evidence for this at least goes back to the theology of the Jews in and after the exile; the most recent evidence is almost contemporary, found in the writings of Marxist and post-Marxist romantics. For these romantics, the fight will be continued especially once everything has been lost. At the visible forefront today we find such furious veterans as Antonio Negri. With his suggestive reflections in the field of "multitude," he wants to unfold a rainbow of micro-oppositions that span an earth allegedly integrated by global capitalism into one unified empire.

Militancy provides one of the most important keys for the configuration of rage and time. With its first appearances the effective history of cumulative memories of rage emerge. It thus belongs to the primary history of what Nietzsche refers to as resentment. This begins to emerge when the vengeful rage is prevented from expressing itself directly and is forced to take a detour through sublimation, internalization, transference, and distortion. Wherever feelings of being set back are subject to the force of deferral, censorship, and metaphor, local repositories of rage are created whose sole aim is a later release and retranslation. The preservation of rage creates a challenge for the psyche of the inhibited avenger to connect the storage of rage with the need to keep it ready for a time that has been deferred but not definitely determined. This can only be achieved by an internalization, which rests on successful divestiture. The Jewish culture of prayer shows how this is possible. In this culture of prayer, the wish for revenge becomes at the same time inward and advances to the most intimate conversation of the soul with God. Simultaneously, the patterns of such inner dialogues solidify into collections of texts that can then be passed down from generation to generation.

More recent defenses of the Psalms by Catholic theologians create an analogy between Jewish prayer and free association as it is practiced on the psychoanalytic couch. These authors refuse the potential need for censorship by arguing that openly stated wishes of destruction possess a measure of authenticity, which attests to a productive therapeutic relationship with Yahweh as the analyst and supervisor. It is thus not legitimate to take away from the humiliated their calls for revenge and fierce accusations against their oppressors. Today this is said to be as true as it was in ancient times because "the Bible, the revealed word of God, already bestows them with rage."[11]

The Psalms represent an authentic creation of a treasury of rage. A treasury is a stock of values that can be drawn on during times of lack. To draw on a treasury of rage means to bring back the conserved suffering of the past for new use today. Such a treasury fulfils its goal when fading rage can be reanimated from the accumulated savings.

Under no circumstances can the accumulation of rage value be limited to human matters and mortal memories. The depository of rage that has been set up by zealots is not merely imprinted into the memories of those yearning for revenge documented in texts. Essential is the conception of a transcendent archive, which operates parallel to the inevitably complete secular archives in which the deeds and crimes of the Jews and their enemies have been meticulously recorded. As we have seen, the God of the Jews was elevated above the gods of the surrounding empires by postcaptivity theology—in terms of both his cosmological competence as Creator and his political and moral competence. Because of these competencies it is expected that he has full access to the records of everyone's life as judge and king of these archives. In particular, he has access to the complete records concerning the lives of sinners and arrogant enemies. In this way the empirical rage fund, which includes the national traumatic memory as well as its corresponding demands for revenge, can be connected to the transcendent archive, that is, to the divine memory of injustice. The pathos of fidelity, which is typical for the religion of the old covenant, thus not only expresses that the alliance between God and the people has to be internalized anew from generation to generation but also underlines the demand that the old debts should not be forgotten as long as they are listed in the book of rage, as long as they have not been paid.

The Auto-aggressive Rage Mass

THE PILING-UP OF JEWISH RAGE—WITHOUT WHICH THE CONCEPT of justice, with its persistent religious tinge, is difficult to grasp—proceeds in almost equal parts in two separate depositories, between which there are complicated transactions. In the first one we can find the already mentioned rage masses, which are mainly directed against external enemies, invaders, oppressors, and believers of other gods. The prophetic books that are listed in the Bible under the heading "words concerning foreign people" include a whole archive of hate discourses and sacral curses. The wish of destruction that is directed at the external world is declined for all cases. It is important to note that in these works it is not just hatred as such that is carefully articulated. Rather, the justifications of hatred, including bad memories, dislike, and religious accusations are hoarded and kept ready in order to be used again when the time comes.

The second collection point is best described as a depository for auto-aggressive quantities of rage. This treasury of rage naturally needs to be stored with God himself. It will mainly be the Jewish people who will suffer from these collections of rage during times of plight. This time the prophetic "words about Israel and Judah" will accompany the exercise of God's wrath against his own people. In God's case, the accumulation of rage proceeds according to a simple principle: by closely observing the lives of his children of Israel, he is filled with such a large rage potential that its activation can literally be only "a question of time." At the crucial moment prophets are needed whose purpose it is to announce the coming disastrous penalty—or identify political disaster, natural catastrophes, and dissipation of the life world that have already befallen the population as signs of penalty.

The auto-aggressive direction of these collections of rage is expressed clearly in the prophetic literature starting with Isaiah. This rage, which operates top-down, is entrusted to selected orators for interpretation. The prophet Ezekiel is assigned by God to announce the following:

> Alas for all the evil abominations of the house of Israel! for they shall fall by the sword, by the famine, and by the pestilence. He that is far off shall die of the pestilence; and he that is near shall fall by the sword; and he that remaineth and is besieged shall die by the famine: thus will I accomplish my fury upon them. Then shall ye know that I am the Lord, when their slain men shall be among their idols round about their altars. So will I stretch out my hand upon them, and make the land desolate, yea, more desolate than the wilderness toward Diblath, in all their habitations: and they shall know that I am the Lord. (Ezekiel 6:11–14, AV)

The people of Israel are regularly compared to a whore who has slept with countless suitors. These suitors will one day be called to form a court and judge the sinner. The consequences of the judgment are described by the prophet in horrible detail:

> They . . . shall *stone thee with stones, and thrust thee through with their swords.* And they shall burn thine houses with fire, and execute judgments upon thee in the sight of many women. . . . So will I make my fury toward thee to rest, and my jealousy shall depart from thee, and I will be quiet, and will be no more angry. Because thou hast . . . fretted me in all these things; behold, there- fore I also will recompense thy way upon thine head. (Ezekiel 16:40–43)

IT WOULD BE MISTAKEN TO INTERPRET THESE THREATENING SPEECHES as mere symptoms of an immature extremism. The harsh tone of this prophetic speech should not divert one from acknowledging how much God himself works on acquiring the qualities of being patient, graceful, and tolerant, even though from a modern perspective these do not seem to be plausible characterizations. In fact, even the most upsetting threats of destruction uphold a pedagogical perspective. The One God begins to understand that faith in him cannot be created overnight, even with his most chosen of peoples. His grace, which is often appealed to, always already contains a reflection on his educational goals, which have been raised too high. Thus in his memories of his acquaintance with the people of Israel he remembers a crucial moment. After the exodus from Egypt, he wanted to destroy his people because they neglected the commandment to celebrate the Sabbath:

> Then I said, I would pour out my fury upon them in the wilderness, to consume them. But I wrought for my name's sake, that it should not be polluted before the heathen, in whose sight I brought them out. . . . Nevertheless mine eye spared them from destroying them, neither did I make an end of them in the wilderness.　　　　　　　　　　　　　　　　　(Ezekiel 20:13, 17)

HOWEVER, IT IS WRONG TO CHARGE MONOLATRIC PEDAGOGY WITH half-heartedness. It includes the partial extermination of that people as well as the most extreme acts of reeducation. The battle over extermination at the foot of Sinai provides an unforgettable example: the recidivist part of the people, the part that followed the Egyptians by basking in front of the golden calf, is denigrated in dutiful zealousness by the loyal portion standing under the leadership of Moses. On the other hand, the educational horror does not have any limitations when it comes to incorporating the rage of the Lord against his own people. Isaiah proclaims:

> Therefore is the anger of the Lord kindled against his people, and he hath stretched forth his hand against them, and hath smitten them: and the hills did tremble, and their carcasses *were* torn in the midst of the streets. For all this his anger is not turned away, but his hand *is* stretched out still.
>
> And he will lift up an ensign to the nations from far, and will hiss unto them from the end of the earth: and, behold, they shall come with speed swiftly.　　　　　　　　　　　　　　　　　(Isaiah 5:25–26)

> Isaiah also crieth concerning Israel, Though the number of the children of Israel be as the sand of the sea, a remnant shall be saved. For he will finish the work, and cut *it* short in righteousness: because a short work will the Lord make upon the earth.　　　　　　　　　　　　　　(Romans 9:27–28)[12]

The auto-aggression articulated by the prophets through attacks on foreign peoples is unflinchingly directed to the moral reeducation of the people in the sense of Deuteronomic right. Because a people of saints does not come into being overnight, nor in a few decades or centuries, most methods of conversion seem to be necessary again and again. This is expressed by the warning of Ezekiel:

> *As* they gather silver, and brass, and iron, and lead, and tin, into the midst of the furnace, to blow the fire upon it, to melt *it*; so will I gather *you* in mine anger and in my fury, and I will leave *you there*, and melt you. Yea, I will gather you, and blow upon you in the fire of my wrath, and ye shall be melted in the midst thereof. As silver is melted in the midst of the furnace, so shall ye be melted in the midst thereof; and ye shall know that I the LORD have poured out my fury upon you. (Ezekiel 22:20–22, AV)

THE METAPHOR INVOLVING METALLURGY AND ALCHEMY AIMS LESS AT the extermination of those who have failed than at their purification and re-creation. Even though the fire of rage burns the majority of those who want to stay as they always have been, there is regularly a remainder of those who can continue the history of religious revolts against political and anthropological plausibilities. Today theologians sometimes still possess the admirable capacity to present such issues in a favorable light. The claim that the God of Israel is precisely not "a burning fire of ethical energy," a fire that aims to ignite the love of one's closest people. He who prefers it a bit chillier stubbornly prepares his own hell.[13]

HYPERBOLIC RAGE:
THE JEWISH AND CHRISTIAN APOCALYPSE

HOWEVER ONE MAY EVALUATE THE TWO CORRELATED DEPOSITORIES of rage in the universe of post-Babylonian Judaism from the vantage point of psychological, sociological, and psychopolitical factors (leaving the question of its spiritual evaluation aside for the moment), it can hardly be denied that they have contributed to the survival of Israel in an age of chronic distress through their offensive, expressive, autoplastic, and military effects. They provide the reason the religious people par excellence could become the bearer of—permit the expression—a complex wisdom concerning rage. Furthermore, together with Greece, Israel was able to become the most important export nation for rage-manufacturing systems.

The ground operation of the prophetic interpretation of disaster is the tracing back of the manifest Jewish misery during times of political distress to the penal and cathartic rage of Yahweh. Sooner or later, this rage needed to reach its own limits. Even during its highpoint, the era of the prophetic authors and the Babylonian and post-Babylonian times of need, its success was always bound to precarious psycho-semantic operations. An atmosphere that constantly oscillated among hope, anxiety, and despair was necessary in order to lead to a widely shared spiritual acceptance of the rather implausible, immodest, and structurally masochistic interpretations of the prophets. The price for understanding the often disparaging trials of Israel as a part of pedagogy of the wrath of God against his own people consisted in an internalization of the expectations of violence that had far-reaching consequences. Additionally, a hyper-moral confusion was to be expected if the boundary between the sentencing of individual sinners (to use the traditional term without placing too much emphasis on it) and collective extermination has been confused again and again. Why should the people as a whole have to suffer because of some individual sinners who were provocative? It was to be expected that the community would cultivate an attitude of guilt as a response to the continuous appeals of propheticism. This attitude was absolutely disproportionate with the alleged transgressions of the members of this community. Yet however developed this prophetic agitation might have been, it failed to secure the interiorization of the auto-aggressive impulses forever. It is thus not astonishing that the traditional prophetic paradigm collapsed in an especially angry, desperate, and protracted situation of suffering or that it was replaced with a completely novel concept.

This happened during the second half of the second century B.C., when the Middle East, including old Israel, was incorporated by the Hellenic tyrannies—also known as the Diadochian empires—as a result of the decaying of the empire of Alexander. At the time of the Seleucidian reign over Israel, the deficiencies of the prophetic, moralistic, and auto-aggressive processing of unhappiness became so obvious that it became necessary to search for new possibilities for dealing with pressing misery. The first one consisted in the development of a massive military resistance, which is connected to the name of the Maccabees (who simultaneously introduced terror against collaborators from their own people). The second consists in the creation of a radically new schema of interpreting world history, which to the present day we refer to as "apocalyptic."

A community of people concerned for their salvation loses interest in political matters when apocalyptic thinking and feeling fill the stage because they believe that world time has entered a rather limited final phase. During such an end time, prophetic moralism becomes pointless. There will not be any future in which the believer could concern himself for his purification. There will not be any offspring to which the doctrine could be passed on. There will not be any more enemies against whom a people would have to stand up.

The second century B.C. is a key era for the larger history of militancy. The spirit of radical dissatisfaction with the existing situation finds itself confronted with a choice that has essentially remained the same since then. The vengeful must choose between the epochal alternatives of the Maccabean and the apocalyptic options. In short, they had to decide between secular anti-imperial revolt and a religious or para-religious hope for the final downfall of the system. Modernity has only added a third alternative, which, however, has proved decisive: a reformist way to apply liberal democratic procedures to overcome, in due time, historically emerged situations of injustice. It is superfluous to explain why the third option presents the only strategy for civilization in the long run.

From the point of view of building a rage depository, the pre-Christian belief in an apocalypse is important in a threefold sense: First, it dissolves the traditional theology of the rage of God, which rested on the equation between the national history of the people of the covenant and the history of penalty. Second, it brings back the accumulated rage quantities from the archive of God into the power centers of politics, and the worldly anger agencies rage against one another to the point that the destruction of the world completely corresponds to the destruction of the self. (This is, by the way, the first implicit idea of a "world war.") At the last, God brings over the worldly battleground a well-ordered between zone of angelic forces and demons. They engage a subtle world war in the skies, beyond human apocalyptic combatants.

At the front of this war on high, a rebellious angel full of pride—Satan, Lucifer, Iblis, or however else he may be called—enters the history of ideas in order to secure for himself the main part for the following one and a half millennia. It should suffice to state at this point that the birth of the devil from the spirit of the apocalyptic warfare would become essential for the future history of agencies of rage. His appearance changes the topology of the beyond in the most decisive way. Wherever there are devils, their residencies cannot be far away. Wherever devils make themselves a home, hells arise, or, to put it differently, archives of guilt in which rage quantities and revenge impulses are preserved for the sake of constant repetition. Europeans can thank Dante's genius for the insight that in this regime, archive and hell are one and the same. Every guilty person is eternally burned alive there for his own personal file.

Through the personification of rage in the shape of the Great Diabolos— "I am the spirit that constantly negates"—a headquarters of rage was created from which infinite impulses came until the threshold of the Enlightenment. By becoming responsible for the concerns of human thymotics, the devil provided great support for the Christian dismissal of human cravings for recognition, aggression, and competitive behavior—*superbia! ira! invidia!* Nonetheless, he provided the most influential expression of the world domination of rage. The doctrine according to which the devil is the ruler of this world gives an impression of the scope of his competencies. The surrendering of the world to diabolic management and the necessarily connected diabolization of the thymotic was accompanied by both a higher valuation of the image of God and downgrading of the human sphere. Since God's thymotic impulses have been largely outsourced to the diabolic epicenter, God fully ascends to the most sublime of spheres. From now on, the assembly of divine qualifications can fully include the most sublime or arcane qualities, such as those depicted in the celestial rose in the highest room of Dante's *Paradiso*. Only as much traditional rage needed to be preserved in God as necessary to proclaim his "glory."

The price for this release of God from his position as executive of his rage is the emergence of a detailed counter-world of evil. This world was not allowed to take on complete ontological independence; otherwise, one would have had to concede the existence of an Antichrist or a second principle, something impossible within the framework of monotheism. However, even in its subordinate position evil exercises enough power to gain respect as the source of countless miseries since relationships between God and adversarial forces are determined through a dialectics of subordination and revolt. Both impulses are characteristic of a world in which hierarchy developed into the dominant form of thought and life. Only in a universe in which everything should be ordered according to one's rank could this interpretation of evil as the attempt to reverse rank assert itself. It does not only characterize the Christian image of Satan, but lives on in Nietzsche's criticism of the reversal of legitimate positions because of resentment.

For my concerns it is crucial that with the discovery of evil—as exemplified in the devil and in the form of religion in general—radically new possibilities of storing and applying rage become opened. Because of its increase in power, the kingdom of evil gains a diversity and colorfulness that is singular in the history of ideas and anxieties. As we have already seen, the didactic, therapeutic, and majestic-political use of threat was not unknown to the older monolatric and monotheistic religious life. However, only with the emergence of evil in Christian theology can we speak of a common history of religion and terror.

Vessels of Rage and Infernal Depositories: On the Metaphysics of Discharge

LET ME END THIS PSYCHOHISTORICAL DISCURSION WITH A BRIEF summary of the Christian doctrines of the wrathful God and the corresponding character of the devil of rage. As indicated, both have their point of origin in the apocalyptic convictions of the epoch of Seleucid, when the Ascidians forcefully articulated the dramatic concept of the imminent end of the world. The precondition for the creation of this new religious archetype was a deepened individualization of faith. Such a change of emphasis became necessary in light of a political and social horizon that did not show the slightest sign of external change for the better.

Apocalypticism is the religious form of abandoning the world. It can only come into being in a situation in which individuals and groups feel themselves to be the impotent spectators of struggles between superior powers. There are good reasons for the thesis that the invention of the spectator during antiquity came to an end with Jewish apocalypticism. Even if the Greeks created the theater and the stadium, and the Romans added bloody gladiator fights to the arena, it was only with the emergence of the apocalyptic idea of the final game of the chaotic world that a form of watching emerged that points far beyond the witnessing of artistic, cultic, sporty, or cruel spectacles.

The apocalyptics invent an irony that reaches deeper than Socratic irony. They imagine themselves to be in agreement with the will of God, who has a different plan for his world than what his earthly children want to believe. Part of this irony is the refusal of existing values; the consequence of apocalyptic sensation is the freezing of any form of spiritual investment in "this world."[14] In the meantime, the political apocalyptics and anarchic millenarians, whom I will address in a moment, dedicate themselves actively to worsening the situation. After the believer has withdrawn his affective investments from the world, he surrenders the world to its own irresistible course, which is aimed at the imminent end. To witness such a process means to become a special kind of theatergoer. Among all kinds of possible spectacles (*Schauspielen*) the end of the world is the only one for which one does not need to invest any resources to get a special seat. It suffices to be born during the last days of humanity and to know that one lives during these days, in order to constantly sit in the first row. If one has taken a seat there, one can be assured of getting one's money worth when it comes to one's anti-imperial, anti-cosmic, and anti-ontological resentments, as long as the play unfolds in the expected way.

The hope of the apocalyptics can be traced back to a simple and exuberant conviction. They expect to experience the downfall of "this world," sooner or later but in any case during their lifetime. Their intelligence is stimulated by the drive to read the signs that announce the intensely desired disaster. This disposition is the breeding ground for the kind of thinking that makes diagnoses based on apocalyptic assumptions, the thinking that transforms things into signs and signs into omens. The apocalyptics' attitude is dominated by a fever of expectation, a happy sleeplessness of those dreaming of world annihilation and hoping that they will be spared. This is the reason that apocalyptics can overlook pretty much all earthly miseries with the exception of one: that the world refuses to follow its destiny and be annihilated. What refrains from being annihilated will one day be called the "status quo." To sustain itself is the vice of the world. This is the reason for the code word of insiders, "the fact that it continues in this way is the catastrophe."

If apocalyptic predictions do not come true, if the announced day of rage does not arrive in due time, then the beginning of the kingdom of God needs to be backdated. In this case, the vengeful apocalyptic impatience with the world and the hope for "what would be different" need to engage in postapocalyptic compromises with the "status quo." In such arrangements, the Christian age started. Thus every introduction to the history of Christianity should be preceded by a chapter called "When Apocalypticism Fails." This explains why Christianity and gnosis are parallel phenomena that mutually interpret each other insofar as both draw their consequences from the nuisance that the world (why not just call it the Roman empire from now on?) has proven to be resistant to its downfall despite the hastiness of the partisans thirsting for its end.

In this light, it becomes clear why Christianity initially appeared as a bold dissolution of apocalyptic constellations of end time (*Restzeit*) and the wrath of God. Initially, Jesus' message was quasi-naturally premised on the assumption that God has lost patience with the world. This is the reason for the warning that the Day of Judgment would soon arrive, although the day and the hour were still concealed. That at the Day of Judgment large parts of humanity will prove to be beyond rescue is not doubted by anyone infected with end-time fever. John the Baptist believes it as much as Jesus himself, and certainly John, the author of the Christian story of the apocalypse. (In this sense, the later father of horror, St. Augustine, should not be thought of as the inventor of awful additions to a teaching that was originally good in nature. He is only the most attentive and most ruthless interpreter of the foundational documents.) If the Kingdom of God is nigh, then the catastrophe must certainly be waiting. From now on the term "actuality" can no longer be uttered without fear and shivers. After the execution of the Messiah, the rescuing catastrophe is equated with the glorious return of the abject. This is how the thesis concerning the wrath of God can be strengthened through Christian premises. Christ himself will appear as the bringer of the sword at the end days, and he will preside over the court of Judgment Day.

If it were legitimate to ascribe "originality" to figures of sacred history, it would characterize the Christian innovation of a new, ingenious dating and characterization of the Kingdom of God. The genuinely new message is that the coming kingdom is already in place, that it exists "within us" and "among us." This invocation sustained *and* suspended the apocalyptic excitement over the coming end. The question concerning the precise date could thus be put on the back burner, which in fact happened in the generations after Christ. This turn initially made the community of Jesus possible. Paul's network of missions followed, and finally the Christian church came into existence. All three are versions of the same manifest idea. From the perspective of spatial extension, this idea can be summarized by the thesis that "the new world appropriated space already in the old world." From a temporal perspective, it entails the proposition that "the coming world is already present in the actual world." That the entire old world deserves to be dissolved and destroyed should not be forgotten for a second, in spite of the consolidation of the church as a sacred establishment. In this respect, the compromise that resulted from the fusion of apocalypticism and messianic doctrine of salvation, Christianity, is nothing other than a long practice for the revolution. As a result of the association of the themes of presence and advent, closeness and distance, present and future are intertwined in a way that has far-reaching consequences. Ever since, it can be said, the course of events has been under the influence of these conceptions and was shaped by the temporal form of Adventist presentism. Nothing comes into being that has not in some sense already been there. Nothing is actual that is not in some sense still to come.

The price that was paid for the historical compromise of Christians between patience and impatience, or love and rage, was, of course, rather high. How high could only be seen by someone knowledgeable about the consequences of the Christian division between the two "empires"—usually distinguished since Augustine as the community of God, on the one hand, and the worldly empires, on the other. The costs are literally beyond what can be counted: throughout the millennia they have been accredited to the account of the enemy. The term "church tax" gains a terrifying meaning in the light of these benefits. It does not only refer to the economic costs of secular groups for the ecclesiastic parallel community but to the psychic burdens that paid for the existence of the church and its transcendent world behind the world. One can rightly speak of it as the most expensive transfer in the history of the global economy.

Postapocalyptic Christianity secured its survival as a church by subjecting the place of its survival, the world or *saeculum*, to a thoroughgoing devaluation. In order for God to acquire his property from the church, the primary world needed to be ceded to a demon who would assume responsibility for it. This devil is correctly addressed according to Christian protocol as the Prince of This World. In the betrayal of the real world, a betrayal ratified by Augustine, motifs of apocalypticism, Gnosticism, and dualism are interwoven in an extremely damaging manner. Voltaire's saying that the history of mankind is tantamount to excerpts from the annals of hell elegantly summarizes the consequences (or at least the side effects) of the Christian dismissal of the world.

For my purposes, it would be inappropriate to provide a detailed history of the conception of hell. What is important to note in this context of the Christian depictions of the Inferno is that the increasing institutionalization of hell during the long millennium between Augustine and Michelangelo allowed the theme of the transcendent archive of rage to be perfected. The introduction of the deceased into this great collection is a metaphysical necessity. From now on, no one will die without a final examination. The transcendent locations are organized, as readers of Dante well know, into three categories: the hell of perdition, the hell of purgation, and paradise. Arriving souls are assigned to the appropriate section by the most authoritative of judges. All three sections share the character of an archive. While paradise and the hell of perdition constitute static archives in which the eternal presence of rage, or beatitude, dominates, the hell of purgation is a dynamic, intermediary realm in which the great multitude of average sinners are tossed through a purifying torture that comprises seven stages (corresponding to the seven primary sins) before finally reaching the gates of heaven. This process is in precise accordance with each sinner's respective and carefully documented files of transgression.

CHRISTIAN FALLACIES: WHY THE SEARCH FOR REASONS FOR THE RAGE OF GOD IS MISLEADING

IT IS NOT SURPRISING THAT THE DIDACTIC PLAY ABOUT THE WRATH of God already required additional explanations at the time of the first Christian communities. Because Christianity presented itself in its first advertisements as the religion of loving one's enemy, forgiveness, renunciation of rage, and warm-hearted inclusiveness, the conflict between its happy message and its furious eschatology quite soon led to irritations. The prominent position of apocalyptic threat speeches in the collection of authentic words of Jesus inevitably leads to a conflict. Even if one does not agree with Oswald Spengler that the threatening words of Jesus presented his real spirit in the most authentic way,[15] it cannot be denied that the apocalyptic fury lends a characteristic tone to his speeches.

The oldest theological documents of the new movement, the letters of Paul, thus already discuss this dilemma in an all but arbitrary way. Subsequent explicators of rage, who are led by Tertullian and Lactantius, also take on the task of making compatible God's *thymos*, or rather his *orgé*, with the other qualities of the most sublime. There are three threads that connect the available explanations. According to the opinion of the authors, these threads only have to be rightly woven in order to understand why the God of the Christians is not only potentially capable of rage but also needs to unleash this rage at the present moment. Each thread corresponds to a theological concept: the first explains the implications of divine omnipotence, the second explains divine justice, and the third explains divine love. The theologians seek to show with sufficient evidence why rage cannot be excluded from the spectrum of divine attributes.

However, the necessity of the wrath of God cannot be justified convincingly from within theology. It does not at all follow from the "qualities" of God, which we know, as negative theology has always told us, only indirectly and by analogy. The nature of the rage thesis needs to be shown exclusively through a functional analysis, from a metatheological perspective, or in the language of psychopolitics. In fact, the Christianization of the wrath of God leads to a transcendent bank for the purpose of depositing deferred human thymotic impulses and deferred projects of rage whose global design lies beyond the conceptual horizon of the employees of these banks. Moreover, the employees were not supposed to understand the way the bank functioned because transcendent payback transactions could only be carried out in naïveté. The bank undertook these transactions in the form of speech acts, which emphasize the existence of divine rage as well as the reasons to take it seriously. Such acts naturally need to be carried out bona fide because this is the only way through which they can unfold the desired effect, which is to threaten the recipient. Exaggeration is an essential part of this effect, while the slightest bit of irony would be its undoing. The speeches about the wrath of God present themselves as counseling in the shape of insistent prayers. From the point of view of theology, these prayers are dogmatic discourses that provide evidence for the proposition of Catholic ontology according to which the actually existing hell is a necessary and indispensable institution. From this perspective there is a closer relationship between hell and the entire plan of creation than between Banco Ambrosiano and the Vatican.

All the theological deductions of rage consist of pseudo-arguments that are of only a psycho-historical concern. They become intelligible when subjected to a functional analysis of dogma, even if some dogmas have been reformulated and presented as the most cutting-edge results of theological sophism up until the twentieth century, though they still allow insights into obscure areas of historical anthropology. In this context, we can think of the modes of world creation of the *homo hierarchicus*, the psychology of deliberate servitude, the mental dynamics of ontological masochism, the economy of resentment and, generally speaking, the cultural and economic preconditions for the preservation of rage.

Only faith provides an asylum for the three stereotypical deductions of rage: from omnipotence, justice, and the love of God. On the open field of logical evaluation, however, these rage systems quickly collapse. The oldest record of a Christian embarrassment in light of the quality rage reveals the fragility of the foundation. It is well known that in the ninth chapter of his Epistle to the Romans, Paul wrote down the first Christian word in defense of the wrath of God. The occasion was an uncomfortable discovery, which after having been made needed to be immediately concealed because of its fatal implications. The discovery was that God's qualities, omnipotence and justice, are not compatible.

One becomes conscious of this dangerous incompatibility the moment one checks God's omnipotence against its ontological implications. It becomes apparent that absolute power creates an access of free decisions (from a human point of view, arbitrary decisions) that cannot be traced back to rational and universally agreeable criteria. Otherwise, God would only be the secretary of the concepts that human reason comes up with. Consequently, the free omnipotence of God is responsible for infinitely more things in the world than could ever be explained by the principle of justice. Examples for this pervade the Old Testament and apologetic literature. God in fact loves Jacob and dedicates his hatred to Esau; if the sources are credible, he prefers Israel and lets Egypt fall by punishing the pharaoh. Of course he could have reacted otherwise in each of these cases, and all others. However, he did not want to act differently than he acted. But why?

The only truthful answer is (according to Paul and his followers) that one is not permitted to ask "why" questions about the decisions of the Almighty. "Who are you, human, that you dare to dispute God?" From the perspective of the architecture of worldviews, God is precisely what functionalists call the foundation of contingency: all logical regresses end with him. The intellect may rest next to this last information: God's will and chance coincide in the infinite. Here we come across the aforementioned secret of discrimination. Theologians call it under their breaths "*mysterium ininquitatis.*" Indeed ,we can only talk of ultimate power if it expresses itself in absolute freedom of discrimination or preferential treatment. Once it becomes realized, expectations of justice and equal opportunity are suspended. Omnipotence stands for unfairness in the realm of the absolute.

Paul understands the implications of his topic and sees that the other indispensable attribute of God, justice, is endangered. Because God cannot be unjust, one must concede that his omnipotence from time to time overshadows his justice. Thus Paul writes in Romans 9 concerning the revealed truth that God himself obdurated the mind of the Pharaoh (*obdurare*):

> Thou wilt say then unto me, Why doth he yet find fault? For who hath
> resisted his will? Nay but, O man, who art thou that repliest against God?
> Shall the thing formed say to him that formed it, Why hast thou made me
> thus? Hath not the potter power over the clay, of the same lump to make one
> vessel unto honor, and another unto dishonor? What if God, willing to shew
> his wrath, and to make his power known, endured with much longsuffering
> the vessels of wrath fitted to destruction: And that he might make known
> the riches of his glory on the vessels of mercy, which he had afore prepared
> unto glory. (Romans 9:19–23, AV)

The ambiguity is obvious: the apostle needs to use the omnipotence of
the creator in order to explain the unequal treatment of different people; yet
he needs to revert to the justice of God, as well as his love, in order to lessen
the intolerability of this omnipotence. That this to-and-fro movement fails
to provide a justification for the wrath of God is self-evident. If countless
human beings have been created to be vessels of rage, this can only be logically
justified by inferring that rage precedes its reasons or causes. In one sense,
God becomes furious simply from thinking that one of his yet-uncreated
creations will one day deny him his due respect. At the same time, he does
create such disrespectful vessels in order to then practice his righteous rage
against them. Whoever then asks how rage can arouse itself against the
heartened sinner, before the predestined sinner has even been born, should
prove whether he is not a vessel that is destined to be shattered.

The solution of the riddle can be found when looking at the vocabulary
of the author of the Epistle to the Romans; for this purpose, verses 9:22 and
9:23 are of particular importance. There God's "glory" (*potentia, divitias glo-*
riae) is emphasized just as much as his will to "make known" (*notam facere*)
his own power and glory and to "show" (*ostendere*) these. One needs to
take these expressions literally. The divine business of rage rests on the need
to expose the power of being able to express rage as forcefully as possible.
According to its depth structure, it is "ostentatious"—only as the show of
power, as fame, and as a demonstration of glory can it be kept alive and its
authority sustained.

This rage show is, however, a mere prelude to a continuously deferred
feature presentation. This fits another aspect of making threats for the sake
of appearance, an aspect that is rarely missing even in the case of the most
profane expressions of rage. In performance, rage announces that in the
end things will be even worse. Rage is in itself an affect that likes to show

itself and to impress others. This starts at the level of animal expressivity, a fact that Seneca emphasizes in *De ira* by mentioning the irrepressibility of physical symptoms of rage. Every interference with its inherent impulse to manifest itself leads to a shifting of wrathful energies.

Here, we are dealing with a shift from the human to the divine level. To the degree that Christians internalize the prohibitions against rage and revenge that have been imposed upon them, they develop a passionate interest in God's ability to be full of rage. They realize that it is a privilege to practice rage, a privilege they renounce in the interest of the one and only furious one. Their identification with this glory becomes all the more intense because it will reveal itself on the day of rage. Christians always fail to imagine the rage of the lord fiercely enough because they are only allowed to let go of the prohibition of rage on the *dies irae* in order to fully enjoy the last spectacle. It is not accidental that the depiction of the Day of Judgment became the paradigmatic topic in the Christian imagination.

The two other derivations of the wrath of God, from justice and from the love of God, equally lead us into rushed contradictions and vicious circles. Simply pointing to the principle of proportionality is sufficient to show that the wrath of God cannot be derived from justice. The principle of proportionality serves as a regulative idea in the domain of what is considered just and appropriate: finite guilt can never lead to infinite penalty. However, because penalties of this kind are used as a threat, God's abysmal injustice (once again: his omnipotence) is used in order to demonstrate his justice. The failure of this argument is obvious. It is only the transition into a performative register that is responsible for the rage-theological intensification. For nothing could create a stronger impression than the imagining and depiction of divine terrors. These enter the game as soon as the conception of unbearable torment is combined with the idea of eternity. Rage, which is depicted as a consequence of justice, in reality obeys a magisterial political logic. It is embodied in an imaginary theater of horror that preserves for eternity that which could not be endured for a second in time. This is the reason fire has a prominent significance for the *terror perpetuus*. The psychopolitical necessity that was already evident for the early Christians, the need to present God at the height of his capacity to be enraged, was little by little reinforced by theological arguments. This is most obvious in the writings of the great polemicist, Tertullian, who had no problem in promising total satisfaction in the beyond via a thirst for revenge stimulated through a renunciation of revenge. I will return to this topic soon.

What remains to be discussed here is the derivation of the wrath of God from his love, and what is interesting about it are the forms in which it fails. For it is here that the dynamics of resentment responsible for the entire domain becomes especially evident. Since Lactantius, apologists for the theorem of rage have inferred from the love of God the fact that he is not indifferent to the actions of humanity. This was taken as a reason to assume bipolarity in his affects. If God would not hate the godless and the unjust, he could not love the pious and the just. Thus God is enraged, *quod erat demonstrandum.*

One who does not want to waste time with the psychological naïveté of this thesis can see how the derivation of the wrath of God from love fails in a more sophisticated way, which is, moreover, almost contemporary. Hans Urs von Balthasar locates the wrath of God doctrine directly with the highest Christian theologoumenon, that is, the understanding of the trinity. He interprets the indifference of humanity to the Trinitarian communication of love as an insult of the honor of God. Rage, then, becomes an adequate answer to this insult. The wish of the Almighty to include all humans in the message of his love is initially to be read as a sign of generosity. However, it becomes alarming if it is accompanied by a magic right to penetration. If one attempts to withstand this right, one becomes guilty of insulting the Trinity. This reveals a barely concealed gender-mythological speculation according to which God is only masculine, while all other actors in the holy comedy have to accept feminine positions unless they are religiously frigid. The concept of insult reveals how the crude regulatory naïveté of the Lactanctic rage theology passes into a more refined erotodynamic naïveté of a semimodern *theo*-psychology.

Balthasar, the most important thymotic among twentieth-century theologians, smartly emphasizes the honor of God: what follows from this concept is, first of all, how the loving God is insulted by the creature that is nonloving or orients its life according to other values. This is admittedly somewhat absurd; on the other hand, the dimension of divine "narcissism" and its striving for glory is emphasized to such a degree that the functional theory of rage seems to be confirmed. According to Balthasar, God has chronic difficulty with the enforcement of his glory, since it has from time immemorial had an occult side. How is it supposed to be possible that the unimpressible at the same time bears witness to the glory of God? In light of this complication it is once more possible to establish a link to the psychopolitical interpretation of the wrath of God: it becomes established from the compulsion to present a power that arises out of impotence.

The entire group of theses concerning the wrath of God, including its ghastly eschatological depictions, can only be reconstructed in the light of a thymotic economy. It is legitimate to let the biblical and Scholastic justifications of the wrathful God rest because of their logical inconsistencies. In reality, the title "God" functions in these discourses only as a place marker for the depository of human savings of wrath and as frozen wishes for revenge. The wrathful God is nothing but the administrator of secular resentment accounts, which are deposited with him or with his subordinate diabolic executives in order to be ready for withdrawal at a later time. The assets emerge through inhibited impulses of rage whose release was circumvented by such moral acts as forgiveness and the renunciation of revenge. The glory of God serves in this context as a guarantee of his legal capacity as executor of the treasury and as administrator over the currency. If he is elevated to the status of the Lord of History, it is because history includes precisely those mnemonic functions without which the stable relationship between rage deposits and rage payments could not be ascertained.

The motif of the *dies irae*, the day of rage, would never have reached its psychohistorical efficacy if the idea of the great payday was not logically connected to the complementary idea of a long phase of saving. What is called "history" gains its definite coherence only by designating the period during which the deposited quantities of rage and intensities of revenge keep the same value. Sufficiently long periods of acquiring rage and depositing revenge have to precede the day of rage. History is the bridge that connects the first deposits with the expiration of all grace periods. For this period of time there exists a strict prohibition of inflation. From the perspective of the criticism of morality, inflation is called a change of values, and precisely this change of values needs to be ruled out.

Assuming that Nietzsche's interpretation is correct, the historical Christians were indeed often people who experienced high resentment tension. They had to reject every change of values that could devalue the historically accumulated assets of rage in the transcendent bank. However, because theologians had a realistic conception of both the inevitability of a change of value and the necessary weakening of impulses of rage and revenge, they compensated the danger of inflation by postponing penalties to eternity. By declaring all sentences to last for eternity, they made sure that no historically conditioned losses or invalidations of rage would have to be accepted. The house of revenge should also not lose anything. In this context, the doctrine concerning the eternity of sentences, which is otherwise the bleakest spot of the religion of reconciliation, becomes understandable as an exceptionally motivated demand. Wherever the preservation of guilt has to exist over a long stretch of time, the recourse to eternity becomes indispensible. In good just as in bad days, eternity is the asylum of resentment.

In Praise of Purgatory

CHRISTIAN THEOLOGIANS AFTER THE MIDDLE AGES NEED TO BE credited for having started to sense the intolerability of their own resentment constructions. Subsequently, they felt compelled to weaken the excesses of their theology of rage. This was reflected in the invention of purgatory. It is probably not overdrawn to characterize the new theology of purgatory, which rapidly expanded from the eleventh century on, as the real innovation of the Christian thought that created history. With it came both an epochal structural change in the processing of resentment and a new logic of transition. It leads to a theory of second chances and third places. Studying these largely forgotten, although well reconstructed phenomena,[16] will reveal, in the mediation forms of purgatorial processual logic, almost everything that, during the twentieth century, was referred to by Merleau-Ponty's cloudy expression "the adventures of the dialectic."

These dialectics make clear the need for a third location between the Inferno and the Paradise. In contrast to the farmers and the monks of the early Middle Ages, who had made the submissive *humilitas* their second nature, the reemerging citizenry made thymotic demands in the realm of religion. These could not be reconciled with the terror of subordinating oneself to the alternatives of salvation or damnation. Christian citizens of newly flourishing European city cultures during the early high Middle Ages were the first to become convinced that inherited eschatologies were untenable. They were the first ones for whom the need emerged to dismantle the problematic binary choice between salvation and eternal damnation. Instead, they introduced a crossover between these two poles. This process of dismantling became all the more necessary when eschatological threats were not primarily addressed to non-Christians, that is, to the members of *gentes*, the "heathens," those foreign to religion, as well as the "insidious Jews," but to the more or less pious inhabitants of Christianized Europe.

The harshness of the tone with which eschatological thinking of the time of the church fathers addressed non-Christians, who were taken to deserve condemnation, can be seen in the polemical writings of the Catharginian Tertullian (ca. 155–ca. 220), most obviously in his treatise *De spectaculis*. Although for the historian of dogma it is a rather embarrassing example of logical Christian thinking, it is of high testimonial value for external interpretations of metaphysical strategies for working through rage. In *De spectaculis* the connection between earthly renunciation and satisfaction in the beyond is revealed in an almost obscene fashion. It is not accidental that Nietzsche and Max Scheler explicitly point to this work in their analyses of resentment. After Tertullian provides reasons that Christians should not be present at heathen spectacles (in particular because theaters are the romping places for demons), he directly discusses the divine compensations for earthly abstinence. He knows that Roman Christians require a certain reserve in order to be able to do without the "games." The chariot races in the circus, the obscenities in the theater, the stupid exercises of fattened athletes in the stadium, and, most important, the fascinating cruelties in the arena, were everyday amusements in Roman society. However, Tertullian offers a compensation for staying away from the Roman spectacles. He erects a divine comedy over and against the earthly shows, a divine comedy that does not merely satisfy the curiosity of its audience but also does justice to the performative character of the glory of God by means of explicit demonstrations of rage. What will provide the highest satisfaction to the redeemed souls in heaven? They are able to dedicate themselves to the view of an exquisite enforcement of sentences:

> But what a spectacle is already at hand—the return of the lord, now no object of doubt, now exalted, now triumphant! . . . Yes, and there are still to come other spectacles—that last, that eternal Day of Judgement. . . . What sight shall wake my wonder, what my laughter, my joy and exultation? As I see all those kings, those great kings . . . groaning in the depths of darkness! . . . those sages, too, the philosophers blushing before their disciples as they blaze together. . . . And then there will be the tragic actors to be heard, more vocal in their own tragedy; and the players to be seen, lither of limb by far in the fire; and then the charioteer to watch, red all over in the wheel of flame, . . . unless it be that not even then would I wish to see them, in my desire rather to turn an insatiable gaze on them who vented their rage and fury on the Lord. . . . Such sights, such exultation,—what praetor, consul, quaestor,

priest, will ever give you of his bounty? And yet all these, in some sort, are ours, pictured through faith in the imagination of the spirit.[17]

Tertullian's statement is important because it reveals an early stage of the process of rage manipulation in a postapocalyptic style. During this stage, the inner censorship against openly revealed satisfaction through imagined horrors has not yet been implemented. More than a hundred years later the church leader Lactantius, in his work *De mortibus persecutorum*, will once again delight in surpassing the real horrors of the treatment of Christians by the Romans through the imagined cruelty of eschatological revenge. Both authors avowedly emphasize the basic trait of otherworldly revenge. It is known that Tertullian is also the first theologian of the Christian renunciation of revenge.[18] He promises that suspended revenge will lead to an infinite satisfaction of the desire to witness revenge in the other world and thus strictly applies the postapocalyptic schema of "only then and yet also now."

This arrangement is based on a juridical conception of the renunciation of rage. Who distances himself from rage here and now needs to be able to rely on God as the bookkeeping avenger. The person who does not attend the spectacles of this world will be presented a much more stimulating spectacle in the other world. The view of eternal torments satisfies the yearning of the apocalyptic for a total administration of the world within one single spectacle. Thus theory and resentment form a unity; pure view takes on the form of pure compensation. Those who have been redeemed not only enjoy the salvific view of God but also participate in the ultimate worldview of God, which looks down on the world that has been judged and destroyed.

WITH THE INTRODUCTION OF PURGATORY, THE CHRISTIAN management of rage gains momentum. To this point it was dominated by the primitive harshness of the choice between condemnation and salvation. This departure was made possible through a logical operation the audacity of which is difficult to comprehend within the context of modern theoretical positions. In order to establish the otherworldly place of purgatory as a third eschatological space, the introduction of a processual moment into the heretofore timeless and statically conceived divine world became necessary. Thanks to this innovation, a middle segment of eternity was reintroduced into time and transformed into a stage for a cathartic sequel to earthly existence. Thus purgatorial post-time was added to existential time. One could claim straightaway that purgatory is the matrix and the pattern of what later was called history, that is, the processuality, which is thought to be singular, in which humanity constitutes itself as a global collective in order to, step by step, emancipate itself from the burden of its local pasts. If it is the case that in the beyond we still find catharsis (or progress), transformation, and "development," then the place of purification becomes latently historical. If human history orients itself against the background of purification (or progress), then it latently takes on purgatorial functions.

To finish this excursion into the history of the religious processing of rage in the Old World, I want to call attention to the increasing similarity of purgatorial practices to formal monetary transactions. Speaking of the creation of a treasury of rage should be taken as merely metaphorical. The transition from masses of rage from the treasury form to the capital form administered by banks can be taken literally, to some extent. As we know, the invention of purgatory soon led to an encompassing system of advance payments for the otherworldly purification sentences, a system that came to be known as the selling of indulgences (*Ablaßhandel*). Thanks to these transactions, the pope and his bishops belonged to the group of the first gamblers in the emerging capitalist monetary economy. Lutheran Christians probably recall that the anti-Roman fervor of the reformer was, among other things, provoked by the excesses of the business with the fear of hell. It supported the illusion that through the acquisition of "indulgences," it would be possible to secure otherworldly salvation. Luther's impulse was reactionary in an authentic sense insofar as he connected his faith and the pathos of grace to the unrelenting slogan "back to the deserved wrath of God" (which was then, of course, compensated by God's grace). As partisan of an either/or decision, Luther abhorred the modern sentiment behind the third way that the Catholic Church had laid out. This third way allowed for a reduction of the negotiable divine amount of rage for sins by making anticipatory payments. This procedure bears more than a superficial resemblance to modern installment buying.

In this respect, Catholicism had already approached modern Mammonism much more than was ever possible for the much referred to spirit of Protestantism and its connection to capitalism. At least it needs to be admitted that the Catholic accumulation of a rage treasury and the establishment of the first general rage bank could not yet fulfill all important banking functions because the transformation of rage treasuries into fully valid, conferrable, and investable capital was not possible under Catholic supervision.

On this level, Christian eschatology did not get beyond the role of a savings bank. The transition to the investment of assets was accomplished only by the later rage organizations of the nineteenth and twentieth centuries.

The modern face of the Catholic system of selling indulgences showed itself in the openness with which the business borders between other-worldly and this-worldly commodities were overcome. This system created procedures to pay off transcendent debts with secular money. During the twentieth century, the atheist Catholic Georges Bataille reminded us of the necessity of a universal economy that does not stop at the commerce of commodities among one another, commodities and assets, or assets and assets. Rather it once again transcends the boundary that separates what is here and what is beyond to expand to transactions between life and death.

With this reference to the stimulation of early-modern financial economy through the business with eschatological anxiety, let me end this excursion to the religious sources of the old European management of rage. We cannot say with Dante, on his return from the *Inferno*, "*E quindi uscimmo a riveder le stele.*"[19] After the return to modern times we perceive a sky darkened by thunderclouds. There is only one spot where it is torn open. There one can perceive the red star of the revolution in the East, which rushes anxiously across the short twentieth century.

THE RAGE REVOLUTION

ON THE COMMUNIST WORLD BANK OF RAGE

> Let the axe dance on their skulls!
> Strike them dead! Strike them dead!!
> Bravo: and skulls fit well to ash trays
> Rage is the grand marshal.
> Hunger is the regulator.
> Bayonet, browning, bomb . . .
> Ahead! Speed up!
>
> —VLADIMIR MAYAKOVSKI, *150 MILLIONS*

CONSIDERING THE ORIGIN, IDENTIFICATION, AND WORKING mechanism of divine wrath reveals a rarely noticed truth: apocalyptic theory allows for a unique frenetic exhilaration. It is ignited by the expectation that everything in the last instance will happen completely differently from how those currently successful believe it will. The apocalyptic's view transforms circumstances and events into unmistakable hints of the approaching end of the untenable old world. However, because this ending is yearned for intensely, even the darkest signs of the age are evangelically charged. While Greek theory exhilarates through the conception of participating in the timeless worldview of the gods, apocalyptic theory is intoxicated with the idea that from now on everything is only a part of a final vision.

After his polemics against Roman spectacles, Tertullian addresses the conversations of those who have been relieved and asks himself: "What sight shall wake my wonder, what my laughter, my joy and exultation? As I see all those kings, those great kings . . . groaning in the depths of darkness!"[1] This combination of image and affect reveals the true psychopolitical character (or one of the true characteristics) of the reversal of positions that lately would be described as revolution. The religiously justified and demanded total transformation reaches beyond the boundary between here and the beyond. It calls for a strict symmetric exchange between actual and future situations. The desire to see the concept of revolution realized according to its geometric meaning can be satisfied during, and only during, this metaphysical maneuver. Tertullian does not leave any doubt that this transformation caused by God's almighty will turns the affect balances of human existence upside down: "Then let us mourn (*lugeamus*) while the heathen rejoice, that, when they have begun to mourn, we may rejoice (*gaudeamus*)."[2] The symmetry of the reversal is guaranteed through deposits of rage which have been stored with God. Once this depository matures on the Day of Judgment, the cosmic evening of suffering will be realized. Suffer in time, rejoice in eternity; rejoice in time, suffer for eternity. The satisfaction of resentment is exclusively secured through the anticipation of the future exchange of positions.

IF A REVOLUTION IS NOT ENOUGH

LATER, REAL "REVOLUTIONS" WERE ACCOMPANIED ONLY BY PHANTASMS of these symmetries. A believer that the last will be first would have to regard the realized revolution as a strict teacher of disappointment. Restif de la Bretonne mentions in *The Nights of Paris* that on July 13, 1789, a group of robbers from Faubourg Saint-Antoine, a "horrifying mob," said the following: "Today the last day for the rich and wealthy has started: tomorrow it is our turn. Tomorrow we will sleep in feather beds and those whose lives we have graciously spared will then, assuming that this is their wish, be able to reside in our darkest holes."[3] Reality would show within a few weeks that the revolution does not lead to the swapping of domiciles between rich and poor. Although there are new appointments to positions of power, at most an increase of preferential positions and attractive offices, the revolution never brings about an actual reversal of top and bottom, not to mention material equality. In the most favorable case, the revolution spreads the spectrum of elite functions so that more candidates are able to secure their profits. The personnel and the semantics change, but the asymmetries persist. If this is avoidable or inevitable? Only an interrogation of history can decide this question.

Since asymmetry is nothing but a technical term for inequality—which is the same as "injustice" from the perspective of egalitarian premises—all revolutions since the French Revolution of 1789 have been accompanied by consequent waves of disappointment and frustration. In addition to resignation and a cynical turning away from yesterday's illusions, these waves often lead to momentous formations of rage, which in turn produced the desire for an extended and deepened restaging of the revolutionary drama.

Since the events following the storming of the Bastille, the ideological and political history of Europe has been marked by the waiting of the disappointed for the second, the true, actual, and all-encompassing revolution. This second revolution is supposed to provide a delayed gratification for those who have been deceived and left behind during the great days. This is why the motto of the past two centuries was: The fight goes on! The use of this motto can be traced more or less explicitly to all dissidence movements from the radicals of 1792 up to the alter-mondialists of Seattle, Genoa, and Davos. After the victorious Third Estate had taken what it deserved in 1789, the losers also wanted to have their due. These losers were the Fourth Estate excluded from the feasts of the bourgeoisie.

The primary guilt for the exclusion of many from better positions was usually not attributed to a structural scarcity of preferred positions. Rather, an argumentative strategy was chosen according to which the combination of suppression, exploitation, and alienation was made responsible for a situation in which good positions were not available to everyone. Overcoming the evil triad would supposedly create a world in which the specters of scarcity and injustice were dispelled. For the first time in the history of humanity, a theater was supposed to have been created whose audience hall would consist exclusively of first rows.

Throughout the two-hundred-year-old tradition of the left, one largely ignored the fact that the motivation behind social utopias was only to a small extent abolishing the privileges of the ruling class. True, Saint-Just, the death angel of egalitarianism, had taught that the power to change the world belonged to the unhappy. But was this reason enough to make the happy minority as unhappy as the miserable majority just to abide by the law of justice? Wouldn't it indeed have been simpler to create misery for 1 million happy people out 20 million French, rather than creating the illusion that it was possible to transform the miserable 19 million into satisfied citizens? The fantastic idea of translating the privileges of the happy into egalitarian entitlements always seemed much more attractive. It could be argued that this operation provided the original contribution of France to the psychopolitics of the nineteenth and twentieth centuries. Only thanks to this contribution was it possible for the French to redeem their soul after the horrible interlude of the guillotine. The price, however, was a certain inclination toward rebellious illusions, which since then has not missed any opportunity to manifest itself. At the last minute, the revolutionary nation stepped back from the abyss out of which resentment against the unhappy was lured, and France displayed the confidence to enter into an offensive strategy of generosity for the sake of the unhappy. The democratization of happiness constitutes the leitmotif of modern social politics in the Old World. It began with the fantasies of the early socialists—"Yes, sugar, herbs for all!"—and reaches to the redistributive policies of Rhenish capitalism.

Given the implications of the "continuing revolution" in terms of illusionary dynamics, it is not surprising that the strongest social-revolutionary impulses always emanated from those activists who spoke in the name of the masses but never forgot their own ambitions to climb the social ladder. Their weakness consisted in ignoring an elementary fact: even after successful transformations, good positions remain scarce and are struggled over. This ignorance of the real is methodical. If one can speak of a blind spot in the eye of the revolutionary, it consists in the expectation, which is never admitted, of reaping the fruits of the change. Is it thus legitimate to claim that revolutionaries are career oriented just like everyone else? It is, though not without qualification. At least initially, revolutionary business stands under the law of selflessness, or at least it appears this way. It is not accidental, after all, that in speeches of praise for the most ruthless functionaries of the overthrow it is said that they did not act out of any kind of ambition for themselves. This, however, only proves that it is possible to combine multiple blind spots. A milieu, revolutionary or not, is always also an alliance for the sake of jointly ignoring matters of fact that are obvious to those who are foreign to the milieu. What is obscured reveals itself afterward in the bitterness of failed aspirants because they were not taken care of while others made their way up. Then the complaint is voiced that the revolution has devoured its children. This is the proof that rage belongs to the renewable energies of those left behind.

Ghostly Exhilarations

PSYCHOLOGICAL RETROFITTING BECOMES INDISPENSABLE UNDER these conditions. During the political crises of modernity, exhilaration makes a pact with revolt in order to simplify the latter's business. This business consists in, from time to time, renewing the illusions that those on top could soon switch places with those at the bottom. Nobody less than Alexis de Tocqueville, an eyewitness of the Paris turmoil of 1848, describes in his *Recollections* an episode that endows the laughter of the humiliated and offended with a prophetic significance. The scene occurs during dinner on a June day in 1848 in a beautiful apartment on the *rive gauche*, in the seventh arrondissement of Paris. Antonio Negri cites it in order to counter what he regarded as Jacques Derrida's far too pacific, or harmless, elaborations in *Specters of Marx* with a more robust interpretation of the revolutionary spook:

> The Tocqueville family is reunited. Nevertheless, in the calm of the evening, the cannonade fired by the bourgeoisie against the rebellion of rioting workers resounds suddenly—distant noises from the right bank. The diners shiver, their faces darken. But a smile escapes a young waitress who serves their table and has just arrived from the Faubourg Saint Antoine. She's immediately fired. Isn't the true specter of communism perhaps there in that smile? The one that frightened the Tsar, the pope . . . and the Lord of Tocqueville? Isn't a glimmer of joy there, making for the specter of liberation?[4]

THIS SIGN OF EXHILARATION IS ALREADY QUITE DIFFERENT FROM THE forced smile that we encounter in Tertullian's fantasy of the Day of Judgment. In a way, it is part of actual turmoil. It is carried on the surge of events, which reminds us from time to time that everything could turn out to be very different from what the well-fed people of success expect.

Since more recent history takes on the role of judging the old world, it executes in its extreme moments the judgment of the present over the past. For a moment the smiling servant secretly but nevertheless clearly joins the side of those revolting. The guests at the full table had every right to fear the verdicts of the worse-off. Later generations do not know whether during this exhilaration it was class hatred or the pleasant anticipation of times of change that were announced through the noise on the streets. Did the maid smile because she was expecting to spend the following nights with one of the warriors? Or did she even believe that soon she would sit at the table herself and that Monsieur Tocqueville would have to serve her? In any case, such a smile no longer needs any apocalyptic pretenses. Actual events allow their interpreters to predict the future out of the rage of the present.

If revolutionary intentions are transformed into a force of action that has to prevail throughout significant periods of time, an explicit psychopolitics of the inner just as much as the outer becomes indispensable. Such a psychopolitics faces the challenge of creating a liquid rage reserve to fend off the depressive temptations that inevitably follow political backlashes—one may think for example of Lenin's "emigration blues" and his increasing nervous neuropathies after the disappointment of his revolutionary hopes in 1905.[5] The correct way seems to consist in working on a secure connection between exhilaration and militancy. In a letter to Marx dated February 13, 1851, Friedrich Engels articulates a part of the psychopolitical prudential rules intended to allow the revolutionary to survive in the midst of the historical "maelstrom." Part of it consists in jealously watching over one's own intellectual superiority and material independence "by way of being *substantially* more revolutionary than the others." Consequently, any kind of official governmental function has to be avoided, if possible, and every party position as well. A believer in the revolution does not need the formal recognition of holding office, nor any acclamation through "a herd of jackasses who swear by us because they think we're of the same kidney as they."[6] This means "no seat on committees, etc., no responsibility for jackasses, merciless criticism of everyone, and, besides, that serenity of which all the conspiracies of blockheads cannot deprive us."[7] This marks the reawakening of the Aristotelian recommendation: "Never hate, but despise often."

In a letter that Rosa Luxemburg wrote to her friend Mathilde Wurm on December 28, 1916, from a prison in Berlin, a letter which has rightly become famous, there are comparable richly orchestrated dynamic figures of affection. They are complemented by a desperately courageous, revolutionary-humanist credo, which has understandably become part of the annals of left militancy. At the beginning of the letter, the prisoner's intense dissatisfaction with whimsy in a letter from another friend is discharged:

> In the melancholic view, I have been complaining that you people are not marching up to the cannon's mouth. 'Not marching' is a good one! You people do not march; you do not even walk; you creep. It is not simply a difference of degree, but rather of kind. On the whole, you people are a different zoological species than I, and your grousing, peevish, cowardly and half-hearted nature has never been as alien, as hateful to me, as it is now. . . . As for me, although I have never been soft, lately I have grown hard as polished steel, and I will no longer make the smallest concession either in political or

personal discourse. . . . Do you have enough now for a New Year's greeting? Then see that you remain a *Mensch*! . . . And that means to be firm, lucid and cheerful. Yes, cheerful despite everything and anything—since whining is the business of the weak.[8]

This singular document makes clear that more than melancholy was prohibited in the stream of victorious bourgeois progress, a fact that was described in 1969 by Wolf Lepenies in his classic study *Melancholie und Gesellschaft* (Melancholy and society). The bourgeois leaders of the proletarian revolutionary movement also issued a prohibition against whining. It was thought that any inclination toward self-pity would deduct energies from the agents of world change, energies that would be lost for the great plan. Against this background it would be interesting to read what Rosa Luxemburg would have written to Jenny Marx. Karl Marx confides to his friend Engels in November 1868 that "my wife has for years . . . lost her spiritual balance. With her lament and crankiness she tortures the children to death."[9]

Almost one hundred years later, with the knowledge of the failure of the Soviet master plan, Antonio Negri attempted to reclaim exhilaration. This time, he does not attempt it in the name of the industrial proletariat, which had exhausted its role as historically efficacious rage collective under a messianic flag. The new subjects of militant exhilaration are from now on supposed to be the poor, the people at the rim of society, the bohemians around the world, which Negri once again appeals to as the "multitude." He claims to have observed a promising smile on their lips, a "poor smile of outlaws," which has once and for all emancipated itself from the existing conditions. His role model is Charlie Chaplin, who in *Modern Times* subversively connected poverty and irrepressible vitality.[10] After saying goodbye to the world revolution, what remains for eternal militancy is, it seems, only the laughter of those who do not have anything to laugh about.

THE EPOCHAL PROJECT:
AROUSING THE *THYMOS* OF THE ABJECT

THE ABOVE REMARKS DO MORE THAN PROVIDE EVIDENCE FOR THE frequently documented connection between forced exhilaration and resentment. The outspoken words of Friedrich Engels, the vehement confession of Rosa Luxemburg, and finally Antonio Negri's hints of the ghostly smile of the servant and the equally unconditional laughter of the underdog—all of these reveal clearly that such appeals to cheerfulness pursue an aim beyond personal moods. It is not at all the case that these authors want to contribute to an anxiously optimistic attitude toward life, an attitude that is at home in the Christian petit bourgeois *juste milieu*. In reality, if the call for exhilaration is of any importance, it is exclusively as a demand for a sovereign attitude. The sovereignty desired by dissidents is, however, not looked for while hovering over the turmoil. The goal is to find it amidst of the battle din of time. It is gained through the deliberate acceptance of a plight that no person capable of rational deliberation would take over. To be sovereign means to vote for that through which one is overburdened.

Militants aim to transform their existence into a center of world-changing rage. They are engaged in a permanent war on two fronts, against happiness and irony. This makes them into inverse romantics who, instead of sinking into world-weariness, want to embody the rage of the world in their person. Just as the romantic subject conceives of itself as the gathering point of pain, where surge not only personal grievances but also the sufferings of the world, the militant subject conceives of his life as the gathering point of rage, where all the unpaid bills are registred and stored for future payback. Apart from the reasons for outrage in the present, all of the unatoned-for horrors of past history are recorded. The strong heads of protest are the encyclopedists who collect the knowledge concerning the rage of humankind. The immense amounts of injustice are piled up in their occult archives, which leftwing historians characterize as the repositories of class societies. This is the justification for the amalgam of sentimentality and implacability that is typical of revolutionary affectivity. If one does not feel the rage of millenia in oneself, one misunderstands what is from now on at stake.

It becomes apparent that after the death of God, a new carrier of rage was needed. If human beings take over this role, they intimate more or less explicitly that history itself needs to secure the coming and execution of the Day of Judgment. The question, "What needs to be done?" can only be raised once those participating take over the mandate to secularize hell and to relocate the court of judgment into the present. While a believer around 1900 would have wanted prayer, "O God, to whom vengeance belongeth, show thyself!" (Psalm 94), he would have to accept anarchists and professional revolutionaries entering his room. The price necessary for the turn to immanence in light of monotheist tradition is that the final horror becomes fully secular, pragmatic, and political. This attitude reached its most expressive form in the Russian terrorists who destabilized the empire of the czar with countless attacks starting in 1878. This "thirty years' apostolate of blood" is summarized in the words that the accused Kaliayev presented to the court: "I consider my death as a supreme protest against a world of blood and tears."[11]

From the perspective of militant activists, the current social conditions—and I am speaking now of a period whose beginning can be dated to the last third of the eighteenth century—provides an outlook lamentable in every respect. On the one hand, it is unfortunate that things are as they are. On the other hand, it is deplorable that things as they stand do not bring forth a much higher degree of outrage. It is obvious that most people lack not only the necessary means to live a humane life but also the rage to revolt against this lack. As soon as one concedes the changeability of the world through human interventions in the natural and social orders, following the bourgeois theoreticians of progress, the second lack inevitably becomes the focus of attention. It is a deficit that activists believe can be overcome by their methods. While assuming that material poverty can be abolished through technical progress and a revolutionary redistribution of existing goods—and in the last instance even an emancipatory reorganization of production—the disciples of unconditional militancy announce that from now on they are responsible for the spread of rage and indignation.

Hence, since "society" primarily suffers from an unforgivable lack of manifest rage with regard to its own conditions, the development of a culture of indignation through the methodically exercised excitation of rage becomes the most important psychopolitical task, a task first taken up during the French Revolution, when the idea of "criticism" entered its triumphal course through the sphere of the existing conditions. The radical habitus of large milieus during the nineteenth and twentieth centuries is attributable to the victory of criticism: the abjection of the "establishment" countless contemporaries was an a priori moral date. The militant currents of the nineteenth and twentieth centuries converged at this point, regardless of whether they followed the anarchistic, communist, international-socialist, or national-socialist rallying cries.

In the more talented militant minds, there is a certain megalothymic sentiment. This sentiment is revealed in the certainty that only generous outrage qualifies one to lead a certain movement. Naturally, militancy is for whatever reason hardly conceivable without a certain dose of thymotic irritability. From now on, however, "to militate" means nothing less than attributing a new subject to human history, a subject designed according to the rule of "rage." To the extent to which militancy connects itself with moral and social intelligence, its agents' complex of rage and pride builds itself up to the level of an authentic megalothymics. The militant human being is not angry only as a result of his own affairs; if necessary, he transforms his personal feelings into the resonating ground of a universally significant upsurge of rage. Whether or not one believes in the ideal generalizations of the (for the most part) well-cultivated and well-fed rebels is initially only a question of taste.

At any rate, the militant idealisms that have become the important and even determining factors for serious politics during the last two hundred years remain totally incomprehensible without acknowledgment of the megalothymic, the *vulgo* and its ambitious and arrogant bearers. They would seem strange even to today's Westerners, members of an age without idea or significant politics. At the same time, they explain why the stronger minds of the opposition were for the most part morally sensitive commoners who, motivated by a mixture of ambition and indignation against the establishment, joined the camp of revolt or the revolution. What Albert Camus said about the birth of the new community out of the spirit of indignation is true for all of these people: "I rebel, therefore we exist"—a sentence whose hardly comprehensible pathos clearly belongs to the past.[12] A few decades later, Heiner Müller let his figures exclaim in a kindred spirit, "The home of the slaves is the revolt."[13]

It is not necessary to explain here in extreme detail why such statements do not fit the taste of the present. They sound like hollow slogans from an almanac for educated losers. For the historian they can serve as proof that the "revolutionary subject" in psychopolitical terms primarily referred to a functioning thymotic collective. Naturally, such a collective could not have presented itself with such a title both because the teachings of *thymos* had faded during the bourgeois century and also because rage, ambition, and indignation never seemed to be sufficient motives to justify their presentation on the political stage. Only slowly was it understood that the noble superstructure would remain mere fiction without an ignoble foundation. The theme of both Virgil and Freud, in which one must stir up the netherworld in order to win over the elevated gods does not just describe trips to Hades; it also points to the political arrangements for setting free those forces that have waited under civilized garments for the opportunity to explode, much like Typhon, the hundred-headed monster that Zeus buried beneath Mount Etna.

The rhetoric of the left was from its beginning confronted with the task of translating the affects of the "dangerous classes" into the language of ideals. It was the mission of revolutionary semantics to gain access to the ascendant energies, to transfigure them with Apollonian slogans. In fact, this connection of the higher and the lower created the obsession of modernity, the *idée fixe* of new times: whoever would make history in support of the degraded and humiliated must go beyond mere postulates. She would have to show that this time the historical tendency was in line with morality. The violence of facts, buried in the relationships of production, was supposed to be subservient to goodwill. It was supposed to help end an entire age of injustice. From now on, to support the revolution meant to participate in the building of a vehicle to a better world, a vehicle powered by its own rage resources and steered by well-informed, utopian pilots.

Work on this project had to start with the support of the rage-driven forces. The formula for this endeavor could have been "*intellectus quaerens iram*," if the doctors of the industrial conflicts were still able to speak Latin. As soon as insight begins its search for rage, it discovers a world of reasons to rebel, and this discovery is the drive for the translation of theory into praxis. However, only intellectuals are affected by the embarrassment that, for them, theory precedes praxis. For praxis-oriented people, the situation has always been the opposite. They discover their battle lines and only then look for the fitting justifications. When Bakunin, for example, stated in 1869 with regard to the stupidity of the sentiment of the Russian people: "We have to stir up this ruinous sleep, this dullness, this apathy by all means. . . . We want that now only the deed dictates the word,"[14] he was actually addressing a future wave of terrorists, who do not feel any need for theories in order to act. For them, assuming that their rage had indeed been directed at something beyond its horizon, the reverse formula was true: "*ira quaerens intellectum.*" On the stage of the real world, rage, indignation, or "the movement" always preceded ideologies. Whatever the fighting heroes brought forward to justify their actions, the justification followed the path that rage was already traversing.

FOR PSYCHOHISTORIANS AND POLITICAL SCIENTISTS IT WOULD BE A rewarding task to retell the history of social movements from the eve of the

French Revolution until the age of postmodern distractions as the narrative of thymotic collectives. Modern militancy looks back on a long succession of rage corporations in the shape of secret societies, terrorist organizations, revolutionary cells, national and supranational organizations, workers' parties, unions of all shades, aid organizations, and artistic associations. All of these are organized according to conditions of membership, rituals, and club activities, as well as their newspapers, journals, and editorial houses. Let us not forget that even for the Russian revolutionaries in exile during the regime of the czar, the publication and secret distribution of their newspapers—in particular the ominous *Iskar*—made up most of their activities. However different these forms of organization and media of communication might have been, all of these rage associations competed against one another to get the main part in the screenplay of history after 1789: the revolutionary subject who would patiently complete the task of emancipation and, *eo ipso*, the task of democratizing all privileges, which the bourgeoisie had left only partially completed.

Gatherings of wrath begin almost without exception with an appeal to "the people." As a reservoir of subversive energy and explosive unhappiness, this mythical force was enlisted again and again for the creation of insurgent movements. For over two centuries, the concrete forms of thymotic collectives emanated from this matrix, from the French clubs of the Jacobins and the *enragés* of the great days, to the English dissenters and the "poor of Christ" (those Wesleyan Methodists who experienced their subjectivization as a calling to become preachers of morality),[15] to the activists of the Russian, Chinese, Cuban, and Cambodian revolutions and the new social movements of global capitalism. None of these collectives could have gained power without the exuberant belief that in its "people" rage and justice had become one.

Early German communist groups also considered themselves part of the incalculably broad spectrum of politico-thymotic formations during the nineteenth century. Heinrich Heine was terrified by these groups, as he records in *Confessions* in 1854. In his visionary poem "Vagabond Rats," he writes about their hooligan-like following:

> They carry their heads equally shaven, as radical as possible, as bald as a rat.

> [*Sie tragen die Köpfe geschoren egal*
> *Ganz radikal, ganz rattenkahl.*]

HE WAS SHOCKED THAT WEITLING, THE JOURNEYMAN TAILOR WITH extravagant utopian ideas, kept his cap on his head during a surprise meeting in a bookstore in Hamburg. With the hysterical immediacy of an actor who likes to show off his pains, Weitling rubbed his ankle on which the chains had rested during his time in prison. Nevertheless, ten years earlier, Heine had honored the psychohistorically important and, in terms of the history of ideas, inevitable nature of these new movements, using a balanced prose:

> The destruction of the faith in heaven does not only possess a moral, but also a political significance. The masses do not anymore bear their earthly plight with Christian patience, but yearn for happiness on earth. Communism is the natural result of this altered world view. It is spreading across all of Germany.

The strongest contribution to the communist cause comes from the moral unacceptability of contemporary society. Society only defends itself out of sheer need, "without faith in its legitimacy, even without self-respect, just like that older society whose morose structure collapsed when the son of the carpenter arrived." Regarding the arrival of French communists, Heine remarked in a correspondent's report from 1843 that he enjoys speaking of them because only their movement deserves "a committed attention" insofar as it "is very similar to the *Ecclesia pressa* of the first century. It is despised and persecuted in the present while still possessing a propaganda whose zealousness of faith and dark destructive will also remind of Galilean beginnings."[16]

INDIGNATION WITHOUT THEORY; OR, THE MOMENT OF ANARCHY

HEINE DIED A DECADE TOO EARLY TO HAVE PURSUED THE UNFOLDING of the tendencies that he had acknowledged to be inescapable. He had sensitively noticed that the merely "fine" arts had surpassed their zenith and that an age of dark moralisms and a-musical struggles cast its clouds ahead. During the course of events, the iconoclastic forces, which did not respect any form of higher culture, shifted from the communist to the anarchic pole. For the anarchists of the 1860s and 1870s, it seemed politically correct to dismiss any form of culture that was in line with the establishment of bourgeois society. The motivation lay in the ever more radically presented hostility against the state and religion, which, *nolens volens*, drew all phenomena of art and education that were indirectly dependent on the social order into its propaganda of destruction. Early anarchism also did not want to take seriously the culture of subversion: for it the only acceptable infiltration of the established order had to start with the gospel of the bomb.

In *The Principles of the Revolution*, the explicit manifesto of violence of 1869, Bakunin laid down his conception of the primacy of destructive actions. He revealed a remarkable distinction in the discontinuous temporal phases in the entire revolutionary course of events: "With regard to time, the concept revolution entails two completely different facts: *the beginning*, the time of destruction of the existing social norms, and *the end*, the construction, i.e. the creation of completely novel forms out of this amorphism."[17] The success of the coming revolution initially depends, according to Bakunin, exclusively on the radicalization of social tensions, through which it is supposed to be possible that increasingly numerous and extreme acts of violence will be sparked, acts that culminate in the complete destruction of the old order. It is mainly those who are furious and raging and, why not, also the criminals and terrorists who dictate the course of events. At this stage, the occupational image of the revolutionary is mapped onto the popular figure of a noble criminal, and Bakunin dedicated a sentimental hymn to the iconic Russian robbers of the forests,[18] as if he wanted to disclaim Hegel's harsh judgment of Schiller's *The Robbers* that "it is still only boys who can be seduced by this robber ideal."[19] According to the doctrine, the ones dominating during this phase are those "persons who cannot manage to suppress the compulsion to destructiveness inside themselves and who, still before the beginning of the universal war, identify and find the enemy and, without thinking, destroy him."[20]

It could be argued that this statement regarding the destruction of the enemy "without thinking," a statement that Bakunin wrote down without much reflection, gained vast empirical content during the following century and a half, even though the innocence of the initial thoughtlessness would vanish quickly. It announces the secret of a habitus of destruction, which was the initially rhetorical and later increasingly practical point of orientation for the extremist subcultures on the left, and later also on the right. In light of this fixation, it is necessary to speak of an anarcho-fascism that anticipated the decisive character traits of the left and right fascist movements *in nuce*, traits that developed fully only later—an exception is the will to domination of the collapsed feudal and bourgeois state. Wherever the nations of extremism arose during the twentieth century, what was hidden in the anarchistic beginnings was fully revealed.

In 1869 Bakunin expressed his hope that those individual actions that were committed out of anger or fanaticism would grow "so to say, to an epidemic passion of youth" until the general revolution would be born out of it. "This is the natural way," in what one might call the catechism of revolt. It follows that the revolution needs to be started with spectacular individual deeds, culminating in the "destruction of people of power." "Furthermore, work is becoming increasingly easier," because from now on it slides down the slippery slope of social dissolution.[21]

The goal of the anarchic work of destruction is revealed in the mysterious word "amorphism": only once the old order is fully dissolved into formless elementary particles is the destructive initial phase of the revolution over. Only then can constructive minds be allowed to get involved in the course of things and start the reconstruction of the world on the basis of egalitarian axioms. What remains decisive is that the reconstruction is made exclusively out of the formless mass of reality particles—without the state, the church, or capital processes. Anyone who thinks too early about reconstruction becomes a traitor to the holy goal of destruction because he is not able to serve it without hesitation. Let me remark in passing that "amorphism" found a technical support during Bakunin's time in the invention of dynamite. The belief that it would be possible to "explode" entire social orders had its pragmatic paradigm not only in the storm on the Bastille but also in the most recent achievements in the domain of explosive material. It was not accidental that the rather material occupational name "*Dinamitario*" was given to an Italian anarchist of the turn of the century. Just as Lenin's communism aimed later to create the synthesis of Soviet power and electrification, anarchism aimed in its time to present the product made out of destructive desires and dynamite.

According to the anarchistic theory of phases, the first generation of revolt is only committed to its objection against the actual conditions. Because the beginning is autonomous with regard to the end, authentic revolutionaries initially have no right to reflect on "the paradisiacal edifice of future life." In the present, all power, all rage, and all hatred need to be mobilized for "the initial course of the revolution."[22]

125

Based on the essence of the law of necessity and full justice, we have to dedicate ourselves fully to the enduring, irresistible, incessant destruction, which
needs to grow like a crescendo as long as there is nothing left to destroy of the
existing social forms. . . .

The revolution justifies everything. . . . The field has thus been cleared! . . .
The victims have been identified by the unconcealed indignation of the
people! . . . It will be called terrorism! . . . So what, to us it does not matter. . . .
Today's generation needs to create by itself a relentlessly crude force and
march the unstoppable way of destruction.[23]

WHAT IS SIGNIFICANT ABOUT THIS DOCUMENT IS THE CONNECTION
of rage and the temporal pole of the beginning. When Bakunin speaks of
revolution, he primarily thinks of the movement that initiates the struggle.
This means that the departure for the revolutionary struggle is conceived
of as a purely inchoate impulse. This impulse is more than a criminal act of
expression because it is located within an incalculable future horizon. The
revolutionary is nevertheless supposed to carry out his actions with so much
expressive momentum that the people can interpret it as advertising signs
of rage against the oppressors. Anarchism openly exposes its origin in the
populism of rage. The true social anarchist dreams about the fusion of the
rampant fury of destructiveness of individual actors with an immeasurable,
latent rage of the people. The anarchist hoped for the manifest explosion of
this rage just as the early Christians waited for the return of Christ. It was
believed that this return could be brought closer by ever again leading the
masses to use violence and terror until these "masses" saw in violence and
terror their own tendencies and wishes. This signified the end of the process
of exteriorizing horror. Christian "masses," which had for centuries become
subdued through their fear of the Lord, would then understand that the
time in which they had no other choice but to internalize metaphysical horror had passed. They were transformed from frightened slaves into anarchic
masters. Finally, these anarchic masters became the terrifying creators of
history. Terror, which had been turned to the outside, is benevolent so long
as it provides proof that the age of sacred intimidation is over.

One should not infer from the comparatively marginal political significance of Bakunin's thinking that it was a mere rhetorical movement, a form
of political prelude to surrealism. The aesthetic reception of Bakunin in
bohemian circles around 1900 should also not distract from his influence

on the creation of an activist habitus. In reality, the forthright philosophy of destruction of the anarchists is one of the sources of the mobilizing and extremist attitudes that could later be observed in the fascist movements on the left and on the right.

The effects of anarchism are nonetheless more indirect. By far the most important effect can probably be located in the indirect influence that Lenin's thought enjoyed. Even though the leader of the Russian Revolution took over the destructive judgments of Marx concerning Bakunin at least on the level of discourse, not to say at the level of lip service (because it is well known that the International Workers Association, also known as the First International, broke apart in 1876 because of an unbridgeable alienation between Marx and Bakunin), Marx secretly remained faithful to the terroristic voluntarism of Bakunin's understanding of the revolution, however much "voluntarism" was a curse in the dictionary of the Bolshevists. In a sense, the October Revolution was a revenge of Bakunin against Marx because Lenin, in the most "unfree" of all possible situations, set up a world-historical monument for Bakunin's doctrine concerning the destructive element of the revolutionary beginning. He then admittedly dedicated himself to the completely un-Bakunian business of the despotic construction of a government.

In February 1875, Bakunin expressed his despair to Elisée Reclus from Lugano, despair about the lack of revolutionary verve among the partially resigned, partially opportunist "masses." Only a handful of steadfast groups, such as the Jurassier (people from the canton of Jura) and the Belgians, these "last Mohicans of the deceased International," could come up with the energy to continue to fight in the present conditions. Now only the eruption of war between the imperial powers of Europe could give wings to the revolutionary cause: "As for myself, my dear friend, I am too old, too sick, and—shall I confess it?—too disillusioned, to participate in this work. . . . There remains yet another hope: world war. . . . But what a prospect!"[24]

CLASS CONSCIOUSNESS:
THE THYMOTIZATION OF THE PROLETARIAT

BY FAR THE MOST INFLUENTIAL CREATION OF A BODY OF RAGE occurred on the left wing of the workers' movement when it increasingly came under the influence of Marx's ideas during the last third of the nineteenth century. Retrospectively, it is clear that the strategic successes of Marxism rested on its superiority in formulating a sufficiently precise model for the powerful historical rage collective of that age. The leading thymotic group was from now on to be called the "proletariat" or, more specifically, the "industrial proletariat." Part of its definition was, according to Marx's thought, a systematic concept of being exploited. This conception was supplemented by an ethically sophisticated historical mission centered around the concepts of alienation and reappropriation. Nothing less was at stake with regard to the liberation of the working class than the regeneration of the human being. This liberation would correct the deformations resulting from the living conditions of the majorities in class societies.

To understand the thymotic tendencies of the early workers' movements it is essential to consider, apart from the impulses received from Christian sects of awakening, Thomas Paine's *Human Rights* (1791–1792), which he presented in response to Edmund Burke's critique of the French Revolution. The point of this work can be summarized in the demand that a lack of property is no longer acceptable as a convincing pretense for political disenfranchisement. Universally conceived human rights formalize a claim to dignity, which the British had hitherto expressed in the euphonic "birthrights." This word was destined to explode the oligarchic equation of property with the capability to hold rights, an equation rooted in political custom.[25] One can hear the echo of the pathos with which Cromwell's Cavalry of the Chosen attacked the positions of the obdurate land-owning aristocracy. The attack of the poor majority on the rich minority, which has dominated the course of political and ideological transactions since the discovery of "mankind," in fact begins at that moment when the property-less present themselves as the party of human beings and want to be the bearers of equal rights as human beings. The way to speak of rights that belong to human beings as human beings gained its full force during struggles over the position on the economic ladder and the preservation of property of the ambitious middle strata of the society. The sum total of struggles on this front has been called class struggle since the early nineteenth century.

The strength of Marxist doctrine was to substantiate the idealist verve of Paine's declaration of human rights with a firm foundation of materialist and pragmatic arguments. This happened at a time when materialism and pragmatism were about to become the religion of the reasonable. Because of Marx's contribution, the justification of human dignity shifted from the Christian-humanist conception of an order created in God's image to a historical anthropology of work. The essential basis for dignity was now taken to be the demand that human beings—as the creators of their own existence—have a claim to enjoy the results of their activities. As a result, there was a semireligious valuation of concepts such as "work," "labor force," "process of production," and others, which when taken together with the concept of the proletariat—initially only an economic term—resulted in a messianic twist. Who from now on spoke about "work" in a Marxist vocabulary did not only meant more than the process of production, which is opposed to "capital" as the exploitable resource for the creation of value. Work thus became at the same time an anthropological, even demiurgic, quantity. Humankind, civilization, prosperity, and the entire realm of higher values go back to this quantity.

It is thus not surprising that the transformed way of speaking about work turned into a rallying cry for thymotic movements of the working collective. The proletariat was challenged to understand itself—in spite of its often emphasized dehumanization and reification—as the true matrix of humanity in general, with all its future potential. On the other hand, this constellation of concepts showed that the enemy of the workers is at the same time the enemy of humankind and thus deserves to be pushed back to the past. In order to clearly draw the battle lines of a civil war of unprecedented extent, the only thing that needed to be made plausible now was the position of the capital-owning class, regardless of its sometimes respectable private moral convictions, as the enemy of the workers. The ultimate war was supposed to release unconditional hostility: the capital-owning bourgeoisie, including its well-fed entourage, as the objective brutes, on the one side, and the proletarians, who were the sole producers of value, together with their escort of hungry offspring as the objectively true human beings, on the other side. In this war, the stakes include the true nature of the producing human being. Because one party, it is said, entertains a merely parasitical relationship with regard to production, while the other party includes those that produce authentically, the latter has to be rightly and inevitably victorious in the end. From this moment onward, to understand the essence of reality meant to think civil war.[26] Because this war was conceived of as a total war, neutrality was not an option.

Only in light of this anthropological background is it possible to understand the success that the concept of "class consciousness" has enjoyed. It is now easy to comprehend that the emphasis is less on "class" than on "consciousness"; the latter is necessarily a property of psychic systems or individuals. Today the concept of "class consciousness" would be replaced by "class communication," provided that the concept of classes can still be used.[27] Under conditions of a civil society marked by capitalism, there is, according to the pure revolutionary doctrine, only one true human class, the producers, which is confronted by the capitalist class of illusory human beings or value-sucking vampires. The labor force, which is the collective destined to struggle, therefore only needs to be convinced that it embodies, in spite of its empirical misery, true humanity and the future potential of the species. From an increased self-understanding, revolutionary shame would immediately emerge, shame that would in turn breed revolutionary rage. As soon as the proletariat discovers that it represents humiliated humanity, it will not be able to continue to accept its current condition. In freeing themselves from their misery—what Hegel would have called the negation of the negation of their humanity—the members of the finally conscious class would start a global storm on the Bastille. By completing the final revolution, the class of the true human being would "overthrow all conditions in which man is a degraded, enslaved, neglected, contemptible being."[28]

It is evident that the discourse surrounding the class consciousness of the workers referred, in fact, to nothing but the thyzmotization of the proletariat. Thymotization signifies the subjective aspect of the preparation for an extensive battle. Class consciousness thus never meant that the industrial worker was supposed to come home after work in order to read Schiller's *Maid of Orleans* to expand a mind constricted by turmoil and sorrow. The expression certainly never implied that workers were supposed to reflect on their misery in economical terms. Authentic class consciousness means consciousness of civil war. As such, it can only be the result of battles in which the truth of the position of the fighting class is revealed.

This being the case, "true class consciousness" would be light-years away "from the real, psychological thoughts of man about their lives," as Georg Lukács explained in a mildly threatening tone of voice.[29] Threatening much more openly, the same author continued to teach that it is not what the workers thought at the time that was of importance for the future but rather what they were supposed to think according to the objective party doctrine. According to the teaching of the strategists of class struggle, no element of the social totality could escape the challenge to develop a true consciousness of its position and function in the big picture, certainly not the proletariat. Lukács admits that authentic class consciousness for the bourgeoisie would be tantamount to an insight into the inevitable nature of its coming downfall. This was, if not a good, at least a sufficient reason that the bourgeoisie fled from its tragic knowledge into the domain of the unconscious and unreasonable. The destruction of reason and the bourgeoisie's insistence that it has a right to the positions it has lost are one and the same.[30] There are only a few individuals who have the moral power to betray their own class, renounce their origin, and join the "standpoint of the proletariat." Only from this standpoint would it be possible, it is claimed, to reconcile reason and sustainability for the future.

For the proletariat, on the other hand, the acquisition of class consciousness turns into a gay science of its mission to be the "leader of history." Unfortunately, such a sovereign conception cannot be acquired overnight and is not free. Only by going through the "infinitely painful path of the proletarian revolution with its many reverses" will the future "subject of history" work its way up to the true concept of itself. In addition, there is the burden of self-criticism,[31] which needs to be carried by activists. Luckily, they don't have to carry this burden alone, without the help of the party, which is always right. According to the self-elected masterminds of the working class, this class was sentenced "with historical necessity" to abide by the revolutionary schedule: "the proletariat cannot abdicate its mission."[32] The principles of this self-study culminate in the doctrine that one gets to know war only by waging it.

If class consciousness would fully live up to its mission, it would have to create class knowledge, class pride, and class rage. The first factor was, according to the conviction of the communists as well as anarchists, already given by the life experience of the worker, however much it still required for its completion the experience of war, self-criticism, and dialectical theory. The second factor could be brought out by appealing to arguments concerning human rights, the anthropology of labor, and political economy. These were supposed to help the members of the proletariat hold their heads up high, as appropriate for their value-creating role. The third factor needed to be fueled and channeled by means of propaganda: "Right, just as the blaze of fire, now forces itself with power to the surface," the *International* visualizes the course of thymotic mobilization. Meaningful eruption only happens after rage has cultivated the proletariat for a long enough time. Complete class consciousness presupposes that the sum of pride and knowledge is multiplied by the rage of the thymotic collective. The mature result of the proletarian process of learning can manifest itself only practically, through militant revolutionary activism.

It is not necessary to explain in detail why the conception of the class of producers as a victorious fighting subject of history could result in nothing but a bad realization of philosophy. The fateful mistake behind its conception goes beyond the adventurous equation of the industrial labor force with humanity. The greater problem is the holistic or organological approach according to which a sufficiently organized association of people would be capable of copying the achievements and qualities of a single human being on a higher level. By way of subscribing to such a misconception, the classical left entered the space of illusions in which the famous substantive collectives and the ominous elevated subjectivities were up to mischief. The class of producers, having become self-conscious, would thus be a giant, comparable to Plato's ideal republic, an organization in which reason, feeling, and will are united to become one monological, dynamic unified self. The craziness of this illusion was instantly recognized by the workers' movement, which covered it up by emphasizing that class consciousness is to a high degree connected to the "problem of organization." The magic word "organization" evoked the leap from the level of "many active individual wills" (Engels) to that of the standardized class will. The unrealizability of an effective homogenization of millions of spontaneous individual wills is, however, already manifested in the superficial belief that the illusion of class cohesion could be upheld through surrogate constructions.

The most far-reaching of these surrogate constructions entered the stage in the form of Lenin's conception of the party. It is immediately clear how the idea of the party and that of class consciousness support each other. Because achieved class consciousness, understood as the proletariat's insight into its position within the social totality, was an impossibility, the party could and had to present itself as the representative of the still empirically premature collectivity. Consequently, the party defended its claim to be the "leader of history." However, because the avant-garde was cut off from its "basis" as long as there was no hope for the loyalty of the masses, it had to entertain the fiction of the essential constructability of the class consciousness of those it was supposed to lead. The practical demand was thus: only the party embodies the legitimate rage collective, insofar as it acts as the representative for the not-yet-mature and operational "masses" in seizing the right to act. The party is consequently the true "I" of the still alienated collective of workers. It is not accidental that the party usually likes to adorn itself with the telling title "organon of the entire proletariat," with the term "organon" meaning "brain," "center of the will," or "better self." For

Lukács the party is confronted to take on "the sublime role of *bearer of the class consciousness of the proletariat and the conscience of its historical vocation.*"[33] The resolutions of the party are nothing but quotations from the idealized inner monologue of the working class. It is only within the party that rage meets intellect; it is exclusively the party intellect that is allowed to start searching for the rage of the masses.

The history of the workers' movement since the days of the Gotha Congress of 1875 documents how rage has found its suitable host within the party. During its long march through modernity, it undeniably managed to make important discoveries. However, the mistakes it has nevertheless committed are revealed in the choice of communist symbols. Foremost there is the official sign of hammer and sickle, which revealed an idiotic antiquarianism already in 1917. The fact that the emblematic tools of conservative German craftsmanship[34] were to appear on the flag of the Soviet Union sufficiently reveals the helplessness of those in charge. A simple act of reflection would have led to objections because industrial workers do not hammer and the proletariat in the countryside has, for the longest time, not touched a sickle. Even more fatal was the choice of symbols by the radical left in Germany, which constituted itself during the final stage of the First World War as the "Spartacus League," using the name of a crucified gladiator slave as its advertisement, as if deliberately trying to draw on the analogy of Christianity while unconsciously citing a tradition of defeat. Only the red star of revolutionary Russia was capable of preserving its secret for a longer period of time. It only revealed its apocalyptic origin as a sign of downfall at the end of the Soviet episode.

The party as the "organon" of the proletariat rested on the fiction of a giant. Because it constituted itself as the "more elevated" subject, comprising individual resolved activists whose synchrony and homogeneity could never be secured (as the constant ideological cleansings showed), it remained dependent on an avant-garde of the avant-garde, which embodied the last concentration of class consciousness and thus, in a sense, its true soul. Given the circumstances, this could only refer to the mastermind of revolution. The inner monologues of the party were supposed to be authentically conducted only in his thoughts. He embodied the true self of the workers' movement insofar as he was the ultimate source of its legitimacy as its center of will and rage. Comparable to the world soul, which Hegel believed he had witnessed from horseback after the battle of Jena and which carried the name of Napoleon, the theoretical and thymotic head of the revolutionary organization would be the vital location of the world. The becoming-human of rage is said to have achieved its destiny in that location—initially it was Karl Marx himself. Far from disqualifying himself from accepting the historical position because of his personality, which was marked by hatred and resentment (as the standard ad hominem criticism of the author of *Capital* has it), he would have been perfectly suited because he was equipped with the necessary qualifications. Not only did he possess the lucidity and the will to power of a born leader, he also possessed sufficient rage to enflame everybody who would follow him. Every successor of Marx would have to be measured by whether he or she was capable of being a convincing incarnation of progressive world rage and a focal point of revolutionary knowledge of the revolutionary process as Marx had been. After the premature death of Rosa Luxemburg, there was nobody else during the early twentieth century who could have contested Lenin's claim to be Marx's successor. He was indeed the man whom God had created out of wrath to be a politician, to apply a characterization of Max Weber concerning the poet Ernst Toller to a more suitable recipient.

One might take this reduction of class consciousness to the party and the reduction of the party to its mastermind to be nothing but romantic hubris. And this is understandable. However, such reductions also have the advantage of thinking through the speculative exaggerations entailed by the concept of classes as well as that of the party. This act of reduction allows one to locate rage and consciousness where they are really situated: in a concrete individual. Such an individual should, of course, not be taken to be an ordinary contemporary human being. He is better understood as an exemplary human being who, by thinking and being enraged, concentrates in himself the just distribution of affects of humankind during the age of class society. In this leader, *thymos* is animated sufficiently to be able to call for a new world order. Seen from this perspective, Marx would be more than the Philoctetes of modern philosophy—some of his character traits recall the foul-smelling Greek fighter whose unbearable vociferation made him intolerable to his companions, so that they abandoned him together with Achilles' bow on the island of Lemnos. Marx also represented a western mahatma, an encompassing soul, who revealed superhuman greatness even when raging. His radically partisan intelligence functioned as the memory device for the learned dissatisfaction of the age.

In what follows I will show that the political party has been dependent on the ideological figure of a leader-mastermind in a way not fully understandable even for him. The dependence is so extreme that the party itself only functioned as a monological machine in which the soliloquies of the leader were continued on a greater level. The head of the revolutionary movement had to project his knowledge and his will as the theoretical and moral monarch of the party. The goal was to transform the party, or at least the central committee, into a collective monarchic "organon." The episodes of discussions within communist movements were always only additions to the essentially monological ideal. Earlier I emphasized that the exemplary militant human being transforms his existence into a collection point for accumulating rage during the time of the advent of the revolution. Drawing the consequence of this observation, it becomes understandable that the resolute "subject of revolution" had to act like a banker assigned to manage a global financial institute. Only thus could the revolutionary subject believe that she was the chosen center of world affairs: in this bank the accumulated emotions of indignation, memories of suffering, and impulses of rage are stored and united to become an active mass of value and energy. Moreover, the revolutionary quantities are made available for reinvestment in the real world. The future will thus be substantively identical to the return on the intelligently invested sums of rage and indignation.

It is precisely these collecting and reinvesting activities that needed to be represented on an extended scale for the creation of a larger militant body. As soon as the transfer from the radical subjectivity of the leader to the members of the party (and the new secret service agents) is completed, a political organism of a completely new type comes into existence. Thanks to its appearance on the market of passions, collective rage is transformed from a mere aggregate of psychopolitical impulses to a form of capital that calls for its utilization.

On the Appearance of a Nonmonetary Banking System

I HAVE ARGUED THAT DURING THE NINETEENTH CENTURY THE concept of the anarchist cell of destruction was a reproduction of the paradigm of the popular Russian band of thieves. Naturally this model could not be publicly defended in front of the anarchists. It is thus no surprise that one comes across in Bakunin's writings on the organization of the anarchist movement para-religious disguises of the criminal business of revolution. This is especially true of the *Revolutionary Catechism* from 1866 and the *Program of the International Brotherhood* from 1868. When studying these documents, one notices the similarity to the secret societies of the eighteenth century and, *eo ipso*, to Christian orders: here as in movements like Rosicrucianism, members seem to be sworn in with bombs to undertake their historical mission. It was thus not by mere accident that the followers of Bakunin have often been compared to the Jesuits. Because Bakuninism anticipated an exclusively destructive revolutionary mission, none of its programmatic writings could tolerate the subtle equation of a coalition of anarchists with a criminal organization. As members of a church of total destruction, Bakunin's followers were released from the task of social reconstruction.

The situation was totally different for the communists who stood up for their faith in the inseparable processual unity of overthrow and reconstruction. Because they aimed for the acquisition of governmental power, anarchic concessions to the romanticism of criminality or lawless counterculture were intolerable to them. The revolutionary government would retain clear qualities of state power through its communist functionaries. This fact was excluded by the paradigm of the noble robber gang or that of the criminal order. The fighters who were motivated by Lenin's idea called for a model of organization that would be capable of satisfying the demands of a long-term politics of change from above. Under the given circumstances, such a model could only be mapped onto the successful institutions of a semifeudal society, in particular the army (from which the concept of a hierarchy of command was to be taken to derive the strictest party discipline), as well as the administrative bureaucracy (which was supposed to provide an appealing paradigm for the socialist party machinery because of its quasi-automatic, selfless efficiency). Enough has been written about Lenin's admiration for the organization of the German mail system. If one wants to immerse oneself into the real socialist philistinism, one should focus on the mechanisms of subordination within the German authoritarian state around 1900. Lenin himself never concealed the fact that he was convinced that the organization of the Russian "potentials of protest" needed to pursue the same path that had been traveled by the state capitalism of the Germans and by the strict organization of the Prussian war industry after 1914.

Neither the model character and paradigmatic influence of late-feudal and bourgeois forms of organizing the army nor the administration of the development of the Leninist party have ever been seriously called into question. Rosa Luxemburg was thus not wrong when she warned early on against Lenin's Germanophile preference for "ultra-centralism." However, the reference to such role models conceals what was genuinely new in organized communism. As already stated, the specific nature of communism can only be understood according to its effective design, more a banking establishment than a military or bureaucratic entity. To dissolve this apparent paradox one needs to dismiss the prejudice that banks exclusively deal with monetary transactions. In reality the function of a bank consists in covering a much broader domain of phenomena. Analogous processes are present wherever cultural and psychopolitical entities such as scientific theories, acts of faith, works of art, political acts of protest, and so on are accumulated. Once a certain degree of accumulation has been reached, they are transformed from mere treasure to capital. If one concedes the existence of a nonmonetary system of banking, it becomes understandable that banks of a different kind, as collection points of affect, can operate with the rage of others just as well as monetary banks operate with the money of their customers. By doing just this, they relieve their clients of the difficulty of having to take their own initiative, while nevertheless promising gains. What in the one case are monetary capital gains are in the other case thymotic premiums.

Such banks generally present themselves as political parties or movements, in particular parties on the left of the political spectrum. The transformation from raging impulses into "constructive politics" can rightly be seen in each camp as the magnum opus of psychopolitics. (Additionally, it could be argued that Niklas Luhmann's theory of social systems and in particular its emphasis on the differentiation of subsystems, such as law, science, art, economy, the health system, religion, pedagogy, and so on, suggest a specific form of regional capitalization as well as a specific corresponding bank formation.)

Economics defines a bank as a collection point for capital (*Kapitalsammelstelle*). Its main task consists in administering the balances of its clients for the sake of the preservation and increase of value. Practically speaking, this means that the deposits of customers, which are fruitless monetary treasures when deposited, are transformed immediately into capital. Consequently, they are invested in profit-oriented forms of business. One of the most important functions of a bank consists in providing a risk buffer, which allows clients to partake in successful investments while protecting them whenever possible against disappointments. This arrangement is controlled by the interest rate, which naturally decreases proportionately to the level of risk control.[35]

In our context it is important to keep in mind that the temporal profile of money is transformed in an important respect through the transition from its treasury form to its capital form. The simple treasury is still fully subject to the preservation of value. By keeping together the material results of past yields and plundering, it has a purely conservative function (not to mention, for the moment, the imaginary values connected to the creation of this treasury). It negates the passing of time in order to secure wealth in a permanent present. If one is standing in front of a treasure chest or if one enters a treasure chamber, one literally experiences what is meant by presence. The time form created by the present treasure is thus the duration sustained by the past, the duration as the continuous present of what has been accumulated—sublime boredom is the reflex experienced.

Capital, on the other hand, does not know the dull happiness of accumulated presence. Because of its dynamic mode of being, it is sentenced to constant externalization. It can only present itself episodically as a virtually present sum, as, for example, on those days when one's balance is to be determined. Because it is constantly occupied with using itself, there is no point in time when it is in full possession of itself. The consequence is that it essentially brings about "futurist" effects. It creates a chronic anticipatory excitement for what comes, an excitement that manifests itself on each new level achieved as a renewed expectation of gains. The temporal form of capital is the short and diverting period of accumulation, which constitutes a permanent crisis. It is thus exclusively the dynamic of capital that accomplishes what Trotsky wanted to entrust to a political leadership because of a confusion of concepts: the "permanent revolution" exactly characterizes the modus vivendi of capital, not the actions of a cadre. Its true mission is to make sure that the extended continuation of its own movements is not jeopardized. It takes itself as called upon to overthrow all conditions in which customs, morals, and legislature stand in the way of its victory march. Therefore there is no capitalism without the triumphant expansion of a lack of respect, which cultural critics have been giving the pseudophilosophical title of "nihilism" since the nineteenth century. In reality, the cult of nothingness is simply the necessary side effect of monetary monotheism for which all other values are merely idols and illusions. The theology of this cult of nothingness can, by the way, also be developed by drawing on the trinity. What is added to the Father is "money," to the Son "success," and to the Holy Spirit "prominence." According to the capitalist logic, the banks have the key role in creating a world that functions exclusively according to money because only these agencies of permanently productive unrest are able to successfully collect and steer monetary currents.

THE IDEA OF A COLLETING POINT AS SUCH IS OF COURSE MUCH OLDER than that of the bank. As is well known, the bank gained its still recognizable outlines only since the early Italian Renaissance. Its history reaches back to the era of the so-called Neolithic revolutions, during which the transition to the cultivation of grain developed simultaneously with the praxis of storing supplies. There was a long line of technical and mental innovations that corresponded to this transition, innovations like the construction of storehouses as well as the practice of housekeeping with scarce resources in stock. (We should also not forget the invention of wars of conquest as a second harvest by accessing the supplies of others.)

The most important reflex in the history of ideas from early agrarian cultures of supply keeping is revealed in the harvest. The peasant form of life is marked by a habitus that penetrates everything: the annual waiting for the moment of ripeness. The consequence of harvesting is the invention of a supply as the basis of communal life within the circle of the year. The archetype of storage imposes on the intelligence of the first farmers and civil servants the operational model of "saving," "dividing the supplies wisely throughout the year," and "redistributing." If the scheme of harvest becomes metaphorically available, all forms of treasure can be stockpiled as supplies. In the beginning this happened to weapons and jewelry and extended to include the treasures of healing, the arts, law, and knowledge. With these resources a culture secures its symbolic survival.

Martin Heidegger suggested connecting the philosophical concept of *logos*, which derives from the Greek verb "*legein*," to the agrarian schema of "*Lese*," which means to pick or to select but also to read and interpret. Consequently, the logical understanding of writings and the interpreting of context would in some sense be a symbolic continuation of harvesting. This suggests that the form of the accumulation of supplies is mirrored in the constitution of the domain of knowledge, in which the seeds of tradition are supposed to ripen during subsequent generations so as to be collected again and again during the harvest of knowledge. In these circumstances philosophers (who are usually exclusively dependent on urban contexts) could still imagine themselves as hybrid peasants.

Heidegger's theory of *Logos* as "*Lese des Sinns*," a reading or interpretation of the meaning, thus remains stuck in a premodern conception of knowledge. By holding on to the ancient and medieval archetype of an accumulated supply or treasure, the thinker refused to accept the modernization of the production of knowledge through research. He sensed a fatal disfiguration of the "originally grown," pretechnical mode of the being of things through this modernization. In reality, research aims at an organized accumulation of knowledge and innovation, notably in scientific academies and modern universities. Contemporary research is thus surprisingly analogous to the unfolding of the banking industry in the more recent financial economy. Scientific academies and modern universities play the role of authentic knowledge banks. Traditional banks cooperate as partners and observers of corporations. In the cognitive domain the managerial function is taken over by research institutions. Once the treasury form of knowledge—as it was embodied by pansophist scholars of the Baroque era up until Leibniz—passes over into the form of capital, it may no longer be accumulated as an inactive supply. The educative rule "earn it in order to own it" is suspended for the kind of knowledge that is made dynamic for the purpose of research. It is no longer an acquired possession but serves as the base material for its extended reproduction, like modern money, which, instead of being stored in chests or under the mattress, returns to the sphere of circulation in order to become productive on higher levels.

This change in the form of knowledge is not an innovation of the twentieth century, though it was during this age that the research institutions began to use terms such as "economy of knowledge" and "cognitive science" in order to claim a right to such concepts as the "knowledge society." The process of knowledge is essentially premised on assumptions analogous to capital production, since the available supply of scientific knowledge has been developed for extended reproduction through organized research. The establishment of scientific academies, which Leibniz wholly supported, is one of the main symptoms of this transition.

For knowledge, research corresponds to investing within the monetary sphere. Research implies the controlled risking of what has already been earned for the chance of future gains. One expects that a graph of such risk operations would depict continuing accumulations in spite of cyclical fluctuations. It is admittedly the case that knowledge capital, just as monetary capital, experiences specific crises in which its future productivity is called into question. The solution for such crises usually consists in what recent sociologists of knowledge refer to as a "paradigm change." In the course of development of such paradigm changes, older cognitive values are destroyed, while business continues more intensively than ever before, albeit with different basic conceptual parameters.

ANALOGOUS OBSERVATIONS ABOUT MORE RECENT ART HISTORY ARE possible. Beginning at the latest in the early nineteenth century (its prehistory dates back to the fifteenth century), there has been a transition from the treasure form to the capitalist form of accumulation in the domain of artistic creation. This transition can best be observed when studying the history of the museum and its changes of function. We know of these processes from the flourishing science of museology as well as through the more recent studies surrounding curating. These disciplines established themselves during the last half of the twentieth century as the national and global economies of the art world, even if the praxis of curating only rarely takes into account its modern theoretical foundations. However, just as workers at a bank can do excellent work without mastering the general logic of the banking industry, the curators of the contemporary art world and culture are capable of making themselves useful without reflecting on the larger movements of artistic capital.

It is mainly thanks to the research of Boris Groys that it is possible to reconstruct with precise concepts the endogenous capitalization of the art system.[36] The endogenous character of these processes emphasizes that what is important here is not so much the interaction of money and art on the art market. Neither is it the so-called commodity character of the artwork, which had a central position in the now almost extinct form of Marxist art criticism. In reality, the art system has been internally transformed into a structure analogous to the system of capital, including the corresponding forms of interaction of entrepreneurialism and banking functions. In this process, the results of past artistic production constitute a stock of capital from which contemporary artistic producers can borrow in order to use this loan to produce new and sufficiently different works. Groys has referred to the capital stock of accumulated objects of art as an "archive." However, in contrast to Foucault's use of this term, Groys does not want to focus ironically on the gray, dusty, dead side of the reservoir, but its living, progressive, and decision-guiding tendencies. In the last instance, only the state or the imaginary International of states qualifies for the position of housing this "archive" because it is the guarantor of culture, whereas private collections can only assure their relative value in reference to public collections and their virtual synthesis within the archive.

The archive is the intelligent form of the imaginary museum. While André Malraux's well-known coinage stopped at the blunt idea of ever-present global treasure, Groys identifies the archive as the epitome of the modernized high culture, a depository with the function of self-investing capital. Thus Groys identifies the reason the contemporary art world is intelligible only as the participation of artists and managers in the restlessly expanded reproduction of the archive. In reality the archive, which is constantly present as background, forces upon the ongoing production of art the necessity constantly bringing about expansions of the definition of art. The results of artistic production are evaluated by the agents of the archive. Whenever there is a sufficient level of differentiation among the stored material, its results will be absorbed into the collection.[37] What was the opposite of art can now enter art's sanctuary. Since this system has penetrated the markets, the popular remark that something has become "fit for the museum" (museumsreif) now means the opposite of what it was intended to mean. Whatever has found its way into the museum or, more generally, into the archive becomes part of the eternal recurrence of the new. However, just like every accumulated stock of value, the archive is also subject to the risk of devaluation or extinction. In particular, the appearance of new artistic genres as a consequence of the development of new media sparks crises, which are usually overcome by the archive through a reevaluation.[38]

FINALLY, THE CREATION OF A TREASURY, WHICH IS THE THRESHOLD of a formal banking system, can also be identified in the religious domain. What Christians have been calling since the first century of their existence the "ecclesia" is not simply an assemblage of people connected by shared doctrines of faith. From its beginning, the concept of the church also referred to a gathering point for pieces of testimony that provided evidence for the reality of salvation within profane time. The ecclesiastical gathering movement began at the latest during the second century with the collection of gospels and apostolic writings. Their condensation into the canonic New Testament possessed a high polemical value early on because the history of the "true religion" proceeded as a permanent defensive battle against aberrations. What was added to the evangelical nucleus as part of a continuous accumulation were the apostolic stories from the early mission. Afterward, the stories of martyrdom from the era of the "suppressed church" were added. The effects of apocalypticism and the enduring expectation of an immanent return were also responsible for these additions. Since then, church history has always remained in some sense a history of martyrdom. The happy epochs of the church are the empty pages of martyrology. (The *Martyrologicum Romanum*, a literary ossuary of the entire history of the faith, encompasses in its new edition of 2001 no less than 6,990 entries. It provides a treasury of testimonies to document Christian willingness to sacrifice from the oldest persecutions through the twentieth century.) What follows are the vitae of saints, the legends of desert fathers, and the countless life histories of the blessed and exemplary. This edifying collection of Christian exempla is completed by the doctrinal treasure of conciliatory remarks (with the "Denzinger" as the ossuary of dogmatism), receiving its voluminous manifestations in the article of the accredited theologians. Finally, the chronicle of bishops and the history of orders and missions add a colorful archive to the glaring treasures of faith.

Apart from the council of the bishops and doctors, authority thus always also means, according to Catholicism, the glamour of the "treasure of the Church." Thanks to a 2,000-year-old accumulation of ever new exemplifications, this treasure must bear witness to the "reality of salvation" as it is present in the *ecclesia*. However, it is questionable whether the Catholic administration of these "realities" is capable of bringing about the effective transition from the treasury to the capital form, because the Church's concern for orthodoxy severely inhibits the reinvestment of traditional values in innovative projects. And yet the idea of an expanded reproduction of the salvation treasure is not foreign to contemporary Catholics. John Paul II answered the challenge of modernity in his own way. In the time of the declining success of the company, an important segment of sacred capital, the family of saints, was increased by more than 100 percent. The more than 483 sanctifications (in addition to 1,268 beatifications) during his term of office can only be appropriately understood as part of an encompassing offensive aimed at transforming the static salvation treasury into operative salvation capital. Church historians have calculated that John Paul II's canonizations alone are more numerous than those of the entire history of the Church since the Middle Ages. Without a doubt, the significance of this pope will be determined primarily based on his role in mobilizing the Church's treasure.

The allusion to this treasure of testimonies makes clear that the historic success of Christianity was advanced through more than the construction of a metaphysical revenge bank, which I have discussed in detail in the previous chapter. Its historical success is also attributable to a process that could perhaps best be described as a construction of a treasury of love, perhaps even as the creation of a world bank of salvation. Its results are shared by those worldly people who do not have any interest in the salvation treasures of the Church but are ready to admit that successful "societies" have to carefully regenerate and reinvest their "social capital." Even non-Christians should be able to understand why the processes that have been laid out here could be interpreted from the internal perspective of the Church as the work of the Holy Spirit. For my purpose it is sufficient to demonstrate the reality of a nonmonetary banking system even in the case of the Church. What is acceptable for works of love should be endorsed for works of rage.

COMINTERN: THE WORLD BANK OF RAGE
AND THE FASCIST PEOPLE'S BANKS

THE FOLLOWING OBSERVATIONS CONCERNING THE INSTALLMENT OF A globally operative rage bank gain more consistency in light of the background of a general phenomenology of "treasure creation" (*Schatzbildungen*) and the transition to regional capital processes. Treasure creation manifests itself empirically as an effect of communication and shapes the fund by organizational means. The critical moment for such transitions consists in the transformation of an assembled value and energy into a quantity that can be invested.

A consideration of rage-treasure creation in the main capitalistic countries during the second half of the nineteenth century makes it self-evident why the chronic liaison of economic misery and the political repression of the "masses" under the grip of capitalism were responsible for the abundance of raw material for rage and indignation. These amorphous, barely articulate impulses of dissidence were initially in the hands of their individual owners. They were for the most impotent until taken up by interested organizations, which collected and transformed them into the corporate capital of a progressive politics of rage-based opposition.

At this stage of my investigation, it can be seen clearly how the political alliances and parties of the old left had to accept the role of collection points of dissidence. It is part of the function of leftist parties to organize the *thymos* of the disadvantaged. They provide the liaison between rage capacities and a desire for dignity, and they grant the struggle a pragmatic, mediated, and political shape. Their contract is based on a promise to their clients to disburse a thymotic return in the form of increased self-respect and a more powerful grasp on the future, provided that the clients refrain from independent utilization of their rage. The gains are earned through the political operations of the rage banks, which extend the existential possibilities of their clients in a material as well as symbolic manner. Because collection institutes pursue diverse strategies for investing rage, it initially remains to be seen how the leftist banks will work with the deposits entrusted unto them.

During the last third of the nineteenth century there emerged at least three distinct styles of operating with rage and protest: the anarchic-terrorist, the communist-centralist, and the social-democratic-reformist (and syndicalist) styles. These naturally present themselves in countless compromises, and their intermixture with forms of collection from the right has led to further complications. For all three procedures it was evident that the initially obligatory regional and national forms of rage collection had a pragmatic and preliminary character. The anticapitalist impulse could maintain the level of its enemy only if it reached the same supranational level as the enemy in terms of organization and operation. This insight led to the internationalist pathos, which has been binding for all authentic parties on the left since the days of the International Workers Association (1864–1876) and the second International (1889–1914; and then again as the Socialist International from 1923 until today).

In historical accounts of the twentieth century, August 1914 was unanimously depicted as the fateful moment of political modernity, for reasons that are all too obvious. With a similar consensus it was remarked that the entry of the imperial nations of Europe into the First World War resulted in the catastrophe of socialist internationalism because the vast majority of the moderate left parties underwent a conversion toward prioritizing national motivations for war in light of the imminent military confrontation. The infamous remark from Wilhelm II's speech on August 4, 1914, from the throne in the Berlin Parliament, that he does not know any parties anymore but only Germans (similar to comments from his second balcony speech in front of the people on July 31) proclaims—and at the same time registers, by focusing on the German example—the complete collapse of transnational solidarities. In fact, there was almost everywhere an integration of primarily social-democratic and accommodated workers' movements in the euphoric mobilizations of nationalistic and imperial states. As the sources prove, the approval of the bonds issued to support the war by the Social Democratic Party created a moral shock for many people affiliated with the left.

In my thymotic terms, the fatality of these processes can be described as a form of an inevitable bank crisis. The rage deposits of the "masses" in internationally operating banking houses are put at the disposal of the polemical deals of national political leadership by the managers. By with-drawing decades' worth of accumulated quantities of rage and dissidence from the frontline against the capitalist order and making it available for the war between imperial nations, the leaders of the moderate workers move-ment committed a "white-collar crime" of unparalleled extent. However, they were able to at least partially apologize for the giant misuse of rage capital by pointing toward the war-mongering enthusiasm of their custom-ers. In fact, even after almost a hundred years, the enthusiastic images of August 1914 remain a scandal not only from a political but also from an anthropological point of view.

Seen from a cultural-theoretical perspective, the shift in rage from inter-nationalism to nationalism means a return to historical formations of polit-ical stress groups that can shoulder the consequences of war. The Second International remained too loosely connected to be able to pull together its members under conditions of real pressure and become an effective war collective (using the terminology of Heiner Mühlmann, a maximal-stress cooperation).[39] It was completely incapable of constituting a political body that could withstand the burdens of war. Under the threat of war, symboli-cally secure Internationalists enlisted almost automatically into the national fronts; for the time being their emotional boundaries were identical with the political collectives for the processing of stress—with the exception of those rare fellows who wore the curse "unpatriotic scoundrel" as a philosophical mark of honor. Since the nineteenth century the capacity for national self-preservation was reinforced through armies of draftees, organized around centers of regular soldiers. By the way, one needed to wait to the begin-ning of the twenty-first century before it was possible to politically organize postnational military units in Europe. The fact that these processes were so cumbersome and so slow gives us insight into the strength of the equation of the nation with the ultimate political unit of survival, an equation that continues to have an effect even today.

The perpetually loose coordination of the national components of the Second International reveal the deep dissatisfaction of the radical wing of the workers' movement after August 1914 as a sign of naïveté or hypocrisy. After all, one could not seriously expect that the majority of the proletariat of France, England, Germany, and so on could remain distant from their respective national mobilizations in a time of war. But from the events of 1917, it is obvious that the "imperialist war" directly supported the radical position. The hope that there would be a world war as the last chance for revolutionary aspirations, which Bakunin had diagnosed in 1875, was realized a little more than forty years later.

For the political processing of popular thymotic impulses, the eruption of war in 1914 constituted a serious break. Its immediate result consisted in the abrupt transformation of the largest portion of anticapitalist rage values into acute national antagonisms. The psychopolitical consequences of this are reflected in the complex of events referred to as the "age of extremes." This age was, first, determined by the Leninist attempt to violently reacquire the rage that had been lost. This attempt needs to be seen primarily as a realpolitik of the revolution at all costs. The second feature was the enduring amalgamation of rage with militant national movements, which stirred up the political scene in Europe after World War I. The struggle for the betrayed rage of the proletariat helped to position the two formations of extremist militancy. Their match constituted the heavyweight confrontation of world politics between 1917 and 1945.

The primary adversary on the left, a Third International dominated by Leninism, seemed for the first time capable of presenting itself with a legitimate claim to become a world rage bank. Bolstered by the victory of the October Revolution, the board of directors and supervisors of this company thought that they could take command of a new organ of collective rage. It would become a unified organization of globally dispersed potentials of dissidence, a unified antibourgeois, anticapitalist, and anti-imperialist politics with high dividends calculated for the activated "masses."

The tragedy of this new collection began during the first days of the Russian Revolution, when it became clear that Lenin's dispassionate sense of reality morally demystified the radical left. More than one generation was necessary to accept this demystification. Already during the fall of 1918, workers in Petrograd were called on to commit massacres against Russian social democrats: "Comrades, fight the right-wing social revolutionaries without grace, without pity. Court procedures and tribunals are not necessary. The rage of workers will ravage.... Wipe the enemies out physically."[40] During the defeat of the sailors, the most loyal followers of Lenin demanded the rule of councils against the monopolization of the revolution through the Bolshevist leadership. It was consequently obvious where the revolutionary journey was headed. The fact that the organizer of the Red Army and the subsequent great hope of anti-Stalinist illusions, Leo Trotsky, excelled in the slaughter of the Kronstadt opposition reveals the slippery slope that the cause of the left in Russia had entered onto. Another sign for its misdirection was the fact that Lenin himself did not feel embarrassed to denounce the large majority of bona-fide socialist insurgents as petit bourgeois counterrevolutionaries during the tenth convention of the Communist Party, which took place at the same time as the slaughter of the sailors.

Lenin had already committed himself publicly to the dogma that the struggle against barbarism ought not to refrain from using barbarous methods. With that turn of phrase he included the anarchistic externalization of horror in communism. The man who in the moment of coming to power had written, "history will not forgive us, if we do not assume power now" and "procrastination is becoming positively criminal,"[41] was obviously not willing to give up the opportunity, even if the crude means of conquest and the monopolization of power were in stark contrast to the noble goals of the overall project. It could have already been anticipated that the revolution had become a constant putsch, which required an ever-more grotesque effort in order to pretend fidelity to the program. By postulating mass terror as the recipe for success for the revolutionary state, Leninism exploded the dynamic liaison of indignation and idealism, which had been the politico-utopian privilege of the left until 1917.

This had far-reaching consequences for what was later referred to as the "political suspension of morality." Every contemporary was able to understand in 1917 that an epoch of states of exceptions had just started. What was also certain was that in times of convulsive beginnings, the indignation of beautiful souls over unfortunate circumstances was no longer sufficient. At the same time, no one was prepared for the culmination of revolutionary exterminism, which almost from the first day of battle entered the scene in full armor. According to Lenin, it was the first duty of the revolutionary to get his hands dirty. Based on an obvious intuition concerning the new conditions, the Bolshevists announced their program in their mouthpiece, the newspaper *Pravda*, on August 31, 1918, with the following words: "The hymn of the working class will from now on be the song of hatred and of revenge!" Explicitly canceling the fifth commandment, "Thou shall not kill," Lenin's teaching led from the necessity of revolutionary brutality to an open break (although it was still presented as provisional) with the Judeo-Christian and civil moral tradition of old Europe. Revealing the consistency of a fanatic convert, Georg Lukács already by 1920 proposed rethinking these new rules for murdering in the name of the Good from the perspective of a "second ethics."[42] The "second" was supposed to mean in this context that although one still remembers the first ethics, that is, the ethics of the Judeo-Christian tradition, which is against killing, one suspends it deliberately in order to enter the stage of revolutionary action without any reservations. The absolute idealism of revolutionary engagement unleashed total instrumentalism in the elimination of obstacles hindering the new. For both Lenin and Lukács it was clear that the revolution was assigned a purgatorial mission. From the logic of the intermediary domain in between class society and communism necessarily resulted the pattern of "cleansing." Because world history had become the world court of judgment, the true revolutionary had to show all the necessary strength against the residues of the past. It is not accidental that the motto of Russian avant-gardism was, "Time is always right." When the future knocks on the door, it enters through the gate of horror.

In less subtle contexts, this political suspension of morality or, more simply, the duty to commit crimes, referred to a simple quantitative reflection: in order to save the lives of millions of human beings, one had to accept that a few thousand people would have to be sacrificed. No person with the power of judgment, it was claimed, could deny this argument. Only a short time later, one could witness how millions were sacrificed so that a few thousand, and ultimately only a few dozen, could stay in power, while being led by a suspicious philosopher-king. The few continued to claim, of course, that they exercised their power in the interest of the most sublime hopes of humanity. The paradox of egalitarianism had never been exaggerated more convincingly than during the heyday of Bolshevism: the alpha dogs of classlessness achieved their plan to accumulate all of the power in their hands.[43]

In addition to these tragic calculations, cruder ones were voiced early on. In Lenin's immediate proximity one could hear theses such as, "When it comes to such a numerically rich people such as the Russians, one may sacrifice one-tenth without much ado, if it would be possible to continue to collaborate with the rest."[44] Lenin's closest collaborator, Zinoviev, the author of these class-genocidal fantasies, certainly would have never expressed these theses if he could not have been assured that the leader of the revolution would have approved of them. Since 1918, the archetype of decimation haunted the decrees of the party leader: if one would eliminate every tenth person here and there, the rest would be almost automatically transformed into a malleable mass.[45] We know about Trotsky as well that while a commander of the Red Army he used even the most insignificant occasion to let every tenth soldier be executed. Lenin's remark that repression would only be necessary during the period of transition from capitalism to communism was never much more than a slogan to suffocate moral concerns. The occasionally added argument that this time it was a suppression of the minority through the majority, which was said to present a promising novelty and was appropriate to the fighting style of "socialist humanism," turned out to be a conciliatory phrase. It was supposed to save the activists from understanding the fatal drift of their project. In hindsight, everyone who does not have reasons for not wanting to know can clearly see why communism, once in power, remained from the first to the last a transition from the bad to worse.[46]

If one agrees that "fascism" was, during its initial phase, an attempt to transfer the energy of the war socialisms into the life-forms of postwar society, it is impossible to deny the following: Lenin's directives from the late fall of 1917 onward initiated the first authentic fascist initiatives of the twentieth century. Mussolini and his clones could only react as epigones to these initiatives.[47] The approaches of the older militant right before 1914, for example, the Action Française, present little more than light-handed bricolages made out of the widely available socialist and nationalist copies. Even Georges Sorel's appeals to the fighting proletariat were only some of the more successful among the commonplace hymns to violence as a remedy for the liberal "culture of cowardice."

The characteristic features of the new political style Lenin introduced, which never concealed its origin in the realism of the First World War, were distinctly revealed in the left-fascist original of this myth. The following factors need to be mentioned here: the latent or manifest monological conception of the relationship between leader and followers; the mobilizing of a constant agitation of "society"; the transference of the military habitus to economic production; the rigorous centralism of the executive staff; the cult of militancy as a form of life; ascetic collectivism; hatred for liberal manners of conduct; compulsive enthusiasm for the sake of the revolutionary cause; the monopolization of public space through party propaganda; total rejection of the bourgeois culture of civility; submission of the sciences to partisanship; disdain for pacifist ideals; mistrust of individualism, cosmopolitanism, and pluralism; constant spying on one's own following; the deterministic mode of dealing with the political enemy; and, finally, the temptation, which had been inherited from Jacobin Terror, to give the enemy short shrift, a trial process in which the accusation already entails the sentence.

On the top of the list of characteristics typical for fascism is the explicit abrogation of the fifth commandment, even if only for the duration of a "time of transition." This time of transition lasts until the class enemy (initially referred to as the "enemy of the people") has been eradicated. Exceptions to the prohibition on killing from the Old Testament had long been granted to Jewish fighters and Christian soldiers, but this time the beneficiaries belonged to a semi-civil elite that did not have to abide by moral laws because it was the avant-garde that practiced revenge in the name of humanity. The expression "professional revolutionaries," which Lenin invented, marked the transition to a praxis of morally motivated amoralism. Albert Camus noted in his clever summary of Hegel's amoralizing influence on the thought of revolutionaries during the nineteenth and twentieth centuries that "all of morality becomes provisional."[48] This reveals the increasing alienation of revolutionary activism from its idealist origins. The pragmatic reasons for the becoming provisional of morality in times of permanent struggles were revealed in the modus operandi of the Russian Revolution, when murder for the Good took on chronic, professional, and institutional traits. After a short period of time, practices of killing became habit, systematized and bureaucratized, without ever losing their erratic character. Because no one was capable of saying whether the moral state of exception would ever come to an end, it is not surprising that after a while there was a lack of voices of protest, which more or less directly recommended a morality that would be appropriate for perpetual war.

The activists were convinced that killing in the service of the great cause meant a tragic surrender of virtue. Some saw in it a sacrifice of their personal morality for the sake of the goddess of revolution. Among the commissionaires the ability to kill was celebrated like a sacred competence that distinguished the revolutionary from the bourgeois.[49] The unwillingness to kill was, in the eyes of the activists, the most obvious sign of a continuing bourgeois indolence. We know that part of the legend of Lenin includes a grain of kitsch, and the paradigm of such kitsch was presented by Gorki's hymns of praise for the revolutionary leader too sensitive for his mission.

The subsequent fascist movements from a nationalist wing were not at all in danger of being too sensitive. They only needed to exchange the declaration of war on the class enemy for the declaration of war on the enemy of the people and the race in order to apply Lenin's model to nationalist movements in middle and southern Europe. Their fury was undeniably not simply imitative. The genuine contributions of the German, Italian, Romanian, Croatian, and other radical nationalist parties for the entire complex of exterminist movements in Europe are, after all, large enough, should one take stock. It suffices to say that common morality is overburdened by the task of evaluating macro-criminal complexes. The statistics reveal that we have to assume that for every execution in the name of race during the twentieth century, there were two or three in the name of class.

The so-called fascist movements in Italy and elsewhere emerged from the antibourgeois models of militant nationalism, which one could also call socialism. These movements can best be characterized, in the context of this investigation, as peoples' banks of rage. Their basic function also made them into collection points of protest that clearly reveal functional similarities with parties on the left while accentuating folk, regional, and nationalist ideals. Their display of anticapitalism always remained a mere façade. The widely noticed similarities between the communist and fascist movements become easily understandable after a psychopolitical analysis: in both cases, there are accumulations of rage that reach the dimension of large banks. Fascism is socialism in one country, without the intention of internationalist additions. Focusing on the collectivism of the front and the egalitarianism of production, it needs to be noted that fascism is socialism without a proletariat,[50] or egalitarianism with a folk basis. Its modus operandi is the melting of the population into one thymotically mobilized pack, which takes itself to be unified in its claim to the greatness of the national collective.

The national banks of rage accumulation enjoyed the psychopolitical advantage of being able to work directly with the impulses of patriotic *thymos* without having to take a detour through universalistic ideas or other exhausting fictions. This had a decisive effect on the success of the militant movements of resentment in the countries defeated in World War I. The effects on Germany were the most significant because the demand for the transformation of humiliation into self-affirmation was understandably the strongest there. Considering that postwar periods have always played a key function in the cultural reorientation of combat collectives, it is possible to understand the fatal drift that took hold of the German right after 1918, when it refused to accept its assigned lesson. Italy also did not take on the task of readjusting the body of rules governing its own culture in the light of its war experience. By opening the door to the Italians to join the winning side in the last minute, the Allied forces allowed them the possibility of skipping the labor of stressful revision and escaping into a feeling of heroic self-elevation.[51]

What needed to happen did indeed happen. It was inevitable that the two major enterprises in the area of the political economy of rage identified each other as competitors. Soon each declared the struggle against the other party its primary reason of existence. The anti-Bolshevism of the fascist movements and the anti-fascism of the Comintern underwent an almost a priori process of entanglement. The so-called fascisms presented their business goals from the beginning in an anti-Bolshevik register because of the temporal as well as substantive priority of communist phenomena: the radicals on the right had the example of the left rival in mind when beginning to copy its formulas for success. What remained troubling for fascist leaders was that their Eastern rival was ahead with regard to the most crucial dimension of the new politics: mass murder. Communism, on the other hand, waited a while before recognizing its chance to mobilize all its forces for the struggle against its competitors from the right.

Actually, Stalin's directives against the radical movements on the right in Europe exerted almost irresistible moral constraints. By presenting himself in front of the world as the guarantor of resistance against Nazi Germany, the leader of the Bolshevists forced upon all enemies of Hitler of whatever orientation "antifascism" as the sole morally justifiable option of the age. In this way he immunized the Soviet Union against its critics from within and without.[52] These critics had to be afraid of being denounced as profascist as soon as they raised the slightest objection to Stalin's politics. The propaganda, which Stalin was responsible for, showed how justified this worry was. It mentioned Trotsky and Hitler in the same breath in order to identify the personified dangers for the fatherland of the world proletariat.

Be that as it may, let's take a step back to observe the formation of revolutionary *thymos* during one of its early stages. Since Lenin's "decrees concerning the red terror" from September 5, 1918, the taking of hostages and mass executions of "antirevolutionary elements" became acts of revolutionary duty. In 1919 alone there are supposed to have been half a million executions. Terror had already reached a massive scale in the year before. The Cheka especially enjoyed publishing the lists of those who had been executed in order to indoctrinate the population according to the general tendency of the new measures. The transition from a revolt against the old rule to terror against one's own people and subsequently also against one's own half-hearted following created a climate that approached the kind of "amorphism" that Bakunin had called for. In August 1918, Lenin, quickened by the activist fever, sent telegrams to the entire country in which he called for mass hangings of reluctant farmers—"do it in such a way that the people will see it from afar and shiver."[53] In the same spirit, Krylenko, the people's commissioner for the judiciary, demanded from his subordinates that they should liquidate obvious innocents. Only such a practice would sufficiently impress the "masses."

The strategy that led to this remark by the commissionaire did not suffer from a lack of depth: would it not one day be necessary to conclude from the quantity of excesses that the project was one of justice for which these kinds of sacrifices were necessary? The Polish poet Alexander Wat revealed the logic of cold-blooded fury in his conversations with Czeslaw Milosz: "But blood in the abstract, blood you don't see, blood on the other side of the wall . . . blood spilled on the other side of the river. How pure and great must be the cause for which so much blood is spilled, innocent blood. That was terribly attractive."[54] Where everything revealed a tendency to be excessive and voluptuous, similar proportions were easy to choose when it came to the destruction of enemies. Osip Mandelstam understood already in 1922 that the Soviet Union was about to transform itself into an oriental despotism. "Perhaps we really are Assyrians. Is this why we can look on with such indifference at mass reprisals against slaves, captives, hostages and heretics."[55] The statistics on executions that historians have come up with provide us with the information that during one week under the rule of Lenin, more people were summarily executed than during the entire previous century under the czar's regime after due process.

These are the parameters for the ambivalent space in which countless *compagnons de route* of real communism became lost. The concept of companionship, it could be argued, is the political form of what Heidegger referred to from the perspective of fundamental ontology as "errance" (*die Irre*). Whenever people "err" they move within an intermediary zone situated in between wilderness and route. Heidegger himself was an eminent witness of this, as a matter of fact, because of his periodic preference for the Nazis. Because errance signals a middle course between passage and drift, the travelers will inevitably get to a place that is different from where they wanted to go at the beginning of their journey. "Wayfaring" (*das Gehen*) with communism turned into an odyssey of comrades because it presupposed what should have never been assumed: that the communist actors were pursuing a more or less civilized road to destinations that could be reached. In reality, they supported a developing dictatorship that used excessive, idealistic, and exaggerated violence to bring about what a liberal state could have achieved in less time in a more spontaneous, more effective, and, to a large extent, bloodless manner.

It was because of the chronological course of events that Lenin failed to learn to use the jargon of antifascism. When Mussolini organized the "march on Rome" in October 1922 (his party had been in the Italian parliament for only one year), Lenin had just returned to his desk after suffering two strokes. When "*il Duce*" elevated himself to dictator of Italy, the leader of the revolution had already died after suffering a third stroke. Stalin's propaganda machine, on the other hand, discovered in due course its epochal chance in the proclamation of antifascism. In reality, both "fascism" and "National Socialism" were for the early Comintern not of primary concern. During the 1920s they were overshadowed by the caricature of the socialist or social-democratic rival in the West. The communist movement had specialized in denouncing this rival through derogatory labels such as "social chauvinism." Furthermore, they attempted to accuse and thus smash it as being "half-hearted, mendacious, and rotten."[56]

This was only possible because hatred of the moderate left had turned into an obsession. In the midst of the chaos of the fall of 1918, Lenin took the time to write an almost hundred-page-long tirade. Writing in a professorial style against the "renegade Kautsky," the head of the parliamentary European left, Lenin voiced the famous accusation that Kautsky aimed for a "revolution without revolution." This clearly shows that, already, Lenin equated practical overthrow with the unlimited exercise of violence.[57] Only those who publicly committed to the duty of fighting social democracy as the primary enemy could become members of the Third International, which was constituted in March 1919. Only after the time for effective defensive alliances against the victorious national revolutionary movements had run out did the communist leadership in Moscow change its point of focus to the rage accumulation in national socialisms. At this point, social democrats and communists were already crowded together in concentration camps.

Reflexes of the struggle for the *thymos* monopoly also entered the thoughts of the more subtle minds of the West. In his reflections "On the Concept of History," written in 1940, Walter Benjamin criticized social democracy for believing that future generations should profit one day from improved living conditions. Orientation to future successes, he objected, cuts "the sinews of [the working class's] greatest strength" because by being educated to practice evolutionary patience it forgets its "hatred and its spirit of sacrifice."[58] With arguments of such a quality, the author of the historical-messianic theses wanted to uplift class hatred, which was cherished by the communists. To understand the power of the left-fascist seduction— and the discreet charm of the theological overinterpretation of past events (*geschehener Geschichte*)—it is necessary to acknowledge that even an author of Benjamin's stature could be won over to such philo-Soviet remarks and the sanctification of violence.

However, the consequences of overinterpretation cheerfully transcending the threshold of indolence are plain beginning in the 1920s, in particular among political theologians. Paul Tillich, for example, took himself to be sufficiently inspired to dare to announce that the decision for socialism would, in a specific period, become equivalent to the decision for the kingdom of God. The "specific period" was for Tillich identical with the era after Lenin's death. In the year 1932 the resolute German protestant himself felt called upon to understand and affirm Stalin's *kairos*.

It has been well documented by the history of religion that when the Holy Spirit blows through, it occasionally reaches high wind speeds. The front man Eugen Rosenstock-Huessy had the honor of demonstrating how it can provide for ordained hurricanes when he told the history of Europe, without further ado, as the epic of the Holy Spirit become creative through revolutions. In the year 1931, this phosphorescent lay-theologian thought that it was appropriate to lecture on the Soviet Union: "We will be recreated and revolutionized by Russia, because the story of the creation of the human being is continued there. . . . In Moscow there are the new dogmatic popes who decide about the salvation of our lives."[59] Such remarks can only be made plausible by illuminated interpreters insisting on their right even under the most difficult of circumstances to interpret world history to the last detail as a history of salvation. Profane observers of such victories over probability reach the conclusion that theology and acrobatics must have one and the same root.

THE THIRD INTERNATIONAL, WHICH WAS FOUNDED IN 1919, PRESENTED itself from the beginning as the executive organ of Leninism, which asserted that its aim was "to connect the truly revolutionary parties of the world proletariat." The Third International proclaimed that it would use its councils to create "its own apparatus," which would be capable of replacing the bourgeois state. Hereby nothing less than a system of proletarian Catholicism entered the world stage. The relationship between the party and the councils was unequivocally modeled on the Roman Church and its local parishes. However, what became clear after a few yeas was that nothing but the promise that the battles would be continued remained from the sparkling promises of the *Manifesto of the Communist International to the Global Proletariat*, dated March 6, 1919. Even the concept of an army of councils, which had been proclaimed in the manifesto, quickly gave way to a conventional military machinery in the hands of a monological party leadership.

By presenting itself as the "International of action," the Comintern underlined its claim to accumulate the dispersed dissidence potentials of the proletarian "masses" in a world rage bank. It promised its customers it would invest their thymotic capital in revolutionary projects in order to use it for the purpose of a global, literally catholic project, which was justified in the interest of "the totality." The successes of this bank would have consisted in the creation of a proud proletariat and in the global improvement of its conditions of living—insofar as effective returns from the thymotic investments of the "masses" express themselves in the transformation of vengeful inclinations to pride and self-affirmations. Why this did not come about does not need to be laid out in detail. It is well known that Lenin assumed that the Russian Revolution would soon function as a trigger for world-revolutionary upheavals, in particular with regard to the German proletariat, which had been assigned a key role by Lenin. This assessment was plausible: there was indeed large potential for protest in the Western hemisphere. Moreover, the German question was without a doubt the most essential one. However, the dissident energies took on the shape of national-revolutionary accumulation movements, in particular in Mussolini's Italy and among the political spectrum on the right in the unfortunate Weimar Republic—and the reasons for this become clear in light of psychopolitical analysis.

The early terrorist turn of the Russian events makes one thing unmistakably clear from the beginning: the new central bank could at no time be satisfied with the real investments of its clients. Because the effective rage deposits of the Soviet proletarians were much too small for the intended project, the necessary assets had to be raised by force from the huge "masses" of the country's farmers. However, nothing suggested that this potential would have accrued to the communist fund because the interests of the rural poor hardly had a common denominator with the marginal Marxist working force, not to mention with the dictating commissionaires.

In this situation the directorship of the massively undercapitalized world bank of rage resorted to the strategy of blackmailing the reluctant "masses" of farmers to deposit their thymotic savings. The managerial secret of the Russian Revolution consisted in procuring the missing quantities of rage in the form of mandatory credit loans. Consequently, the Soviets created enormous amounts of exploitable anxiety, which was connected to the extorted willingness to feign support for the projects of the revolutionary rage bank. With regard to this point, the analogies between the Catholic politics of redemption and the communist version of the gospel are impressive.

The greatest success of the Russian Revolution was probably its ability to enforce a broad current of simulated assent. It is thanks to this that it was discovered that class hatred, which is the precondition for legitimizing revolutionary politics, does not necessarily need to be present—as little as institutionalized religion always presupposes true faith. The affect could just as much be brought about by artificial means, whether by agitation and measures for the sake of mobilization or through the enforcement of applause for the projects of the party. Instead of basing his theory of the simulacrum on contemporary cultural life, Jean Baudrillard could have derived it just as well from investigating communist power.

Because the extortion of assent by way of instilling fear was by itself not able to support the Soviet developmental dictatorship, it was necessary to create a catalogue with positive images into which those that had initially only been passively affected by the revolution could invest their own ambitions and fantasies. This task was taken up by the directors of Bolshevik psychopolitics not without a sense for thymotic realities. In order to create the necessary degree of collective pride, they activated some of the most powerful mythic models of modernity—the Prometheus complex ranked first, which has always been characteristic for the technophile disposition of bourgeois modernity, then pride in the great achievements of Soviet technology and its urban development—think of the cult surrounding the Moscow subway—and finally the figure of the athlete who defends the honor of the collective through his achievements. The turning of industrial achievements into sport went so far in Soviet ideology that in the case of the famous Sakharov workers, those intense athletes of plan fulfillment, the figure of the proletarian was equated to a winner of an athletic competition in a stadium. And nevertheless it was impossible for the artificially ignited rage of the Komsomolets, the members of the youth organization who had been sworn into Stalinism and who deliberately signed up for the battle of production, to let one forget about the shabbiness of the conditions. The vulnerability of the functionaries to the slightest bit of critique betrayed the instability of the situation. At times a seemingly harmless and substantively fitting remark, such as the statement that Soviet shoes would be of an inferior quality, sufficed to have its author confined to one of the countless prison camps.

The decisive characteristic of the new affective economy consisted in restraining the clients to the institute of accumulation. Because of the abolishment of any opposition, they could no longer take out their rage assets from the party to deposit them in a different corporation. If the bank had paid back the loans of fear to thus allow their clients to make a free decision, the Soviet investors would have withdrawn their assets from the Communist institutions in order to invest them in less despotic projects. Because the situation was as it was, closing one's account would have meant breaking with the party—and suffering the consequences. This coercive manipulation of investors through the revolutionary system of restraining customers has received the not unfitting, although otherwise questionable, name "totalitarianism." "Totalitarian" refers to the retransformation of the customer into a slave of the corporation.

All this explains why the red terror was never simply a necessary bad feature of a "time of transition"—independent of whether this period was conceived of as an episode or as an epoch. The Soviet regime was in principle dependent on the steady regeneration of horror. Without the confiscation of thymotic potentials of large strata of society, the Bolshevist cadres would have been able to remain in power for barely half a year. One should therefore certainly not make Lenin's stubborn character exclusively responsible for the success of the rigid line, however often the abnormal intolerance of the party and revolutionary leader has been documented by its witnesses and victims. The suppression of any form of opposition was in reality a simple business necessity if the party did not want to give up its claim to be the sole representative for the thymotic energies of the "masses." This is why the collapse of the Communist system was imminent when its universal autohypnosis faded away. As long as it stayed in power, it had to confiscate all means of expressing self-respect. Since there is an evident connection between property and self-respect, the destruction of property was the most secure way of humiliating the comrades of the Soviet empire.

If the system was supposed to rule successfully, no non-Bolshevik nucleus for *thymos* articulations was allowed in the country. In order to implement the monopoly of communism with regard to rage, pride, and the dissidence assets of the populations it covered, it was absolutely necessary to cut off the individual as well as groups from any access to alternative sources of self-respect.[60]

The long-term consequences of these psychic expropriations are still atmospherically present in the post-communist universe, even today after decades of thaw and de-Sovietization. Because of a despotism to which the rage expropriation, the breaking of pride, and the destruction of the opposition over many generations were endemic, a climate of deeply destructive humiliation was created in the reigns of Lenin and Stalin, a climate that recalls Oswald Spengler's dark diagnoses about the fellahs emerging from devastated civilizations. Its common reality was popular resignation. The political regime was tolerated as a vicious addition of destiny to the terrible Russian winters. If one wanted to trace back the Soviet climate to individual contributions of actors, one would discover, among other things, a civil servant such as Lazar Kaganovich, one of the most monstrous creatures of Stalin, who demanded from revolutionaries with a solemn tone of voice that they surrender their self-respect and their sensibility.[61] In this atmosphere the Russian people were transformed into a collectivity of passive mystics for whom the state made it easier to abandon themselves. The artist Ilya Kabakov evoked the general attitude of the Russian "society" before and after Stalin's death in an autobiographical conversation with Boris Groys: "The Soviet Union was accepted as one accepts a snow storm or a climate catastrophe." "In spite of the nightmare of the life back then we had the sweet feeling that everyone was living this way."[62]

The re-thymotization of post-Soviet "society" turns out to be a protracted endeavor because of the scarcity of psychic and moral resources. Initially it could only get under way via nationalism—a rather novel idea for Russia.[63] People who know about the contemporary situation observe that Russian "society" does not currently indulge itself in consumerism without limitations, as one might expect, but that it is committed to a daily *bellum omnium contra omnes*. The return to self-affirmative lifestyles happens in the form of a generalized mobbing. This diagnosis allows for a promising prediction. In a country in which everybody had lost respect for everybody else because everybody witnessed everybody else in situations that were humiliating, the flourishing of a meanness of all against all could resemble a sign of recovery.

ACQUIRING RAGE THROUGH WAR BONDS

THE ABOVE CONSIDERATIONS HAVE ELUCIDATED WHY LENIN'S PROJECT of revolution was marked by a severe lack of thymotic capital. The unavoidability of this lack resulted from the historical situation. True, there was not a lack of affect against czarism around 1917. Furthermore, it can be assumed that there was a large reservoir of aspirations for democracy, self-administration, permissiveness, and the redistribution of land. However, these tendencies, which could be aroused and increased easily, were far from harmonized with the coercive capitalist conceptions of development that were characteristic of Leninist theory during the period of transition. In the language of revolutionary insiders, these features were verified by pointing to the still missing "class consciousness." Of course these circumstances could not have remained unknown to Lenin. In order to keep his visions coherent, he was thus dependent on the expectation of an imminent proletarian revolution in Germany, from which he expected an increase in the insufficient Russian capital base. When this revolution failed to materialize and when its weak beginnings fully collapsed after the execution of its leaders, the need for alternative mobilizations of *thymos* in Russia became urgent.

I have already referred to the constitutive role that terror plays in acquiring common consent to the goals of revolution. Not long after the terror was established, a cultural-revolutionary front was added to it: the mass production of desired attitudes through the most intensive forms of propaganda, in combination with the monopolization of education (thanks to teachers and curricula), both of which were indoctrinated with Bolshevist ideology. The height of the Russian artistic avant-garde coincided with these campaigns. It was only with the new, rigidified cultural politics after Stalin's coming into power that this was put to an end. Yet more influential was the creation of combat-stress collectives, which brought about the desired state of thymotic homogenization by way of a shared perception of enemies.

Within the framework of psycho-political logic, one can claim without exaggeration that the Russian Revolution was rescued during its first years by the counterrevolution, just as the Chinese Revolution owed its triumph ultimately to the Japanese, who, following the invasion of China from 1937 to 1947, created the conditions under which the weak communist reserves were enforced by the massive influx of patriotic emotions. After the victory of his troops, Mao Zedong did not create a mystery surrounding the fact that Chinese communism would have been a lost endeavor without the Japanese attack—he was humorous enough to explain to his Japanese visitors that China owed their country eternal gratitude for the invasion.

Observations such as these confirm the suspicion that thymotic realpolitik follows completely different laws. The directors of the new world bank were condemned by stress biology and cultural dynamics to look for support where it could be most easily discovered: in the sources of pride, rage, and self-assertion of the nationally synthesized combat communities. From the beginning it was thus necessary to widen the capital basis of the world bank of rage—apart from anxiety bonds from terror—through the mobilization of a patriotic thymotics. It was not accidental that Lenin liked to conjure up the image of Russia as a "besieged stronghold." Although the Soviet experiment was conducted in a postnational horizon, the conception of a threatened fatherland was an indispensable matrix for the renewal of combative energies. At least the concept of the fatherland was always also interpreted from international perspectives because the Soviet Union, the "home of all workers," was a hybrid body, encompassing at the same time a territory and an idea. The ominous concept of "socialism in one country" did more than provide an emergency solution (*Notlösung*) in light of the persistent deferral of the world revolution. It entailed the concession that the desperately needed thymotic reserves could only be drawn from a seriously threatened combat-stress collective.

The war against the national enemy, to be sure, has always possessed the advantage of high plausibility. No one knew this better than Karl Marx, who sternly commented on the political adventures of the Paris communists of 1871 (who attempted their coup against the bourgeois government of France in the middle of the war against Prussia): "Any attempt at upsetting the new government in the present crisis, when the enemy is almost knocking at the doors of Paris, would be a desperate folly. The French workmen must perform their duty as citizens."[64] A civil war can also provide extreme motivation if the front against the enemies within has been clearly morally demarcated. Because the Bolshevists no longer had a sufficiently external enemy at their disposal after the end of the civil war in 1921, they had to internally refinance their thymotic war bonds and open a new front out of the spirit of pure mobilization.

With this operation the darkest chapter of the tainted history of revolutionary rage transactions began: the intentional redirection of "mass rage" against the affluent farmers of the Soviet Union, in particular those of the Ukraine, who gained notoriety under the name of "kulaks." They are still the largest collective of genocide victims in the history of humanity—at the same time, they constitute the group of victims that can do the least to struggle against the forgetting of the injustice committed against them.

According to Marxist teaching, the Soviet leadership should have regarded the peasantry of the country as a productive class that was, to a certain extent, analogous to the proletariat. Because it belonged to a preindustrial universe, however, it formed a category of producers of the wrong kind, producers condemned to fall. Thus the peasants of Russia and the other Soviet states entered the radar screen of the revolution in a twofold sense—on the one hand, they embodied a shocking backwardness, which could only be eradicated by means of forced modernization; on the other hand, they were the producers of the food that the revolutionary elements claimed for themselves from the first day of the riots. Lenin himself determined the rough tone of the politics concerning the kulaks by consistently situating the independent farmers in the first row of those "classes" to be executed, next to the bourgeoisie, the clergy ("the more representatives of reactionary clergy we can shoot the better"), and the Menshevik reformers. It was only after a return to financing compromises (in the context of the new economic politics after 1921) that most of these groups were allowed to breathe a sigh of relief.

This was finally finished when Stalin around 1930 turned back the wheel to an exclusive command economy. From that point onward, the "destruction of peasantry as a class" became the main priority on the revolutionary agenda. Because there was no arrangement in regular Marxism for using repressive measures against the peasantry as such, Stalin picked up Lenin's directives and had to extend the schema of the struggle between bourgeoisie and proletariat to such an extent that it now included a class struggle that had not been predicted: between the poorer and the less poor, sometimes even affluent strata of the rural population. The latter suddenly enjoyed the questionable honor of being declared a substitute for the exterminated bourgeoisie—even straightaway becoming a representative of "agricultural capitalism." Consequently, the new mobilization was directed against those farmers who were still able to continue with their business in a relatively successful way in the midst of the general economic disaster (from 1917 until

1921 the number of deaths from starvation in Lenin's empire climbed to more than 5 million). It is understandable that these "big farmers" were not excited when the functionaries of the revolutionary countries seized their harvests. Their hesitation in having to deliver their means of subsistence was identified as sabotage and was punished accordingly. The ominous collectivization of agriculture under Stalin pursued the goal of simplifying the confiscation of yields by starting with the production.

The "de-kulaking" during the early 1930s, which led to up to 8 million starvation deaths during the harsh winter of 1932–33, meant a psycho-political caesura in the business conduct of the rage bank management. From 1930 onward in Stalin's politics with regard to the kulaks, the dark aspects of popular *thymos* prevailed as the essential driving forces in the revolutionary rules of business: resentment, envy, the need to humiliate those who were allegedly or truly better off.

If it is appropriate to describe the history of events in the Soviet Union as a drama of the lost innocence of the revolution, the application of hatred against larger farmers—and after 1934 also against so-called midsized farmers (those who owned up to two cows)—marked the transition of the Stalinist U.S.S.R. to an open psychopolitics of dirty energies. In its course, the "class" of those semi-starved was sent into battle against the "class" of those barely able to survive—with the pretense that this would be the most contemporary form of revolutionary struggle in the fatherland of the world proletariat. Stalin himself provided the justification by contributing a new "class analysis" from the vantage point of somebody who was riding on the witch's broom of solitary illumination: according to this justification, it was legitimate to call for a "liquidation of the kulaks as a class" in the name of the Marxist classics. A kulak or "great farmer" was identified as somebody who produced enough in order to provide for his own family and a few laborers—with an occasional surplus sold at markets or in the city. This injustice against the working masses was not in the future allowed to remain unpunished. To avenge it, a demonstration was needed to show what "terrorism in one country" was capable of achieving.[65]

The reason behind the events was concealed in the random broadening of the concept of "class struggle." Suddenly it was no longer mentioned that the bourgeois epoch had "simplified" class oppositions in terms of a clear opposition of bourgeoisie and proletariat, as the *Communist Manifesto* stated. After Stalin had elevated the kulaks to the rank of a "class," and by calling them "counterrevolutionary," this class was ordered to be liquidated overnight in substitution for the barely existing and quickly extinguished bourgeoisie. From that point on, it was evident for everybody who wanted to know that every form of "class analysis" entails the demarcation of fronts at which the executioners confront those to be executed. Mao Zedong also came up with a new "class analysis" when inciting the Chinese youth against the "class" of the old during the great Cultural Revolution.

It is important to realize that we are not merely talking about terminological finesse here. If one continues to speak about classes after Stalin and Mao, one makes an assertion concerning the perpetrators and the victims in a potential or actual (class) genocide. As smarter Marxists have always known, "class" is a descriptive sociological term only at the surface level. In reality, it is primarily strategic in nature because its content materializes only through the formation of a combat collective (a confessional or ideologically formed maximum-stress-cooperation unit).[66] If one uses it affirmatively and, *eo ipso*, performatively, one makes an assertion stating who is justified to extinguish whom under which kind of pretense.[67] Class thinking ranks far above race thinking when it comes to the release of genocidal energies in the twentieth century.

What lends disturbing significance to the processes initiated by Stalin's improvisations is the ease with which the leaders of the Soviet Communist Party were able to induce in countless participants the intoxication of a resentment that unites its bearers to serve as accomplices in extinguishing devalued "classes." Research has provided vast information on the motives of Hitler's willing executioners; Stalin's armies of helpers remain hidden in the catacombs of history. What genocidal excesses in the name of class in fact reveal is the extent to which what sociologists refer to as "social ties" are also always woven out of a hatred that binds the disadvantaged to the seemingly or actually advantaged. When envy dons the gown of social justice, there arises a pleasure in belittling others, a pleasure that is already halfway to destruction.

The Bolshevist system would never have recovered from this defilement—which could hardly have been exceeded even by the Moscow trials—if Stalinism had not been rescued by the war that Hitler carried into the Soviet Union. The fury of idealizing, which its agents and sympathizers shared, would never have sufficed to compensate for these darkenings (*Verdunkelungen*) of the Soviet experiment as a whole, if there had been an appropriate and timely enlightenment concerning the events in the country. The anti-Hitler imperative of those years was responsible for the fact that interest in not perceiving overshadowed the horrors of Stalinism, in particular for Western party supporters and sympathizers, who insisted on their high-minded immunity to the facts. For countless members of the New Left in the Western world, the phase of wishful blindness was to last until the Solzhenitsyn shock of 1974. Only with the appearance of *The Gulag Archipelago* and the works of the *nouveaux philosophes* was it possible for a modified perspective to come about, although some spokesmen of the eternal militancy were still then content with modernizing their protection of ignorance.

After July 22, 1941, it was once more proven in the battle of the Russians against the German invaders that it is possible to set free the most powerful cooperative energies in a collective through provoking the national *thymos*, even if this collective had just suffered the most severe humiliations on the internal front—perhaps precisely then because the war between nations can bring about a certain recovery from ideological infamy. It was thus initially consistent that Stalin's propaganda referred to the war against Hitler's armies as the great patriotic war—in deliberate analogy to the "patriotic war" of the Russians against Napoleon in 1812. The bitter irony of history was only revealed when the heroism and willingness of the Russian people and its allies to suffer entered into the books of "antifascism" after the battle was won.

As Boris Groys has demonstrated, communism constituted itself as a mobilizing power exclusively within the medium of language.[68] It is thus not surprising that its successes consisted mainly in the enforcement of a strategic codification of language (*Sprachregelung*). For good reasons, these successes went far beyond the sphere of Soviet dictates. In the entire sphere of influence of Stalinism and beyond it in the New Left, the ingenious self-depiction of left fascism as antifascism became the dominant language game of the postwar era. This had long-term effects that can be traced to the present in dissident subcultures of the West, most importantly in France and Italy. It is not an exaggeration to identify the flight of the radical left to "antifascism" as the most successful maneuver of language politics in the twentieth century. That it remained, and remains to this day, the source for highly desired confusions follows from its premises.

The continuation of the game by the Western left after 1945 happened primarily because of the need for an encompassing self-amnesty. The so-called attempts to work through the past to search out the "sources" of fascism remained subordinate to this imperative—whereas the tracing back to Lenin's initial contribution remained blocked through a prohibition on thinking. It can be easily explained why the left needed this act of amnesty. Considering the devastating results of Stalinism, they needed to cover up, justify, and relativize an excess of mistakes, failed opportunities, and illusions. Well-meaning companions knew what they did not want to know— and did not hear anything during the critical times. (Sartre, for example, knew about the 10 million prisoners in Soviet camps and remained silent in order not to break with the front of antifascists.) Their always problematic cooperation with the manipulators from Moscow, their acting blindly with regard to the first signs and the true extent of red terror, their one-eyed sympathizing with a communist cause that had been deeply compromised in theory and praxis long ago—all of this strongly called for understanding, romanticizing, and forgiveness. The left's absolution necessarily had to be granted by its own people and from its own *fundus* because independent instances, which could have pardoned them, were not available.

It is not correct to say that the far left in Europe after the Second World War concealed its emotions from itself. By perpetually raising its antifascist convictions, it proclaimed for itself that, apart from its basic historical legitimacy, it had intended grandiose plans and possessed the right to continue where the revolutionaries before Stalin had stopped. A higher moral mathematics was invented according to which someone has to be taken to be innocent if he can prove that someone else was even more criminal. It was thanks to such strategic reflections that for many Hitler served as the savior of conscience. In order to distract oneself from the affinities of one's own engagement with the ideological premises of the most extensive acts of murder in the history of humanity, historical mock trials were staged, mock trials in which everything pointed towards the private first class of the war, to the person who completes the history of the West. Thanks to totalizing forms of cultural criticism—for example, the tracing back of Auschwitz to Luther and Plato, or the criminalization of occidental civilization as a whole—it was attempted to cover how closely the West was affiliated with a class-genocidal system.

The smart redistribution of shame did not miss the intended effect. In fact, a point was reached in which almost every form of critique against communism was denounced as "anticommunism," which, in turn, was denounced as a continuation of fascism by liberal means. Although after 1945 there really were no publicly committed fascists anymore, there was an abundance of paleo-Stalinists, former communists, alternative communists, and radical innocents from the most extreme wings, who held their heads as high as if the crimes of Lenin, Stalin, Mao, Ceausescu, Pol Pot, and other communist leaders had been committed on planet Pluto. The thymotic analysis makes it possible to understand these phenomena. The same human beings, who have convincing reasons to be too proud to engage with reality—*"on a raison de se révolter"*—sometimes, for less convincing reasons, are too proud for the truth.

Maoism: On the Psychopolitics of Pure Fury

IF ONE BELIEVES THAT THE CONTROL OF THYMOTIC ENERGIES through the Stalinist management of rage reached the ultimate degree of realpolitik cold-bloodedness, one is disabused of this belief in a twofold manner by Maoism. The first lesson consists in the invention of a new kind of guerilla warfare that Mao Zedong advanced as China was confronted with a major challenge during the time of civil wars between 1927 and 1945; this kind of guerilla warfare later served as a source of inspiration for the many "liberation armies" of the Third World. The second lesson can be learned from the notorious cultural revolution of the 1960s. We have to remind ourselves that the struggle between social classes was replaced by the unleashing of the hatred of stoned adolescents against the older generation of tradition bearers. Here as well problems of rage management were at the heart of the matter. Mao's politics was from the outset characterized by a methodical substitution of collective fury for missing revolutionary energies, which was provoked by the military-political leadership.

Mao Zedong's fame is primarily connected to his astounding achievements as the strategic head of the civil war, which lasted twenty-five years. What was at stake in the struggle was the question of who was to have power in postfeudal China. The protagonists of this epic battle, the Kuomintang and the communists, initially cooperated from 1924 until 1927, then again from 1937 until 1945, first against the warlords in the provinces of the country, and later against the Japanese invaders. Between 1927 and 1936, and between 1945 and 1949, they confronted each other, at times seemingly and at other times in reality, as fierce adversaries. Mao's military apprenticeship began with the resistance of the communist troops against the dictatorship of the national-revolutionary general Chiang Kai-shek, who seized complete power after his notorious strike in Shanghai against the (until then) allied communists. André Malraux chose as the background plot for his 1933 novel *La condition humaine* the attack of the Kuomintang fighters against the communists of Shanghai to depict a scene that was permeated by hatred and active despair. In light of this background, the idea of an absolute engagement gained focus, an idea that was about to cast its shadow over the European intelligentsia in its Sartrean variety after 1945.

Mao Zedong's strategic intuitions started with the assumption that the diffuse antifeudal rage of the Chinese "masses" of peasants constituted an insufficient basis for the mobilization of the ascetic-heroic troops he required. Because for Mao the organization of an industrial-proletarian movement was never an option—China was in this respect even more underdeveloped than Russia in 1917—he was faced early on with the problem of how to create an efficient machinery of war from only agrarian energies. The solution consisted in the conception of a guerilla doctrine designed for the war of small mobile troops against the massive units of the government. It rested on the easy, albeit effective principle that uses the superiority of the adversary as leverage to increase one's own forces. Mao observed that the brutality of the official military apparatus, which was led by Chiang Kai-shek, created enough despair in the agitated mass of the rural population that with appropriate guidance they could be prompted to defend themselves against armed invaders on their own ground.

By drawing the ultimate consequences from this, Mao understood that for the weak, total mobilization was the key to success. He preached that this could not, of course, come about through a "revolutionary agrarian war" alone. A national war, he taught, was much more capable of bringing about the desired great mobilization—for which the Japanese invasion of 1937 was supposed to provide the desired conditions. Sebastian Haffner has explained that in the history of the war, the significant turn was the invention of the "total guerilla," which was a clear reference to Goebbels's hysteric proclamation of a "total war." Mao proved nothing short of the fact that guerilla warfare can be taken to its specific extreme.

In a lucid commentary on Mao Zedong's writings about the theory of war, Sebastian Haffner exposes the exploitation of national war for the purposes of strengthening the revolutionary guerilla as Mao's epochal innovation. Its basic principle is the integral mobilization of radicalized fighters who confront a superior power of only moderately motivated troops. What makes the difference is the resolution of the leaders to cut off every possibility of escape for their own troops in battle in order to expose them to a situation of absolute stress. In this way, the war was supposed to be projected onto the molecular level. Even the smallest village that had been involved in the war had to transform itself according to the will of the commander into a reactor of despair, willing to sacrifice itself. Mao's apposite slogan is "China's strength lies in her very poverty."[69] The revolutionary war of the people wanted to be a daily plebiscite for excess.

While war, according to Clausewitz, is "an act of violence" in order to "force an enemy to fulfill what we wish for," Mao starts with the axiom that war is nothing but the procedure "to preserve oneself and to destroy the enemy." This is the definition of war of the biopolitical age, which sees the world stage as inhabited solely with competing life complexes. In this connection competition is not understood as an appeal to the judgment of the market about what is the most suitable product but as the contest of destruction on the battle ground of vitalities. Thanks to this intensification, a way was discovered to overcome the amateurish traits of the terror transactions of Bakunin's revolutionaries and replace them with a resolute exterminism—as one otherwise only knows from Hitler's conception of race struggle and its realization through the fascist state (or else from Lenin's and Zinoviev's hardly concealed imperatives, for the sake of the global decimation of populations).

A conception of "growth" is connected to Mao's total guerilla warfare, which enables initially weak fighting cells to corrupt the body of the enemy only bit by bit and secretly, steadily multiplying themselves at his cost. One could call it a model of war constructed according to the paradigm of cancer. Mao's strategy thus possesses great similarity to political oncology. To use Sebastian Haffner's words, "The essence of Maos's warfare" "is to overgrow the enemy, to overgrow him to death."[70] Mao's bizarre preference for an unpopular "protracted war" was rooted in the insight that revolutionary cells required substantial time for their destructive growth in a large country.[71]

These few pieces of evidence make it clear: Mao Zedong had at no point in his career been a Marxist, however much he attempted to keep up the appearance of revolutionary correctness by drawing on Leninist rhetoric. With his belief in the possibility of the great leap of China out of feudalism to communism, he rather resembled a conceptual artist who wanted to fill the empty space of his country with a grandiose installation. Hereby he added an East Asian counterpart to the "*Gesamtkunstwerk* Stalin" of whom Boris Groys has spoken in his recontextualization of Soviet avant-gardism.[72] Mao emerged as a mystic voluntarist whose convictions were rooted more in a primitive ontology of continuing struggle than in a developmental theory of a Western sort. The basic assumptions of the Chinese revolutionary leader could best be described as a frugal form of natural philosophy in which the theme of bipolarity sets the tone. The peasant Mao was, typologically speaking, a neo-pre-Socratic of the Eastern school. He translated conventional Taoist intuitions into the jargon of political economy with which, it has to be noted, he engaged only on a superficial level. He knew almost nothing about property, industry, the banking system, or city culture. About peasants he taught that there were large, middle-sized, and small ones and that the latter constituted the large majority, which was why one needed to seize control of this group. One can understand partially why this mixture of Marx and Lao-tzu left a deep impression on many observers and visitors. Some Western enthusiasts such as the young Phillippe Sollers, who never felt ashamed of his misjudgment, thought that Mao was the Chinese embodiment of Hegel. With a little bit of distance one sees, however, that he was a crossbreed of two kinds of platitude that could only be united in a man of greatness.

The Moscow branch of the world bank of rage needed to become aware of the activist Mao Zedong rather early. At a time when the world revolution in the industrialized countries did not advance a single step forward, news of other battlefronts was followed meticulously, including those in feudal and agrarian China, which had been ravaged by chaos and promised to become more of a burden than a pillar of support for the Comintern. It was more because of speculative reasons than sympathy that Mao's initiatives were strongly supported by the Comintern, which also supported the activities of Chiang Kai-shek because Moscow's society enjoyed seeing itself pulling the strings of competing puppets. Nevertheless, Mao remained for Moscow an embarrassing partner because his successes exposed the secret of combatant voluntarism, which had also been the driving force behind Lenin's initiatives. If one took Mao seriously, one understood sooner or later that the October Revolution was only a coup d'état that wanted to retrospectively prove itself to be a revolution. Mao, on the other hand, was the dramatic advisor of an unprecedented peasant war that cumulated in the acquisition of power by a peasant general.

After the victory of the Chinese Red Army, Mao's mobilizing psychotechnology had reached its limits because the creation of a state and a modern economy, whether hierarchical and state-directed or property-based and entrepreneurial, follows completely different laws than those with which it is possible to drive thymotically distinguished combatant communities into a state of fury that promises victory. The story of the statesman Mao Zedong, it follows, needs to be recorded in the form of a report of the failures of an excessive mobilizer. The strategist Mao remained convinced even after 1949 that the principles of total guerilla warfare could be applied more or less unchanged to the swift creation of a Chinese industry. This fallacy led to the sequence of events from the ominous "Great Leap Forward" (1958–1961) to the Cultural Revolution (1966–1969, and de facto until Mao's death in 1976), and finally to the polite marginalization of the Great Steersman.

As the leader of the national bank of revolutionary affect, Mao was convinced after the creation of the People's Republic that he would be able to regulate infinite credit if he could succeed in amalgamating rage, despair, and revolutionary pride, the mixture that had supported him in the most surprising ways during the civil-war era. In order to advance the industrialization of China, he announced the "Great Leap Forward" in 1958. Every independent observer could interpret it as nothing less than the deliberate psychotization of the entire country. However, what characterized China already back then was the liquidation of every form of internal independent observation, so that Mao's attitudes and statements meant law and eternal truth to 600 million people.

Under these circumstances, the biggest prank of human economic history could be presented as the outflow of an elevated politics of genius: a huge propaganda apparatus advertised for years the idea that China's welfare and the glorious revolution would succeed if—together with the forced collectivization of agriculture—the production of iron was relocated from the cities into the villages. Hundreds of millions of clueless, astonished, and reluctant farmers were forced together in unfamiliar cooperatives. As a result, their motivation and ability to work weakened abruptly. At the same time, they saw themselves confronted with the task of constructing primitive furnaces in order to increase steel production in the country overnight using only local methods. At the time, this was one of the most important indicators of economic ability. The officially proclaimed goal was to surpass the per capita production of England within fifteen years. The results of these frenetic activities, which quickly turned out to be useless, were put into remote dumps and piled in steel mountains. Should there ever be a de-Maoicization in China, one would have to declare these hidden surrealist mountains of rust world cultural heritage sites. (A de-Maoicization of China is, of course, an implausible hypothesis: politically, because Mao Zedong's icon is an indispensable means of integration for the current and future leadership of the country; culturally, because the persisting Sino-centrism almost categorically denies an enlightenment of the Chinese about their own history by better-informed foreign Chinese or non-Chinese.[73] Then again, a formal de-Maoicization is no longer on the agenda because China, with its new economic politics, has for a long time turned its back on the dreams and nightmares of Mao's epoch.)

In spite of the complete senselessness of this form of production, a senselessness soon recognized by the leaders, the mobilization of the workers continued incessantly. Movie images of that time show countless rural Chinese workers in front of a limitless horizon, chasing here and there in a hectic ballet between the smoking chimneys. The neglect of agriculture was accepted by Mao and his followers as an inevitable side effect of this new adjustment of priorities. The burlesque of the Great Leap cost, according to current estimates, between 35 and 43 million lives (or, according to more conservative estimates, approximately 30 million); in some provinces, 40 percent of the population died from starvation and exhaustion. This is the only mass destruction of human beings through work that did not require camps. The fact that the Chinese leadership also insisted on the creation of its own gulag confirms the rule that no fascism, once it has seized power, passes up the chance to be gratified by cracking down its enemies through the dehumanizing act of crowding them together.

Several years were needed before the party leadership was ready to concede that its campaign had failed—until the end it was impossible to find anyone willing to risk telling Mao about his mistakes. The only exceptions were Marshal Peng Dehuai, who had personally attacked Mao at the conference of Lushun in the summer of 1959 because of the obvious debacle (and disappeared immediately after that), and some journalists, who suffered harsh repressions as an immediate consequence. The other members of the cadre were silent or withdrew into diplomatic illnesses in order to keep out of Mao's way at the crucial conferences. Mao himself, when being discreetly reminded about the high toll of his directives, is said to have stated that the corpses could also be useful because they would fertilize Chinese soil.

The culmination of Mao Zedong's mobilizing technology was reached between 1966 and 1969 when the leader, in the meantime marginalized, wanted to seize power again by discovering a new, easily activated rage capital. Similar to Stalin, who staged a false class struggle between the poorest and the less poor among the peasant population of the Soviet Union by tapping into vast resentment reserves, Mao discovered in his empire a new "class position"— between the young and the old, or between the living elements of the movement and those that were in a state of bureaucratic torpidity. The deliberate intensification of this "opposition" was supposed to help Mao draw once again on his conception of total guerrilla warfare. Apparently his quasi-natural-philosophical doctrine of an eternal war of oppositions was suited to transform any structurally caused social difference into a starting point for a civil war that could be declared as a class struggle. Hereby the great director proved himself to be, until the bitter end of the Cultural Revolution, what he had been from the beginning—a nationalistically minded warlord with left-fascist principles and imperial ambitions. He stayed the man who constantly required new combative pretenses in order to remain in power. He also stayed the man who dismissed all such pretenses without hesitation as soon as the circumstances required, or allowed for, such measures.

For Mao it was sufficient to identify a random new resentment collective in order to set it on its designated enemy—this was enough to present the conflict as the contemporary form of "class struggle." The apposite "class" comes into being only in the context of the fight Mao sought in order to destroy the apparatus of the party around Liu Shaotsi, who had dared to push him to the side after the debacle of the Great Leap. In the Chinese teaching of prudential strategies, the method Mao chose is called "killing the enemy with a foreign knife."[74] Mao discovered his instrument in a flood of infuriated adolescents who, following the call of their leader, left their schools and universities in order to spread physical and psychological terror across the entire country. The catchphrase for this deployment of rebellious youth into villages was once again referred to as the unity of theory and praxis.

In Mao's famous Beijing encounters with more than a million euphoric students and Red Guards from all provinces, he explained the assaults that he expected from them. Is it not always the point of such gatherings that the people are given the opportunity to read the mind of the ruler? The public humiliations of scholars, who were chased around market squares wearing hoods of shame, who were beaten and forced to accuse themselves and, in countless cases, even murdered, belong to the memorable scenes of the Cultural Revolution. Even today one discovers ceramic sculptures in Beijing

flea markets that reveal the social-realist style of that age. They depict a pro-
fessor who kneels beneath the boot of a red guardsman with a sign around
his neck saying, "I am a stinking number nine," an intellectual.

THE NIGHTMARISH RIOTS OF THE CULTURAL REVOLUTION—WHICH
were trivialized by Western observers as upheavals—happened almost
simultaneously with the student movements in Berkeley, Paris, and Berlin.
In these cities, there were engaged groups that took the little information
that they had about the events in China and its causes as a sufficient reason
to present themselves as Maoists. Some coquettish admirers of Mao from
back then, who have since forgiven themselves as if nothing happened, have
continued to be active political moralists. Having reached the age to write
memoirs, they depict, not without justification, Western Maoism and their
participation in its *performances* as a sad late form of surrealism.[75] Others
think that it is beneath them to forgive themselves and continue to announce
that they are convinced that they were and are right—only the course of
events, they claim, has taken a wrong turn (especially after the "Thermidor"
of the treacherous Deng) and allowed "restoration" determine the future.[76]
In 1968 Paris seemed to be firmly in the grip of the radical arts and culture sections of newspapers (feuilletons). President Pompidou, a man of the
center-right, was depicted as embodying the empowerment of right-wing
radicalism. The culture sections did not conceal their sympathies with the
events in China, the country of wall newspapers, the Mao bible, and the
slaughter of scholars. Once again, the *mal français* sparked the division of
the world into revolution and restoration, a global epidemic, even though it
was primarily limited to academic circles. When, after the political thaw of
1972, an American president visited the People's Republic of China for the
first time, many members of the New Left in Europe and America were hor-
rified to think that a being of light such as Mao Zedong could shake hands
with a villain like Richard Nixon. In the same year, André Glucksmann
expressed his conviction that France would become a fascist dictatorship in
Les temps modernes.

Jean-Paul Sartre was a master in the sublime art of not being willing
to learn. For a long time he transformed his previous sympathy for revolutionary violence into a self-tormenting exercise. And yet he was also an
eminent representative of a generation of fakers, tormenting themselves on
bed of nails, downplaying themselves in order to pay for belonging to the

bourgeoisie. Even today, it hurts Europeans with a remainder of historical tact to see again images from 1970 of one of the greatest intellectuals of the century, the author of *Being and Nothingness* and the *Critique of Dialectical Reason*, serving as a street vendor for a radically confused tabloid of the Maoist *gauche prolétarienne* in order to step in for, as it was called, the threatened freedom of the dissidents of France.

Such snapshots belong to the final phase of a learning cycle that spanned two centuries. In its course, the European left, fatigued and indefatigable, searched for procedures to lend a voice to the rage of the disadvantaged, a language that was supposed to lead to appropriate political action. The more grotesque the images, the better they helped to illustrate how deep is the abyss that separates rage from the incompatible principle of appropriateness. Looking at these principles reveals the paradox of revolutionary politics in general. Revolutionary politics has always devoted itself to the task of determining the right measure for something that, by itself, strives for what is "without measure."

THE MESSAGE OF MONTE CRISTO

THREE YEARS BEFORE THE PUBLICATION OF *THE COMMUNIST MANIFESTO* in 1848, the French public was infected by a novel that occupied its attention for almost a year and a half. From August 1844 until January 1846, *The Count of Monte Cristo*, the greatest rage fable of world literature, was unraveled in front of the eyes of an enchanted and insatiable audience. Alexandre Dumas's continuing narrative appeared in episodes in the *Journal des Débats*, and the book version of 1846 was more than 1,500 pages long. Hegel had declared that the appearance of a hero whose travels in the world are recorded by an epic is no longer possible in the modern "world condition." But here that very situation was presented, even if in the less artistically respectable genre of the light novel. Mass culture made possible what high culture had not been allowed to do for a long time—a modern *Iliad*, the hero of which, the young sailor from Marseille Edmond Dantès, was denounced by enviers and careerists and innocently imprisoned in the dungeons of the ocean-pounded rock Chateau d'If in order to spend the time after his escape fulfilling his pledge of revenge. His martyrdom had started during Napoleon's exile to Elba in 1814—after a decade of regenerative retreats, voyages, and preparations for revenge, the path of the resurrected led to Paris in 1838, at the height of the July monarchy, when the financial world of the upper-middle class had once and for all taken over the power from the old aristocracy.

The title and the plot of the novel did not leave any doubt that Dumas wanted to tell the story of a messiah who returned to practice revenge. It is not accidental that the work of Edmond Dantès's spiritual mentor and prison companion, Abbe Faria, which the hero discovers at the end of his campaign in his former prison cell, is prefaced with the motto "You will pull the dragon's teeth and trample the lions underfoot, said the Lord."[77] In line with this oath, the mysterious count wants to demonstrate "how much, nowadays, with a fortune of thirteen or fourteen millions, a man could do in the way of harm to his enemies."[78]

As a master of mass entertainment, Dumas understood that nothing has such an intense effect on the public as a profane story of salvation. Perhaps Dumas was the first to see the mission of mass culture in displacing the myth of the eternal recurrence from heaven back to earth. The wrath of God was to become human rage—and waiting for transcendent retribution was to become an immanent praxis, which was to be sufficiently cold-blooded in order to prudently reach its goal but also heated enough in order not to let go even a little bit of the call for retributive gratification. Here rage was explicitly described in terms of its thymotic nature—the elimination of the unbearable lack of suffering, which rules in a world full of injustice without atonement.

Seen from this perspective, Edmond Dantès embodies the world soul of the bourgeois era. He knows in a clear and self-evident way what the political transformers of his day still had to search for. He is the human being who has found his struggle. He is infused by a motivation that eradicates every ambiguity. If one lives for rage, one possesses that simple, apodictic "in-order-to," which Kierkegaard took to be the difference between an apostle and a genius.[79] While the genius always has to wait for new ideas—ideas being unpredictable enough to change direction at every opportunity— the apostle knows every time exactly what needs to be done. What the left Hegelians postulated on the other side of the Rhine in philosophical terminology was realized with all its consequences by Alexandre Dumas in the world of the novel. *The Count of Monte Cristo* provided the French pendant to Marx's *Theses on Feuerbach*. It unfolded a grant narrative apparatus with the proposition: "So far the abject and the offended only showed lenience based on various pretenses with regard to the villains of this world; the point is to take revenge on them."

The transition to practiced revenge presupposes that the revenger knows from the beginning where he needs to search for the evildoers. Dumas completely lives up to this law from the great history of revenge. From the first day of the plot his villains are clearly identifiable—all of them bear the faces of the ruling class in the era of the reign of the bourgeois king. In a sense they are consistently "character masks of capital"—in no case is their guilt reducible to their class position. They are led by the small scoundrel Caderousse, who plays the part of the tale teller in the betrayal of Dantès— he embodies the eternal henchman who senses his own advantage in every regime, no matter if it comes in francs, rubles, or dollars. He is followed by the corrupt judge, Villefort, who knows the innocence of the accused and yet sentences him to life on the prison rock in order not to jeopardize his own career. He is also an embodiment of the timeless opportunist. It is not surprising that he was successful in advancing to the position of attorney general. And finally there are the two directly responsible authors of the conspiracy against the young captain, Fernand and Danglars. The one planned the conspiracy out of jealousy and the other out of envy for his career. The first advanced under Louis Philippe to the position of general and the second became a successful banker, embellished with a purchased aristocratic title. The spectrum of these careers is instructive: in contrast to the Bourbon reaction, the arrivistes of the July monarchy are not bound any longer by the fatal alternative of *rouge* and *noir*. The quantity of good positions has increased dramatically. The city of Paris vibrates with new chances. The possibilities of advancing have multiplied so that, for the first time in the history of old Europe, a majority of the people who advanced to the top were new to the position. With the depictions of these figures, Dumas expresses the conviction that evil in the relationships among people does not ultimately originate from social structures but from the hearts of corrupt individuals. No political transformation can do anything against timeless infamy—only rage, calmly followed through to the end, allows one to reestablish the unsettled balance of the world. This is why popular literature has the task of depoliticizing the rage of the disadvantaged and redirecting it to its "natural" objects, the unambiguously identified villains. True satisfaction, if we can trust the gospel according to Monte Cristo, does not lie in the victory of a collective of humiliated individuals, nor of those offended over their former masters. It comes about only as a result of the rage of a chosen victim against those who have messed with his life.

Only one time, at the height of the rage action—which Dumas reserves for the end—does an appearance of tensions connected to class struggle break into the count's revenge against his enemies. In the end of his missionary work, Dantès does not rest content with ruining the banker Danglars by manipulating option trading. He has to advance his campaign to the point of destroying the capitalist personality as such. Thus Monte Cristo seeks symbolic revenge against the entire spirit of the bourgeois era. Danglars is arrested on behalf of the count by a gang of Italian robbers under the command of a certain Luigi Vampi—a picturesque bandit who reads Plutarch's *Life of Alexander* during his free time, which probably means that he is a university dropout. The banker, who has difficulty understanding the significance of his abduction, is held in a remote cave. He only understands his situation bit by bit: in his cell the prisoner is forced to select his meals from "Luigi Vampi's menu." For each meal from the alternative restaurant the prisoner has to pay a certain price, "as it is appropriate for every true Christian." The prices, however, are exorbitantly high, so that the penny-pincher sees himself forced to spend his entire fortune, with the exception of a symbolic remainder, for his daily livelihood. He spends five million francs in twelve days, which amount, it is told, the count immediately passes on to hospitals and poorhouses.

The reader who follows the downfall of Danglars understands how wrong Marx was in claiming that the proletariat did not have to realize any ideals.[80] There is a proletarian idealism that, in a sense, argues for successful rage. In such cases one experiences the completed cruelty as the realization of a sublime mission—just as with the popular call for the death penalty.

The demand for rage crosses a threshold in these scenes, which have been painted with pleasure. Beyond this threshold there is no hope for further increase. After hardly two weeks, when Danglers, now white-haired form his ordeal, tumbles out of his prison, everything that could be achieved under the auspices of secular law has been realized. The highest satisfaction is granted from the destruction of the bourgeois character. The principle of the corrupt career is unveiled by this destruction; the careerist suffers the penalty that he deserves. If one attentively studies the menu of the robber, it becomes clear that it is nothing more than a popular commentary on the concept of exploitation. The novelist transforms the millionaire into a wretch through the reversal of the relationship of exploitation; the devil experiences with his own body what it means to sell one's life day by day for the simple purpose of self-preservation. He has never needed to sell his labor power in order to survive, but now he must sacrifice his buying power to prevent starvation. The moral lesson of the scene is obvious: every vampire lives with the risk of encountering a superior vampire sooner or later.

Monte Cristo aims to completely suspend the domination of capital over the desires of citizens. This change is not supposed to come about through the expropriation of the means of production as the Marxist vulgate wanted, but rather through the discovery of a treasure that surpasses even the greatest wealth from industry or banking transactions. Thus the treasure hunt of work, profit, and redistribution turns out to be the deeper phenomenon. With this demonstration, I leave the political and economic scene and dive back into the world of fairy tales. However, is it not the case that the deeper layers of every criticism of political economy are only touched by the criticism of the fairy tale of enrichment? Is it not the case that all monetary fantasies rest on one theme, namely, that the hero is supposed to find a way to spend his means without losing his liquidity? The person who has been truly blessed by Fortuna is not supposed to lack the miraculous manna, even if he has charitably given it to the people. It is precisely this effect, which the mysterious count has embodied since he began to haunt the discussions of Paris society like a phantom.

It is not really surprising that such a story ends with a pious lie. After the count settles all outstanding accounts and, according to his strategic plan, disposes one by one of all the people responsible for his suffering, he declares himself free of the will to revenge in a sentimental farewell letter and acknowledges that he, just as Satan before him, succumbed to the temptation of wanting to be just like God. Now, however, having overcome the desire to preside over Judgment Day himself, he will return to human standards. In the future he wishes to be a normal man among men or, even better, a rich man among rich people. He takes leave of his friends by reminding them that "all of human wisdom is entailed by the words: wait and hope!"

The audience had good reasons for not wanting to hear about the man any longer. It is fully justified to let go without remorse the privateer who has become dull. One more member of the satisfied class does not change the condition of the world. Of what concern is the destiny of a deserter who abandons the sublime cause of disaster as soon as he has satisfied himself?

He who violates the pledge of allegiance to the spirit of revenge has lost his entitlement to our attention as readers. The reader continues to stick, with good judgment, to the one who has not been converted, who after his resurrection from the dungeon insists on the execution of his rage as one insists on a sacred legal title.

THE DISPERSION OF RAGE
IN THE ERA OF THE CENTER

Conservatives start with frustration, progressives end
with frustration; everybody suffers from the age and
can agree on that point. The crisis becomes universal.

—NIKLAS LUHMANN, *PROTEST*

IF ONE WANTED TO EXPRESS THE STRONG CHARACTER OF THE
contemporary psychopolitical international situation in one sentence, it
would have to be: We have entered an era without rage collection points of
global perspective. Neither in heaven nor on earth does anyone know what
work could be done with the "just anger of the people." The sacred *fureur*,
from which Jean-Paul Marat, one of the most vicious and greatest agitators
of 1789, expected the creation of a new society, leads today to nothing. It
creates only dissatisfied noise and brings about hardly more than isolated
symbolic actions. However large one realistically needs to conceive of the
contradictory potentials of the present, be it in the countries of the center
or those at the peripheries, they no longer unite in the historically known
forms of radical parties or in international oppositional movements, which
put pressure on the bourgeois center or on an authoritarian, that is, quasi-
liberal state. Vagabond dissidence quantities do not seem to know anymore
whether they still have a task to fulfill. Here and there, there are protest
marches under banners,[1] burning cars expressing the rage of declassified
immigrants, and opportunist waves of indignation transforming traditional

nations of culture into debating clubs in which one scandalizes for weeks about illegal Hitler comparisons and dubious free flights for ministers. At times isolated and more sophisticated political projects or networks of regional significance (which enjoy talking themselves into having global significance) emerge. However, nowhere do we find an articulation of a vision that would provide perspectives for an accumulation capable of action—I will comment on the special case of radical political Islamism later.

The dispersion of forces is in stark contrast to the ubiquitous rumor that the world is increasingly interconnected by new media. Might it be the case that networking itself designates only a state of organized weakness? In large parts of the Third World, if one wants to continue to use that term, just as in some countries of the former Second World, the outrageous circumstances appear to be in no way less dramatic than the situation of the English working class in the nineteenth century according to Friedrich Engels's daunting depiction. One is led to believe that the sum total of suffering, misery, and injustice on earth, which could potentially spark rage, would be enough for ten eruptions when compared to the situation in October 1917—especially if one considers the significantly improved conditions of information—and yet attention to these energies remains modest. There is hardly any constructive use of psychopolitically relevant affects. *Thymos* fields do not manage to stabilize themselves. It seems that rage does not want to continue to learn. It does not reach the level of knowledge, and knowledge does not reach it. Indignation cannot provide for a global idea anymore. Apparently the traditional left parties are one dimension too stupid for their own ambitions, if they are not too sluggish to express their ambitions at all. Intellectuals enjoy citing one another. If the ambitious do in fact lead the conversation, they have more important things to do than take care of the debased and insulted. In the East and in the West all that remains of the hopes of those who used to be revolutionaries, reformers, transformers of the world, and redeemers of classes are mere "petrifactions"—to call up a bizarre phrase of Heiner Müller, bizarre because hopes usually wither, not petrify.

After Theory

THUS THE "AGE OF EXTREMES" SEEMS TO BE OVER—PASSED LIKE A spook that, in retrospect, no one any longer understands what made it powerful. Radicalism is only important in the Western Hemisphere as an aesthetic attitude, perhaps also as a philosophical habitus, but no longer as a political style. The center, the most formless of monsters, consistently understood the law of the hour. It made itself into the protagonist, even solo entertainer on the posthistorical stage. Whatever it touches becomes, just like itself, docile, characterless, and despotic. Yesterday's agents of extremist impatience have become unemployed and are no longer offered any parts to play in the zeitgeist. What is called for now are resilient bores. What is expected of them is to sit around big tables to come up with the world formula of compromise. The relentlessly soft center creates hybrids out of everything.

At the moment it is still difficult to understand the significance of the caesura. For at least a century, the sense of reality has done what was necessary to situate itself at the extremes—probably because it always retained proximity to wars, because it saw war everywhere and wanted to see it everywhere. If one lived during the age of extremes, one witnessed a condition in which, as Hobbes noted, "the Will to contend by battell [*sic*] is sufficiently known."[2] What appeared to be peace was inevitably unmasked as the false face of war. Every act of mediation, every reconciliatory gesture appeared as treason against the harsh reality of the extreme. Now, however, everything that is one-sided and exaggerated is smiled at as if it would reveal a lack of ability to understand the conditioned and meditated character of every position. "Being-there" (*Dasein*) and "to be in the midst of things" (*In-der-Mitte-Sein*) mean the same thing today. Heidegger would probably say: to exist means to be put into mediocracy (*Hineingehaltensein in die Mittel-Mäßigkeit*).[3]

These remarks are roughly synonymous with what modern historians, columnists, and unemployed specialists of the Soviet Union mean when they speak of the postcommunist situation. It may legitimately be proclaimed: pretty much everything that rushed by the audience during the last decades under the heading of "*post-*" ultimately culminates in the conception of a postcommunist situation (which has existed in reality since the last years of the Brezhnev era). Because the Soviet experiment was undeniably the defining political event of the twentieth century, its formal end around 1991 signified the decisive caesura from which the objectively important later datings take their departure. The inflation of the prefix "post-," which has lasted for about two decades now, symbolically expresses that future energies of the culture of rage and dissidence inexorably fade away.

The thesis that we are living "after theory"—to cite the elegant title of an essay from Terry Eagleton's pen, an essay that does not do full justice to the topic—is only sensible if one also applies it to the postcommunist situation.

Because "theory," as it is evoked by some of its disappointed lovers, is meaningless without being related to the communist utopia. If one engaged with social theory during the heyday of Marxist influences, it was necessary for substantive reasons to focus on the large picture—not in the mode of academic contemplation, to be sure, but as a participant of a military briefing and, when it became serious, even as a member of the war council. "Theory" could turn into a discursive praxis of authoritative radicalism because it signified, either explicitly or discreetly, the consultation of the world revolution. That was the reason it could be recognized by its messianic vibrato even in the driest lecture. The interest in it resulted from the mostly concealed but never repudiated suggestion that there could be something like a logical Comintern— a philosophical, sociological, and psychoanalytical supervision of the great act of revenge in the name of world history. Once this specter is discontinued, the drama and the theory are also at once finished. He who says "after theory" truly intends "after politics." One lives "after politics," if one can no longer believe that what can still be done contributes to "the revolution." The presentist adventism, which had instilled its form into the prerevolutionary and revolutionary forms of life, thus disperses. While activists were permeated by the certainty that the present would be filled with the traces of the coming, today's disenchanted live out of the conviction that the future has already been there—and nobody can bear to think of a second visit.

While exercised at a certain level, "theory" was a radically romantic affair because, like a cultural secret service, it spied on the unconscious of the class "societies" in order to find out what became of the impeded desire of human beings for the Other. The dossiers of these services thus always mentioned alterity. This amalgam, prominent during the Indian summer of the critical-theory version of neo-Marxism or as a theory without epithet in German and Anglo-American universities (while France added its resources of Jacobinism and formalism) was nothing but an apocalyptic semiology that contributed to a science of the crisis of the "establishment." It provided the accessories necessary to observe a great politics—one always ready to interpret the emerging signs of the end of the world and the revolution of the world or the sad failure to materialize either.[4]

After the world bank of rage closed down its business operations, countless ideological agencies have been drawn into the maelstrom of competition. Only a few, such as Noam Chomsky and some recent monotonous thinkers, have been almost as successful in their reconstructions as earlier generations—even if only in outsider markets. This does not mean that other contemporaries have sunk into states of peevish inexpressiveness. It is not at all the case that we have to become silent when we want to address the *mal d'être* of our days just because the East is no longer red. To the contrary, it is astounding how quickly the contemporary intelligentsia wanted to adapt to the situation, a situation in which there is no universally functioning depot capable of collecting rage, indignation, dissidence, subversion, and protest. And certainly there is no emission center for future projects that could convincingly transcend the actual world system. And still: wherever one evokes among intellectuals of the old school the rediscovery of the political, there is a form of homesickness or nostalgia for the old days in which one wanted to believe that the day of rage would soon come.

Although the Soviet Union appeared since Stalin's death in 1953 as a morally extinct colossus, and although it had lost every attraction for dissident fantasy, its factual existence served as a guarantee that the principle of the left possessed a sort of secular manifestation. Although Jean-Paul Sartre was never a formal member of the Communist Party, he could commit himself "to the leading role of the Soviet Union" still in 1952. Just like the Roman Catholic Church itself during the periods of the grossest perversions bore witness through its mere existence to a transcendental mission, the disenchanted "Eastern bloc" provided a foundation for the moral and ontological postulate that there have to be domains of possibility pointing beyond the capitalist world system. The spirit of utopia possessed more credibility than today in demanding a field "left to the establishment" in which potential worlds could flourish. Back then, no one would have fallen for the simplistic slogan, "A different world is possible." The other world was in the midst of us, and it was horrible. What was called for was another otherness—in this situation the word "alternative" started its career. Of course, the complete absurdity and rottenness of "realized" socialism was apparent, but as long as the rotten and absurd complex continued to exist, the simple "that" of its existence provided a reason to believe that a nonperverse realization of its justified motivations would be possible. Not all dissident potentials were already condemned to the art world's late-night programs and pantomimes; the horizon was not yet narrowly constricted to amusement parks for erotically excited last men.

APART FROM THE EPISTEMOLOGICAL BREAK WITH THE OLD EUROPEAN monological conception of truth, responsibility for the currently dominant unlimited pluralism mainly belongs to the end of the dogma of homogeneous evolution, which had still characterized the European Enlightenment—in that regard it is an heir to medieval logic. The illusion ended that one could control one's age from a single metropolis, whether called Moscow, Paris, Berkeley, Frankfurt, or Heidelberg. In the meantime, the "multiplicities," the differentiations, the singularities are so prominent that their media could forget that they belong to one common "humanity." In 1951, Albert Camus wrote with regard to the passed horrors, "Disaster is today our common fatherland." Contemporaries do not want to hear about common fatherlands beyond their own spheres of interest. Even the negative utopia, the anticipation of a global natural catastrophe, is incapable of creating a transcending horizon of binding departures. The spirit of de-solidarization, whether private, local, national, multinational, or imperial, reaches so deep that every unity wants to be certain that it will be spared, even if the others are swallowed up by the maelstrom. The next years will show how dangerous this multi-egoistic situation is. If it belongs to the lessons of the twentieth century that universalism from above fails, the stigma of the twenty-first century could become the failure to cultivate a sense for common situations from below.

These changes ruin the moral, rhetorical, and doctrinal basis of the traditional left. Previously successful language games have become implausible as what could be commonly taken for granted has changed. The prudish gynecological images with which Marxism got intoxicated have totally lost their footing in reality. Who could seriously repeat the phrase that the means for the realization of the classless "society" would grow "from the bottom" of the bourgeois "society"—in order to one day break free, and why not with the help of a bloody C-section by the name of "revolution"? It would now be just as ridiculous to continue using the outdated metaphor of a "primal ground," as if truth and the future could hide down there, ready for the big leap to the top. The conception of a hidden "society" beneath "society," of a secret world of cellars and tunnels where the subversion of the bourgeois edifices was planned for the future, is a totally empty conception. Only abstruse "sleepers" wait under the cover of normality for the day of being activated. The deep bunkers built today—for example, for the secret nuclear-weapons programs of expansive middle-tier powers—could be all kinds of things, but not incubation cells for happy futures.

Today the decline of a mythology of cellars and the underground extends so far that even steadfast partisans of the communist idea such as Antonio Negri have had to give up the old totem of the left: the groundhog. In a universe made up of surfaces, Negri claims, this being, which digs in hidden places, has lost its political significance. It is to be replaced by the snake, a creature with a rich gnostic past life that adapts perfectly well in the horizontal dimension to the flat, transparent shape and color changing world.[5]

Let us return to the irony of the situation: after 1991 there was nothing left to understand of what had already been hidden for alert observers of the Soviet experiment after 1918 and Lenin's decrees concerning the red terror, for the sympathizers with the left opposition after 1921, for those stuck with utopian defiance after 1956, and for the special-needs students of history after 1968.

The art of reading for "deconstruction," the representative of radical critique, could only remain on the stage by clearly distinguishing itself from the myths of the underground. It is not concerned with digging down into the impossible depth of texts and institutions in order to attach dynamite to the "foundations." It carefully points to the instability and ambiguities of seemingly solid constructions; it reveals the indeterminacy of allegedly clear binary oppositions; it makes manifest the hidden self-contradictions of coherent discourses. As a new version of the dream analysis of texts of any kind, in particular those of the old European metaphysics, it is, although its defenders often claim the opposite, an upgraded version of hermeneutics, which dedicates itself with a critical apparatus and heightened pathos to the task of provisionally letting everything be what it is.[6] Starting with this result, it is also possible to understand the complicity between deconstruction and American mass culture: the latter is also committed to the mission of not touching "what exists." Its means is the incessant evocation of the dream of a worse world next to which the existing world looks like a realized utopia, worthy of being defended by all means.

It would be possible to gather many observations following a similar tendency in order to always repeat the same fact: after the resignation of the Eastern opponents from the world civil war in between 1917 and 1945, and since the end of the Cold War between the two primary nuclear powers, the ideological pendulum, which used to swing to the extremes, has almost reached a standstill. Where everything is pulled to the center, gravity wins. Graffiti artists from Berlin understood: Being puts consciousness out of tune (*Das Sein verstimmt das Bewußtsein*). "Being" now refers to the gravitational forces of the unified center. Only what possesses the power to draw down is real. What could be more obvious in this situation than that the new unhappy consciousness diverts itself from Being just like in the old days? Precisely this is the signature of an age that wants to be everything but critical. The intelligentsia has, for the most part, turned away from criticism to opt once again for the primacy of religion. Desecularization gains ground every day. The need for the life-serving illusion has wrestled down "truth"—what this transition means for the process of civilization in the long run cannot be predicted today. Criticism was, it is important to realize, the consequence of the ontological assumption that fictions can fail because of facts. Now it is the facts that fail because of fictions—because in the future, facts themselves are supposed to be only successful fictions.

Future historians will confirm that the last third of the twentieth century was dominated by the motif of a return to the center—a center that could never fully decide on its motivations and philosophical implications. These historians will identify the unwillingness of the intellectual to identify positive values in the center or middle positions as one of the symptoms of the crises of that epoch—the ongoing romanticism of radicals blocked the learning processes that could have prepared for the problems of the twenty-first century. They will have to reconstruct how the decay of Western democracies came about after they more and more committed themselves to a neo-authoritarian, partially even neo-belligerent turn after 1990, and even more strongly after 2001.

Returning to today's perspectives, the horizon seems still relatively open, although nobody would believe that it provides for positive medium-term outlooks. What characterizes the situation is not the real decrease of available quantities of rage among the excluded, ambitious, unsuccessful, and vengeful. Their quantity necessarily has to be higher under free circumstances than in the past authoritarian systems of the East in which a climate of discouragement characterized the atmosphere. The mark of the situation is rather the loss of the function of symbolic institutions responsible for the political accumulation and transformation of dissident energies during two centuries of conflict. This raises the question of how our time will interpret the formula *ira quaerens intellectum*—indeed, whether is it at all possible today to revitalize the liaison between indignation and adaptability that constituted (or at least co-constituted) politics for two hundred years?

THE EROTICIZATION OF ALBANIA;
OR, THE ADVENTURES OF THE POSTCOMMUNIST SOUL

IT SEEMS AS IF IT IS NOT ONLY RAGE, DISSATISFACTION, AND GENERAL being-against-it that cannot be addressed anymore. Psychic economies have for some time found themselves altogether condemned to privatize their illusions.[7] The age of the serial reproduction of self-deception has also begun. Consequently, it could have been predicted that those liberated from communism during a critical period show a significantly higher susceptibility for designer illusions.

Seen from a functional perspective, the postcommunist situation implies, as I have already stated, a return of the command economy to the property economy, that is, the replacement of the medium of language with that of money.[8] In psychopolitical terms the conversion corresponds to the transition from a dynamic system of rage and pride to a dynamic system of greed—or, in terms of this psychopolitical analysis: a turn away from the primacy of thymotics for an eroticization without limitations.

The essence of eroticism cannot be understood from the perspective of the special case of the sexual libido and its aesthetic triggers, as recent social psychology assumes. Rather, eroticism is based on the stimulation of the idea of lack and all types of feelings of insufficiency. It articulates itself in corresponding actions of wanting to have and wanting to achieve: no phenomenon of recent psychohistory serves better as an illustration than the reception of the ur-capitalist idea of money that creates money in the countries of the former "Eastern bloc." Marx, who often quotes Hegel inappropriately, could have claimed that all comedies of history happen twice: the first time they are bloody, and the second time ridiculous. It would be interesting to read how the author of *The Eighteenth Brumaire* would have commented on the great investment of fraud with which the proletarian populations and peasants of Eastern Europe were deceived for seventy years about their assembled rage and their aspirations for respect and pride. One would like to know just as much how Marx would have glossed over the waves of corporate criminality which went over the former "Eastern bloc" countries after the breakdown of the communist regimes.

The wave began shortly after the memorable day of December 25, 1991, when the red flag over the Kremlin flew for the last time. The earliest manifestations appeared in postcommunist Romania, which after the execution of the dictator Ceausescu in 1989—also on December 25—took its first steps on the unfamiliar stage of democracy and market economy. Starting in 1992, a hitherto unknown gold fever infected the country, caused by an invasion of allegedly new investment systems, the most successful of which was called Caritas, a name that inspires confidence. The agents of these systems—in Romania alone there are said to have been roughly 600 such conspiracies against probability—promised to finally communicate to their customers a sense of the pleasures of capitalism. The investment games fascinated large parts of the population by promising fantastic profit margins—during the initial phase of the wave it was a common occurrence that the "invested" money increased its value by factor of eight within a few weeks and months. Within a year, Ion Stoica, a fifty-year-old business-man and the initiator of Caritas, became the hero of the nation. Factory worker, unemployed, or employee—those who could invest the remainder of their money could enjoy the benefits of enormous premiums. Many put a mortgage on or sold their houses to acquire the necessary liquidity. For two years, Stoica deluded exhilarated investors about the true nature of the enterprise by providing high yields on a regular basis. The "earnings" were, of course, not returns from regular corporations but rather, as is typical for pyramid schemes, came form shifting the assets of later investors to the accounts of those who had entered the scheme at an earlier point. Up to 20 percent of the Romanian population are said to have bought into this popu-lar and widespread investment game. In the spring of 1994, the yields slowed down and, shortly afterward, the system collapsed. Countless people faced immense debt. It took a concerted effort on the part of the government to prevent a national uprising. For those who were deceived, it could have only been a cold comfort that Stoica was sentenced to six years in prison.

In spite of this deterring episode, the spirit of the blessed Charles A. Ponzi (1882–1949) was soon to go around countless other postcommunist countries. In 1919, in Boston, Ponzi, an Italian adventurer who came to the United States in 1903, launched the first investment scheme. He went on to become a multimillionaire in less than a year, though afterward he spent most of his time in various prisons and died in Rio de Janeiro after a long, poverty-stricken odyssey. During his better days he was celebrated by his enthusiastic supporters as the first get-rich-quick financier of the twenti-eth century. His system, which was based on the trade of postal reply cou-pons (which pretended to use differences in value between American and Italian stamps), was seen by its sympathizers as the most elegant money-creation machine of all time. Since then, there have been countless attempts all over the world to make a quick fortune with the help of the so-called Ponzi scheme. In the footsteps of Ponzi, the Russian Sergey Mavrodi became the sixth-richest man in Russia with his pyramid scheme MMM, which collapsed in 1994 after at least 5 million of his compatriots invested enormous sums of money in it. Being the sixth-richest person in Russia meant something in the empire of new billionaires. In order to evade legal prosecution, Mavrodi let himself be voted into the Duma by his followers, who worshiped him like a savior. After his immunity as a congressman was abolished, he disappeared somewhere abroad, without a doubt because he was convinced that the days of such a talented man would be too valuable to be spent in the prisons of the new Russia.

During the same year, the spark went over to Poland, the Czech Republic, Bulgaria, and Serbia. From Poland it is said to have passed to Albania. It is part of the instructive moments of de-Sovietization that it was precisely the poorest country of Europe that became the most extensive laboratory for postmodern rip-off capitalism. A young businessman from Hamburg with a questionable reputation was partially responsible for the destruction of the illusion in Eastern Europe. His system, which was propagated with sectarian psycho-techniques, went by the name of Jump before being renamed Titan because of an acute danger of being exposed. This Ponzi scheme was once again refurbished and, thanks to the Polish manager of Titan, brought to Albania. However, it is said that it was practiced there as only one among at least a dozen Ponzi schemes. There the managers of the intensely propagated game trend were successful in plunging most of the country into greed psychosis from 1994 to 1996. The idea that money would multiply itself if merely lent to an "investment society" permeated the entire population, which had for decades lived under the dictator Enver Hoxha in severe poverty and confinement from information. One of the indirect consequences was the ignorance of the public with regard to the Romanian affair, which had been carried out only recently. Until the end of 1996 more than half of the 3.3 million Albanians had made "investments" in the pyramid schemes, which were carried out all over the country—many of them pledged their houses and farms to real banks. Here as well profits of up to 100 percent were promised and, for some time at least, also paid. During the final nervous phase of the game, 40 to 50 percent per month was paid out—enough of an incentive to downplay the signs of a reasonable hesitation. The Albanian pyramids also became so attractive because they were advertised on national TV—a fact that was misinterpreted by countless investors as a proof of seriousness.

When the schemes collapsed in January 1997, a frustrated panic broke out. Upset investors accused the state and the government of failing to undertake the necessary measures to protect the investors—which was correct, because those with positions of responsibility had ignored warnings from the World Bank. Groups of those negatively affected spontaneously set police stations on fire, while gangs of angry workers and employees stormed the weapons caches of the police and the army and took approximately 600,000 small arms. In subsequent years, the rate of murder and homicide skyrocketed in Albania, five times as high as before—the majority of the weapons could not be recuperated. It seemed as if state structures deterio-rated overnight: several provincial cities fell into the hands of insurgents, who were recruited primarily from members of the oppositional socialist party. The capital, Tirana, became an arena of civil-war scenes. For a couple of weeks there was no regulatory authority in sight, probably because a large portion of the civil servants had joined the protests. Many policemen who had deserted could only be convinced to return by being promised a tri-pling of their salaries. The Albanian president, Sali Berisha, whose Demo-cratic Party was obviously affiliated with the managers of the pyramids, felt impelled to resign from office.

At the height of the upheaval, the masses, who were driven by a mix-ture of defiance and vengeance, stormed schools and universities as well as countless factories and public offices. They took everything they could and destroyed the remainder in blind anger. Western observers who visited Albania shortly afterward reported that they had never seen such a degree of destruction, even in countries devastated by war. Public buildings were looted to the last doorknobs; families sat in cold apartments beneath a rug and stared for the whole day at images from Italian TV commercials. Many Albanians attempted to leave the country out of fear in overloaded ships and scruffy fishing cutters and even on rafts. Within a few days the har-bors of Brindisi and other Italian Adriatic cities were flooded with refugees. European foreign ministers were, as usual, incapable of coming up with a realistic agreement on the quotas for the admission of this "invasion of the despairing" to the countries of the European Union. The fact that, within a relatively short amount of time, the situation normalized was mainly attrib-utable to the newly formed government's admission that the government had been partially responsible for the debacle. Moreover, the Albanian central bank could rescue significant sums for the investors by freezing the pyramid accounts; another portion of the losses was supposed to be made up by the national budget.

The processes of these schemes and their effects are symptomatically important because a message about capitalism as such is concealed in the infectious energy with which the wave spread through poor countries such as Romania and Albania—at least a message about the exterior view of the system as it presents itself in the daydreams of people excluded from free markets and the private-property economy. Apart from revealing aspects of human nature, the Romanian and Albanian tragicomedies presented the mythic essence of the capitalist conception of wealth: the idea that the money used as capital possesses the property of a self-multiplying *fluidum*—or that money as capital is a powerful amulet that promises the constant arrival of happiness assets to its wearers.

This phantasm does not lack support, even though the serious interpreters of the market economy, or rather the private-property economy, have for a long time warned about short circuits resulting from a purely speculative usage of money and referred to detached casino capitalism as a danger for the global economy in general. Indeed, the party that creates real value within the capitalist complex does not tire of emphasizing that the process of creating prosperity rests initially and, for the most part, exclusively on the artfully directed synergy of private property, cash generation, labor, organization, and innovation, while all other transactions, in particular the purely monetized economy, will never be more than smoke rings in virtual space. The party of easy gains, on the other hand, continues to hold onto the belief that enrichment is nothing other than the natural reward for engaging in speculative risk. For them, it is not labor and effort that result in wealth, although the necessity of labor and effort is not completely denied. According to them, the true significance of wealth consists in demonstrating the sovereignty of Fortuna, who chooses those she favors and leaves the others with nothing. In a less mythological way of speaking, this means that who wins is right and who loses should not complain.

The mistake of the Albanians was thus not a complete misunderstanding of the facts of speculative capitalism. Rather, the Albanians succumbed to a late-socialist dream image that suggested to them that under the capitalist system there could be a first prize for everyone. In their willingness to distance themselves from the phantom of socialist pride and, like the other members of the free world, prioritize desire, they committed themselves to the new circumstances without ulterior motives. Because of their inability and unwillingness to come up with a realistic conception of where the desired gains were supposed to come from, they remained prisoners of their own past. It is beyond doubt that the feeling of being cut off from wealth and its distribution for too long played a role in the storm after the Ponzi schemes. After half a century in a dictatorship that spoon-fed them

THE DISPERSION OF RAGE IN THE ERA OF THE CENTER

grandiose phrases, the people finally wanted to take part in the satisfying injustices of the affluent world—even if someone else would have to pay the bill for the fantastic increase of their input. Just like everyone who followed the call of the popular Eros, the awakened Albanians were convinced that this time it was their turn to bring home the beautiful bride.

REAL CAPITALISM:
COLLAPSE DEFERRAL IN DYNAMIC SYSTEMS OF GREED

NOTHING COULD HAVE BEEN MORE MISPLACED IN LIGHT OF THE Albanian mishap than the sarcasm of some Western observers toward "Shqiptar capitalism." In reality, only a few party supporters of regular capitalism are likely to be able to define the difference between the economic system they favor and a simple pyramid scheme. It cannot be denied that the phenomenon of a gain that one did not earn—or, more generally, of income without effort—is highly valued by long-time players of the capitalist system. For the imaginary of modern national economies, the magic and irrational aspects of an uneven distribution of wealth have a significance that would have to be called archetypical, if the term did not have misleading depth-psychological connotations. The modern property economy attracted a shining aura of happiness fantasies from the beginning, so that the term "Fortuna capitalism" would have been more appropriate. Non-European users grasped this imaginary dimension of the new economic processes within a short time. If the modern property and monetary economy—which is often called, with a slip of the tongue, capitalism—exerts, beyond cultural boundaries, a fascination that even overshadows its practical advantages, then the imaginary dimension derives without question from this source. Furthermore, the belief in the returning Fortuna, who promotes her beneficiaries via banks and stock exchanges, needs to be understood as a post-Christian reinterpretation of Protestant fantasies of being chosen—with the danger of thus disclosing the merciless essence of Calvinism, whose true face is expressed in the mystic obscenity of the feeling of closeness to God when time has come to an end.

The preconditions for the objective commensurability of regular capitalism with a Ponzi scheme can be located in the undeniable fact that both models are credit-based systems of growth that are, for good or evil, dependent on extended reproduction. Both share a tendency to collapse, the regulation of which becomes constitutive for the system dynamics as a whole.

In the case of a pure Ponzi scheme, the collapse needs to occur relatively suddenly (or it needs to be brought about consciously) because the number of momentarily recruitable payers necessarily becomes zero after only a few rounds—which is why, even with good camouflage, it is hardly possible to extend a game longer than a few years. Ponzi himself could extend his games for about nine months, his Eastern European successors for two years at most. Regular capitalism, which is based on industry and banks, distinguishes itself, on the other hand, in that its players respond to fluctuations of interest rates with economic growth, which is primarily caused by the synergy of market expansion, product innovation, and technical rationalization. Its modus of "fleeing ahead" is thus elastic, long-term, and familiar with crises. Its mode of operation includes creative and civilized behaviors. At times, it does not even shy away from revolutionary culture advances. To the amazement of its agents, the capital process has so far showed that it is capable of controlling tendencies that signal collapse even over larger volatility and stagnation phases. Today it can look back on a more or less coherent developmental process of approximately ten human generations, if one follows Immanuel Wallerstein in assuming that the global capitalist system had already emerged around 1500.

With regard to the achievement of the essentially ahistorical or purely futuristic capitalist system, it needs to be stated that it did bring about a historicality of a special kind. Its general tendency was made mystical with the singular concept of "progress." This does not really change the ironic relationship between capitalism and the past. The entrepreneurially run world needs the past basically only to leave it behind.[9]

Especially after the vanishing of the so-called socialist alternative, capitalism confronts today's players and critics with a high standard of seriousness. This can be summarized by the thesis that capitalism provides a growth model for, in principle, an inexhaustible future power. In its name, it is expected that its actors participate in a life of permanent technical change, penetrated in all its domains by commodification and money transfer. The truth is that the future of the game does not look as promising as its boosters relentlessly claim. It suffices to read the popular term "sustainability" as a neurotic symptom of the self-doubt of the status quo. As the word demonstrates, the more thoughtful among today's economic experts already have a clear idea of what is incompatible within the system.

In fact, even non-Ponzi schemes (i.e., the regular national economy in particular and the global economy in general) are imbalanced systems that continuously have to cope with a significant degree of internal threat. Consolidated capitalism can only compensate for its inherent tendency toward collapse (the first manifestation of which was the overproduction crisis that Marx describes) by taking the bull by the horns. What for today's customer is a proof of genuine business principles is rooted in the refinement of steering instruments whose key mechanism needs to be identified as an "art of central banking."[10] This amounts to a process of making the unserious serious—expressed differently, a technology of decelerating breakdown. By raising and lowering the primary interest rates, a central bank pursues the task of minimizing the endemic risks of a crash by adjusting to an acceptable level the stress incurred by the interest rate. By making regulatory decisions, it orients itself according to the actual and expected results of economic achievements, that is, according to the sum total of the effects of market expansion, product innovation, and increased productivity. In this context, the notorious phrase "jumpstart the economy" means nothing other than decreasing the risk of insolvency for the units that are in debt. In the case of professional steering mechanisms, the pressure to settle debt on all levels of economic activity does not need to spell doom for the entire system, even though many businesses and private households might crash. In the big picture, liability stress advances the economic process to new rejuvenations and increases.

The compulsion to expand and innovate, which is characteristic of the capitalist method of production, thus traces itself back to the artfully confined but never fully eliminated Ponzi factor.[11] The capitalist-economic complex constitutes a global network of operations to relocate mountains of debt. But even the best-compensated Ponzi scheme cannot achieve more in the long run than postponing the moment of its demystification—at the very least until the moment in which the path of expansion is blocked because all new players who can be recruited have already entered the game. This might still be a distant possibility for our contemporary world, so that a final rush is for the moment not justified. The indeterminacy of the moment of disappointment can still be interpreted by the participants of the game, with a certain degree of justification, as the essential openness of the future. Nevertheless, those buying into the game should know the opinion of a minority of experts who claim that the openness effect—the unlimited ability to perpetuate the game under its present conditions—can hardly be sustained for more than a few decades. Other interpreters believe that the game will continue for a longer period of time, especially those who are optimistic enough to predict the exhaustion of fossil energies only for the twenty-second century.

During the almost one hundred years since Charles A. Ponzi's Boston coup of 1919, his psychological assumptions have not in any way been falsified. It can be assumed that in general they characterize the psychomotor skills of the capitalist mode of production with a high degree of accuracy. In fact, a certain level of decision making based on the greed dynamic remains indispensible for the morally inconspicuous and economically solid manifestations of the system. These basic decisions are motivated by strong tendencies of expansion that occur in the psycho-semantic economies of the players in increasingly more intensive ways—usually via a detour through cultural media, such as novels, theater, films, and TV. Mass media synergistically create a climate of increasing liberalization, and this wins over the long course against conservative reactions.

Because the quantitative expansion of monetary processes cannot be distinguished from qualitative changes in forms of life, ensembles of capitalist players have to adapt to a permanently revisionist climate. What has been referred to as the zeitgeist since 1800 cannot be imagined without the money spirit. However much one attempts to point out the polarity of money and spirit in the conservative milieu, in the big picture those poles are converging. The expectation of adaptation is manifested in the demand for "mobility" and "lifelong learning" with the aim of making professional biographics flexible and, at the same time, allowing for the highest possible degree of consumerism during old age—this is the point of the most recent introduction of propaganda for a California-style retirement capitalism in Germany. As much as serious values seem to be required in this constant movement, the global tendency of the game requires a continually increasing level of frivolity in player populations. Even under the most favorable of circumstances—when the welfare-state satisfaction of a population has been largely successful and the containment and stimulation of a capital economy has been running smoothly in a country for a long enough period of time—the system requires the integration of a growing portion of the population into more risky greed activities and offensive acts of carelessness—a circumstance only remotely captured by the expression "consumer society." "Consumption" here refers to the willingness of clients to participate in credit-based pleasure-acceleration games—with the danger of spending a large portion of one's lifetime stuck with repayment. The secret of the consumerist lifestyle is concealed in the evocation in its participants of a neo-aristocratic feeling of the complete appropriateness of luxury and extravagance. Under capitalism, an aristocrat is someone who does not need to reflect in order to know that he or she deserves only the best.

Greed is the affect that refers to the ontological assumption that it is possible to sustain a permanent asymmetry between giving and taking. If taking gets the upper hand in a capitalist player for a long enough period of time, one usually calls it success. The common understanding of success sees it as a phenomenon of overcompensation—often accompanied by a tendency to repeat the unlikely. Stabilized overcompensation creates claims to elite status. Those who have been chronically overcompensated develop the talent of taking their premiums to be an appropriate toll for their effort—or, in the case of a lack of effort, for their mere eminent existence, or even for their physical appearance. Part of a fully developed greed system is typically also the elevation of being good-looking into a good reason for expecting overcompensation. It is characteristic of the unfolded greed culture that its agents assume that they will be compensated most for what they are responsible for least. It is not accidental that the "lookism," this religion of ingratitude, is on the rise globally. Youth culture has been announcing the good news for a long time that in order to be successful, it is enough to look like someone who is known through the mass media that sustain that very culture.

The capitalist form of eroticism unfolds bit by bit the paradox of an "overcompensation for everyone." Through it the human right of greed without limits is proclaimed. Consequently, the market of appearance becomes the market of all markets—in it potential objects of desire are transformed into greed subjects by the drug of overcompensation. It is easily understandable why the last "class antagonism" under capitalism will be between those who are overcompensated and those who make a normal amount of money or very little. The reason this divide is nearly synonymous with the antagonism between the beautiful people and those who cannot earn with their appearance is somewhat more sophisticated. A definition of the word "people" in advanced capitalism would involve the mass of those excluded from overcompensation. These masses are certain not to get anything for their mere appearance.

THROUGH THEIR BEHAVIOR, THE ELITES OF GREED ADMIT THE potential for permanent lotteries—or at least for sufficiently long phases of success to provide the lucky ones with surpluses for the rest of their lives.

Generally, acute greed is accompanied by the feeling that one deserves more luck than one has so far received—one of the reasons it is not possible to determine internal limits for activities that are driven by greed. Few aspirants of Fortuna were willing during the capitalist centuries to state with Andrew Carnegie, "I have had far beyond my just share of life's blessings."[12]

With regard to the unlucky Albanians and their initiation into the spirit of speculative capitalism, it needs to be noted that overall they could be lucky that things did not turn out worse. Apart from the approximately 2,000 bankruptcies of smaller companies, their nationwide losses turned out to be far less dramatic after the crisis than one would have feared. Those who escaped learned that the restructuring toward private property of a command economy could not be achieved through mere speculation. They learned what is a known fact for veterans of capitalism: everyday creation of value possesses a special kind of inertia that one cannot rush unpunished. If one wants to create wealth, one usually has to work for a while and abstain. However much the dream of making a fast buck is indispensable for the moving dynamic of capitalism, it presupposes a regular entrepreneurial culture and a disciplined work world, which combine to take on a road that is only a little bit steep.

As already stated, regular capitalism, which knows how to content itself with profit rates earned in the real economy, is marked by the tension between the burden of interest and an increase in productivity—including all the psychopolitical factors without which the transformation of a given population into consumers capable of increasing demand does not work. While the pyramid crises in Eastern and Southern Europe could be traced back to an acute greed psychosis—and therefore to a sudden and rough eroticization of affective economies—it was necessary to instill deeper, more discreet, and chronically effective forms of eroticizing "society" during the subsequent consolidation phase.

By now we are in a position to understand why the psychodynamic modernization of "societies" moved by money bears the face of eroticism: nothing less is on the agenda of economic modernity than using contemporary psychopolitics of desire imitation and calculating greed to replace the (only seemingly archaic) thymotic control of affect with (only seemingly irrational) aspects that are incompatible with the market. This transformation cannot be achieved without a far-reaching depolarization of populations—and also without the progressive loss of the meaning of language in favor of the image and the number. In particular, classic leftist parties, insofar as they are active as rage and dissidence banks, have to appear in this new climate as dysfunctional relics. They are condemned to struggle with ugly speeches against images of beautiful people and tables of solid numbers—an impossible task. Modernized parties of social democrats à la New Labor, on the other hand, move within the element of capitalist eroticism as sound as a bell—they ceased being pride and rage parties and acknowledged the primacy of appetites. Through the introduction of a Western culture of the standardized image, a depository of illusions is provided to the postcommunist nations that addresses simultaneously erotic longing and the necessity of waiting.

In the course of the transformation there is, from the standpoint of moral history, a singular stimulation of wish rivalries between the participants of the generalized games of desire. In Western populations the structural transformation of desire took many centuries to come about—with a significant acceleration during the nineteenth century. This time has been characterized as the century of the operetta because the eroticization of the bourgeoisie and petit bourgeoisie, which the zeitgeist called for, created its most effective medium in this genre.[13] The courtly and early-bourgeois social orders caused currents of rivalry and severe contests between the participants in court intrigues and leaders of trading concerns. Both were systems of action that were already characterized by emotional "modernization," notably by the consolidation of commerce and an intensification of the *liaisons dangéreuses*, that is, strategic interactions. There was no historical formation, however, in which such a high degree of greed- and envy-driven competition was required as the unfolded "society" of mass consumption, which—after a more than hundred-year prelude—expanded triumphantly according to Euro-American models during the second half of the twentieth century around the globe.

These processes reveal that all modernizations culminate in a more or less dramatic revision of the form of morality authoritative since antiquity. Because today's systems no longer presuppose combative collectives but eroticized populations, they refrain from demanding the cancelation of the Old Testament's fifth commandment—one of the most characteristic traits of left fascism, which, as we have seen, returned in National Socialism. These two formations of thymotic affect modeling called for resolute fighters and child-bearing mothers, not ambitious lovers and luxury consumers—in fact, British followers of the Communist International sang this song in the 1930s: "Let's liquidate love / Till the revolution / Until then love

202

is / An un-bolshevik thing."[14] The primacy of combative values was self-evident for the activists, while Eros figured under the disdainful heading of "bourgeois luxury." As long as killing enjoyed a priority over loving, the spirit of revision was primarily directed against the fifth commandment.[15]

In the advanced sphere of consumption, on the other hand, loving, wishing, and enjoying become the most important civic duties. Nowadays, the abstinence provisions and the prohibitions against envy in the Ten Commandments are what have to be bracketed and replaced by their reversals. While the tenth commandment states, "Thou shalt not covet thy neighbor's house, thou shalt not covet thy neighbor's wife, nor his manservant, nor his maidservant" (Exodus 20:17), the first commandment of the new authoritative law states: *"Thou shall desire and enjoy whatever others present to you as a desirable good!"* The second commandment reinforces the first: it is an imperative to exhibit oneself, which, in diametrical opposition to the rules of discretion of the tradition, elevates the open display of personal enjoyment to the status of a norm.[16] *Thou shall not make a secret of your desires!* It would be short-sighted to think that the effects of the exhibition principle are limited to the world of advertising and night clubs—the reality construction of subjective capitalism is in fact fully built on competitions for visibility. Visibility designates the possibilities of stimulating envy impulses in the worlds of commodities, money, knowledge, sports, and art. In order to compensate for the dangerous effects of the two disinhibition commandments, the third and final commandment needs to claim: *Thou shalt not make responsible anyone else but thyself for potential disappointments during the contest for access to the objects of desire and privileges of enjoyment!*

Dispersed Dissidence:
The Misanthropic International

THE FOREGOING CONSIDERATIONS PRESENT A VARIETY OF CONDITIONS attesting to the impossibility of collecting and organizing contemporary rage and dissidence quanta in the neocapitalist heartland. The most important factor preventing this has already been referred to in passing: in the present, no movements and parties are visible that could once again take on the functions of a world bank for the utopian-prophetic use of thymotic impulses. In the absence of a successful collection point of rage with a perspective on what needs to be done, we are thus at the same time missing the theoretical standpoint from which consultations concerning truly global matters could be carried out. Even though for years there has been a flood of moralizing remarks about the so-called globalization of the public sphere of the West and the newly industrialized countries, the sum total of the discourses does not suggest in the least the emergence of a new "*organon*"—unless one is willing to accept the global sociological divisions of the Pentagon and its staff members, concerned with the so-called war on terror as such. The same circumstance is expressed by the thesis that, at this moment, there are no forms of positive apocalypse whose popularization would be capable of translating the potential collapse of currently successful social and economic systems into attractive visions for the time to come. Neither in Davos nor in Porto Allegre during recent years was there a convincing conversation concerning postcapitalist models. Put differently, this only proves that capitalism wants to be the entire culture. Thus it erects itself as the intransient horizon of the present. What comes after it has to be, according to its self-conception, only always again its own restless metamorphoses and euphoric exaggerations. Only the discourses of the solar movement and related antisystemic approaches contain projections that reveal a level of temporal depth, projections that confront the dominant system with its inevitable end because of its dependence on fossil energies. Some of these projections only identify the reasons for the transition to a non-fossil-energy regime, while others advance to a horizon beyond capital economy.[17]

The second main reason for the devaluation of vengeful impulses in the affect economy of capitalist democracies has already been, at least indirectly, touched upon: contemporary conditions, at least according to their general direction, defeat most variations of fundamentalist thinking—including the young Hegelian figures who present themselves as the practical realizations of a thinking that "gets to the roots." All forms of bearded theory have been excluded from the canon of the present. Typical bearded theories commented on the worldviews of their enemies from the standpoint of ideology critique (and operated on a second-order level of observation) but continued to use naïve semantics to support their own cause—which puts them near the crudest systems of faith. They create the connection between thymotics and extremism, on the one hand, and extremism and monologic thinking, on the other.[18] If rage cannot lead to insight under such conditions, it is only surprising for those who have themselves invested in the business of naiveté.

A third reason for the diffusion of rage and protest potentials can be located in the change of its collection media and its organizing myths. While class-conscious proletarians of the late nineteenth and early twentieth centuries already had the possibility of integrating local suffering and struggle into the epic of the workers' movement, perhaps even into the grand narrative about the advent of the revolution, today's rage carriers do not have a convincing narrative that could provide orientation or assign them a vital place in world affairs. In this situation, the return to ethnic or subcultural narratives is not surprising. If the latter are not available, they are replaced by local we-they constructions. Insofar as the dissatisfied of postmodernity cannot abreact their affects in different locations, the only available option is to escape to their own mirror image, which is provided by mass media as soon as scenes of violence attract public interest. The quick mirroring of self-inflicted excesses in the press and TV images may provide a momentary satisfaction for the actors. In some instances it might even symbolize a satisfactory proof of existence. However, it is precisely in such episodes that the medium wins over the content. This shows once again that the instruments of the "bourgeois public sphere" cannot function as collectors or as accumulation and cultivation media for thymotic subjects (which means that they are incapable of moderating the transformation of rage into pride and hope). It is beyond doubt that modern mass media possess the potential to initiate affective epidemics—topics that could spread according to the principle of viral infections. At the same time, the media neutralize topics in order to subject all events to the law of standardization. It is their democratic mission to create indifference by eradicating the difference between major and minor matters.

Finally, a fourth motif for the political regression of the left culture of rage results from the conversion of money-directed civilization to the primacy of eroticism. The new commandment to love prescribes the love of goods that your neighbor enjoys as if they could become your own. Apparently this extensive commandment of enjoyment is hardly easier to live by than the Christian commandment of charity. Erotic pressure on the actors in a greed-dynamic "society" necessarily leads to a situation in which ever more irritated and isolated individuals find themselves surrounded by impossible offers for relationships. Because of chronic impositions of love, which have to result in failure because of limited means of access, an impulse to hate everything emerges, a hate that belongs to the siege by pseudo-objects. While collective systems of affect convert revolt into participation within the paradigm of postmodern irony, those dissident, angry, socially isolated, and linguistically impoverished impulses are captured by numbness. In this situation the vandalistic relationship to impossible objects imposes itself as the most plausible one. Vandalism could be described as the negativity of the ignorant and thus as a form of rage that has given up once and for all any striving to understand.

THERE WAS NO EVENT IN THE MORE RECENT PAST IN WHICH THIS mechanism expressed itself more explicitly than in the Paris *banlieue* riots, which flamed up in late October 2005 and spread within a few days according to the rules of the media-rewarded imitation game to numerous cities or metropolitan areas in France. It was fully obvious that the unexpected explosions of violence by a group of exclusively male adolescents with Islamic Arab and Christian African origins were riots for the purpose of abreaction and provocative vandalism fun—that affective cocktail that the political hermeneutics of the hegemonic French center-left culture does not know how to deal with. Consequently, the Paris feuilleton was content with accessing the available language games, which are happy about every occasion in which they can quote themselves. ("They set cars on fire—we apply our favorite theories.")

One thing was certain during all of this: none of the political parties could, nor wanted, to offer itself as gatherer or transformer of the emergent dirty energies. Yes, vague commitments to the obligations of a republican pedagogy could be heard, but nothing that would have pointed to a new strategy of a political use of rage. The only quick-witted interpreter of the psychopolitical situation was the then minister of the interior, Nicolas Sarkozy, who bluntly referred to the rioters as "rabble" (*racaille*) who needed to be washed away with a power hose. Not only did he violate the rules of political *beau parler*, he also made clear that in line with the attitude of the new moral majority in the country, this time there would be no attempts of political integration, only uncompromising practices of elimination. It is possible that through this verbal outbreak a new paradigm of political semantics was born. The spokespersons of the center-right would thus have understood the postrepublican imperative according to which politics should not mean anything beyond a system of measures for militant consumer protection. On the rhetorical plane, the transition from social therapy to disposal of the abject is unmistakable—it expresses a current agreement between the conservative anxiety of a large stratum of the society and the neoliberal principle of being relentless, which the wealthy elite admits to.

This alliance is confronted by a left that is not capable, in either its postcommunist or its social-democratic form, of developing appropriate measures of rage collection and its investment in thymotically lucrative projects.[19]

The weakness of the circulating ad hoc explanations for the unexpected eruptions of violence in France is revealed primarily by the fact that most of them attempted to identify the riots as mere momentous symbolic actions, though the interpretations of the symbolized affects varied significantly: depending on the inclination of the interpreter, they ranged from helpless anger through a subsequent need to revenge chronic humiliation up to manifestations of pure "pleasure in evil." No less misleading is the allegation of some rightwing politicians that the burning of vehicles and buildings as well as other acts of vandalism were planned, if not also controlled actions.

In reality, the escalation of the violence goes back to occasional creations of rage objects, which were rewarded through feedback in the French mass media and with high attention and incentives for imitation. Assuming that this reconstruction of the events on the crucial night are fitting, the triggering event consisted in the sudden dissemination of a rumor that the police had driven two suburban adolescents to their deaths on October 27, 2005. This suggestion (which turned out to be only half-true because there was no direct connection between the deaths of the young men and the persecution by the police) was sufficient to evoke a primitive us-them scenario among the numerous adolescents who were present. It quickly spread to other locations. The national police were naturally on the "they" side, as was, for understandable reasons, the eloquent minister of the interior. A confused complex arose that comprised people, symbols, and institutions in which the strangeness and hostility of the French environment crystallized.

The formation of a negative object was, in spite of its vagueness, sufficiently articulated to evoke, in numerous adolescents and for several weeks, the belief that there was a real battle scene on which one could play. During the course of the riots in the streets of Clichy-sous-Bois, Le Blanc Mesnil, Aulnay-sous-Bois, and so on, one could witness a form of theatrical collection with a high power of attraction, even though there was no political management giving orders. An appropriate interpretation of this phenomenon transcends standard sociologies; it rather appears as if only the swarm-logical, medialogical, and mimetological descriptions would be capable of casting light on the rhythm of the events. At any rate, what was decisive for the rapid escalation of the riot was that the typical action on the fighting scene, the random burning of parked cars, presented a long-rehearsed pattern, not to speak of the initiation qualities of a ritual. Through a strong influx of new players, the pattern of a communion suddenly entered the spotlight through destruction.

In a sharp commentary for the newspaper *Libération*,[20] Jean Baudrillard captured the essence of what was so scandalous about the scandal: it was only through the November riots that the French public became aware that in a series of cities in their country, an average of ninety cars were set on fire every night—during the course of 2005 alone there are said to have been more than 9,000 car burnings, of which approximately 2,800 took place during the *banlieue* riots and their provincial imitations. The peak of these pyromania games was reached during the night of November 7, when more than 1,400 cars burned across the entire country. Furthermore, the statistics for 2005 mention that until November, there were 17,500 arsons in garbage containers and almost 6,000 vandalistic acts against public telephone booths and bus stops. Although the sociology of the perpetrators presents a somewhat more complex depiction of the chronic attacks, there is a high measure of similarity between the actors of the acute riot and those of the chronic kindlings. In every case, we are dealing with the same angry young men into whose double misery of unemployment and excess adrenaline the explosive insight into their social superfluity was added. It would be careless not to want to understand that they are the potential recruits for any war, which provides them with a perspective for breaking out of the prison of their involuntary apathy.

Considering the daily arsons, which remained beneath the attention threshold of the media for years, Baudrillard sarcastically speaks of an eternal flame that burns in honor of the unknown immigrant, comparable to the flame at the Arc de Triomphe. The wild flames bear witness to the psychopolitical disasters of French "society," which cannot manage to communicate to large portions of its Arabic and African immigrants and their children a consciousness of belonging to the political culture of the country. However, this is a mischaracterization of the situation; what is at stake here is not the French "political culture," whose splendors remain unseen by the angry adolescents. Rather, at stake are attractive social positions, which are impossible to get for the offspring of immigrants. When he asks, "Belonging to what?" Baudrillard already presupposes, with a provincial consciousness of detachment, that the republican ethos has vanished as a political force in French civil "society." Régis Debray articulated a related diagnosis with a mediological-cultural-theoretical accent by diagnosing, not without a sense of melancholy, the lack of an effective civil religion in France. If his diagnosis was correct, it would suggest nothing less than that the country has irrevocably entered a situation that bears not only post-Gaullist but also postrepublican characteristics. Baudrillard, on the other hand, reaches the provocative conclusion that the majority of the French already behave like insecure immigrants in their own country, immigrants who are plagued by resentment. They can only assert themselves as indigenous by discriminating against other immigrants.

The excessive thesis according to which "society" has become a phantom collective to itself points to the psychopolitical consequences of capitalist eroticization.[21] It is quite likely that a more patient view of the democratic-republican reserves of political culture in France would prove that its regenerative capacities are in a better state than the witty pessimist commentators would have it. This is confirmed by the protest strikes throughout the country that forced the government of Prime Minister Villepin in March 2006 to withdraw a law that loosened the job market for entering workers (*Contrat premier embauche*), a law that had already been passed by the national assembly. Then again, the protests prove that the French adolescents are at home in an illusory bubble in which they protect privileges as if they were basic rights. The current level of subversive mass eroticization also illustrates, to be sure, how strongly the traditional thymotic ensemble of people, nation, party, and confession has been weakened, partially even destroyed, through the politics of desire in popular capitalism. Through this politics, every individual is turned into a consumption citizen who—unless uplifted by family, cultural, and cooperative counter-forces—is increasingly fixed to poisoned loneliness within a doomed irritation of desire. When the French voted no in the referendum in May 2005 to the European Constitution, they engaged, following Baudrillard, in an act that, according to its political and gestural content, constituted the exact equivalent of the riots of the nonintegrated in the suburbs. In a large majority, they behaved like ballot-arsons. They responded to the praised object, Europe, hardly less scornfully than the *banlieue* adolescents responded to the attractions of the French Republic.

These observations, which are the basis of Baudrillard's and Debray's diagnoses, converge in a dark zone. They reveal an amorphous negativism whose phenomenology has been investigated sporadically for a long time while its therapy, as well as its politics, stagnates. In his 1993 essay *Ausichten auf den Bürgerkrieg* (Expectations of civil war), Hans Magnus Enzensberger cited a social worker from the *banlieue* in Paris who vividly described the vandalistic dynamic:

> They have already destroyed everything, the mailboxes, the doors, the stair-cases. They have demolished and looted the polyclinic where their smaller brothers and sisters are treated for free. They do not recognize any rules. They smash medical and dental clinics to bits and pieces and destroy their schools. If they are provided with a soccer field, they saw off the goal posts.[22]

ENZENSBERGER INCLUDES THESE OBSERVATIONS IN A PANORAMA OF scenes of shabby violence, which he sums up under the title "molecular civil war." The typical gesture of this "war" and its "warriors" is the aimless dev-astation of the terrain, which only seemingly resembles "their own." Such behaviors constitute, according to the author, an answer to the dark insight that speaks from all the images from the crowded camps and dismal sub-urbs: "we are *too many*." This dubbing has to upset its bearers. If these fig-ures, until then often inconspicuous and marginal, finally want to take the "abolishment of the superfluous" into their own hands while lashing out blindly, they do it because "they secretly count themselves among them."[23]

The signs of a "molecular civil war" initially increase almost unnoticed: more garbage on the streets, smashed beer bottles on the avenues and side-walks, discarded needles in parks, monotonous graffiti everywhere "whose sole message is autism." In time, the symptoms of destruction reach a critical threshold: smashed school furniture, cut wires, public telephones that have been made useless with pliers, cars set on fire—now it becomes clear that a basic language of disgust has put up a sign for itself. However, these are not traces of a "civil war." To speak of a civil war, formed parties of fighters would have to face each other as confrontable realities. Instead, waves of pre-objective negativity enter the picture as vandalistic impro-visations, which attest to the inability of their bearers to act as citizens, even as fighting citizens. As Enzensberger lucidly remarks, in all of these features is an element of "anger about what is in fact," a form of "hatred against everything that functions," a grudge against the circumstance "that forms an insoluble amalgam with self-hatred."[24] At this time he had already attested on television to a complicity among all forms of practiced vandalism, which function "like one single huge graffiti" scribbled on the wall by vengeful semilunatics who know how to get on the evening news with the help of a few beer bottles filled with gasoline, a lighter, and willing cameramen.

What I have referred to as the language of disgust with how things are describes an epidemic of negativity in which the spread of what in former times was called "cultural malaise" advances to a riot in a failed civilization. This form of negativity has little in common with the forms of morally articulable and politically collectable rage that I have addressed so far. Retrospectively, this spreading disgust makes clear the extent to which the traditional left—especially its Bolshevist wing but also its more liberal forms—can be blamed for anthropological and political negligence since it had always assumed that its members as well as the so-called masses indiscriminately affirmed a natural and ambivalence-free human community in large social associations.

The least that would need to be said about these primarily sociophobic assumptions is that they rest on a one-sided perspective. Realistically speaking, no social politics would ever possess the slightest prospect for success if it did not understand that the goal of social organization has to be to restrain the molestation of human beings by human beings. The collectivist remains of the twentieth century have violated this precept by inventing an unprecedented sadism of constipation: the most extreme maliciousness of the camp universes, as they have been created by Lenin, Stalin, Hitler, and Mao, does not so much consist in the fact that human beings were reduced to the status of "bare life," as Giorgio Agambcn attempted to show in an exaggerated interpretation. Rather, the camp rests on the intuition that hell is always other people as soon as they are mutually forced into unwelcome proximity. In *Huis clos*, Sartre merely replaces macro-hell with micro-hell. If one shoves one's enemies together into a state of total coexistence, one is responsible for each individual being burned in the small flame of induced hostility against his kin. Only saints survive camp situations without being dehumanized. "Camp" is only a conventional name for the modern forges of misanthropy. Without considering the occult misanthropist substrate—which is only minimally concealed in the conviction that there is no need for human beings to be concerned for other human beings (Céline: "One asshole less")—the exterminist excesses of the more recent past would remain even more obscure, defying all previously attempted historical and psychological explanations. The proposition *homo homini lupus* loses its plausibility when considering these aspects. He who speaks of the twentieth century as the century of wolves still thinks too innocently.

The xenophobia of the right is only one of the signs of the misanthropic element, which cannot become visible as long as it persists in concretely identifiable forms, which are, *eo ipso*, its pseudonyms, its ideological garments. Taking offense only at the political and ideological costumes of social disgust misses the essential misanthropic message. The more obscure aspects of the misanthropic mood are systematically ignored. In reality, the sociophobic-misanthropic tendency is endemic to the left as well as the right. In all opportune idioms it rages against the imposition of coexisting with whomever and whatever. It is only with the epidemically amorphous vandalism that the negative primordial soup surfaces. With it a primary, unblended, and unmitigated misanthropy, the abysmal aversion to the social world and society, and even to the existence of the world in general, becomes identifiable as radical behavior. Hereby it becomes apparent how misanthropy itself is the special form of an amorphous negativity that could be determined with concepts such as misocosmics or misontics: animosities against the world and what exists in the world as a whole. It brings out the aversion to the imposition of existence and coexistence as such.

Rage is encountered in mollusk-like upsurges of this kind at the zero point of articulation. After its relapse to the level of diffuse universal aversion, it relinquishes any kind of collectability, transformability, and cultivatability. It simply no longer remembers anything concerning the close connections among sensitivity for values, legal sensitivity, and a capability for indignation—the matrix of democratic cultures of irritation. It now seems sunken to a sub-thymotic level from which point there is no initiatory power to redeem one's own value and claims.[25] At the "foundation" of the darkest form of rage, there lies, diffuse and inarticulable, the desire for an end of humiliation through the real. We are dealing with an extremism of fatigue—a radical apathy that refrains from any attempt at form or cultivation. Its agents would in reality prefer not to lift a finger, as if playing dead could be the means of escaping the prison of failures. When they try to smash whatever happens to get close to them, it happens as if in a foreign tongue of gestures, the meaning of which not even they believe. To these extremists of tedium, their own massive quantity means nothing. They do not want to know that they could perhaps be the strongest of parties—if they could unify and take action for something in their own interests.

This International of human tedium exists in continuous self-dissolution. Every night it decays in millions of isolated anestheticizations; every morning it formlessly erases itself and all its concerns from the day's menu.

No constitutive assembly would be able to provide form and content to this excessive protest against the actual state of affairs. Wherever fragmentary gatherings occur, one recognizes the theses of the actors in broken glass, wreckage, and burned metal the day after. It is not surprising that the members of this impossible International do not feel addressed by the thought of an organized gathering at all. Every form of purposive cooperation with them would mean a step toward transcendence, not being weary, not being vanquished. Not taking this step is their most intimate revenge against the status quo.

The Global Theater of Threats

TO END, ALLOW ME TO ENGAGE IN A PANORAMIC VIEW IN THE STYLE of a world-historical investigation to look back at the fate of the thymotic during the last two hundred years and situate it against the background of the two monotheistic millennia. What will become clear is that the two most powerful organs of metaphysical and political rage collection in Western civilization, the Catholic teachings concerning the wrath of God and the communist organization of antibourgeois and anticapitalist rage masses, have not mastered the challenges of the time and the change in mentality.

Catholicism only survived the advance of modernity for the price of a reluctant accommodation to the present day, an accommodation that lasted for more than two centuries. During this long period it indulged in gestures of denial that in some aspects closely resemble the theocentric antimodernism of an Islamist type, which we know from contemporary sources. During its period of defiance it ravaged the hubris of the moderns longing to make religion into a private affair. It rebelled zealously against the tendencies to create a deliberately lay state culture or one that was distanced and neutral with regard to religion. However, the change in the basic attitude of Catholicism could not be avoided, even though it was not brought about before the second half of the twentieth century. It brought with it a profound theological conversion: in order to be able to make peace with modernity, Rome needed to distance itself from what before seemed to be nonnegotiable antihumanist and antiliberal traditions, which were rooted in the absolutism of God's law. The transformation reached a point at which Catholic theology defined itself as an "organon" for a more profound justification of human rights. Naturally this brought with it the surrender or degrading intimidation of the believers through apocalyptic threats and dreadful *Dies irae* pronouncements. Subsequently, the time-honored teachings of the wrath of God and images of a revenging Judgment Day at the end of time were withdrawn from within the Church—they have been degraded to the status of curiosities that one inspects as one would a metaphysical horror genre, assuming that one can still find an interest in them.

When it comes to communism's attempt to create a global collection point for thymotic energies with globally convincing human dividends, the disappointed and exasperated elderly witnesses of that spooky epoch are still too close to it to explain why any thought of an "improved" taking-up of similar experiments means for them pure stupidity. In the eyes of those who were born later, the communist adventure already appears like a dark curiosity. It seems to be as gothic as the forgotten Catholic eschatology.

I have addressed the themes, procedures, and promises of the two big rage collectives in the second and third chapters of this book. The effects of its dissolution were addressed in the first chapter, in which the free-floating rage in the early post-Christian situation was sketched out, and this fourth chapter focuses on the political homelessness of rage in the postcommunist situation. I did not pursue the possible and actual relationships between Catholicism and communism—in fact it would have been plausible to portray communism as the secularized form of Christian rage theology, even as a materialistic translation of the idea of the kingdom of God. Let us thus rest content here with the remark that communism did indeed share many characteristics of a second Catholicism. If in 1848 it was claimed with a tone of triumphant satisfaction that a specter was haunting Europe, which terrorized and frightened all governments between Paris and St. Petersburg, this phrase signaled that one was in a situation "after the death of God," a situation in which the function of the world's court of judgment—apart from numerous other professions of God—had to be passed on to secular agencies. Under the circumstances, early communism was best suited to claim this heritage. The "spectral" character of this movement, which Jacques Derrida highlights in *Specters of Marx*, to which I have repeatedly referred, was, to be sure, not so much attributable to the fact that communism presented a rationalist utopia, as Derrida suggests, that is, a thought that could never emerge as a manifestation of flesh and blood. What made ascending communism spooky and what lent it the power to attract the paranoid reflexes of its adversaries was its ability, which could be detected early, to convincingly threaten the status quo with its downfall. When it had lost its capacity to threaten, it was finished as a ghost as well—and no animation of philosophical congresses will provide the hollow pumpkin with new haunting power.

After the collapse of communism the business of world-directed revenge and, generally speaking, the business of a universal balance of suffering had to slip out of the hands of human agencies. Consequently there were good reasons the Catholic Church could present itself as authentic after the fall of communism, even as the soul of an authentic and spiritual communism. To see and seize this opportunity was Karol Wojtyla's theatrical message. The Catholic message, of course, includes the return to the classical mor- ally conservative attitude according to which the man of the present would need to free himself from rage and revolt in order to rediscover what he had lost as a consequence of the events of 1789: patience and humility. What is most of the time overlooked concerning these recommendations is that highly praised virtues stand on shaky grounds if they are not supported by the threatening force of a convincingly delivered theology of the Day of Judgment.

These remarks suggest that Hegel's figure of a cunningness of reason still has a certain pragmatic appeal, however ascetic the expectations of a hid- den reason in history might be today. If one had to step back to sum up the achievements of communism, one would most importantly mention its external effects, which many times surpassed its internal effects in terms of productivity. These external effects were, to be sure, so paradoxical that they were hardly ever addressed. It is not necessary here to once again call to mind the much-appreciated efforts of the Soviet Union in the war on the armies of the National Socialist invader. The most important external effect of communism unfolded only after 1945, when an unprecedented chance opened up to expand the European welfare-state system against the back- ground of the saber-rattling regime of Stalin and its Middle and West Euro- pean outposts.

It is ironic that the communist world bank of rage achieved its most important success in the form of an unintended side effect. By accumulat- ing a truly intimidating political and ideological threat potential, it helped its former main adversaries, the Western, moderate socialists and social democrats, to reach the high point of their historical ability. It made it easy for the parliamentarily integrated socialist parties in Europe to extort an unprecedented amount of concessions from the liberal and conservative managers of capital in redistributing wealth and extending social networks. Within this constellation, it seemed plausible to the social partners of the

Western world to transform large parts of their national industries, in particular in France and Great Britain, to government control.

If it is correct to say that sovereignty refers to the capacity to convincingly threaten someone, then it is also true that the Western workers' parties and unions achieved their highest effects of sovereignty because of an indirect threat of class struggle, which they were able to include in the negotiations of the bargaining parties without having to clench the fist themselves. It sufficed for them to consider the realities of the Second World to make it clear to the employers that social peace has its price. It can be asserted without exaggeration that the social achievements of postwar Europe, in particular the often-cited Rhenish form of capitalism with its extensively extended welfare state and the excessive culture of therapy, were presents from Stalinism—grapes of wrath that, it needs to be said, could only ripen and taste sweet after being exported to a freer climate.

The expenditures for social peace in the West needed to be recalculated from scratch when the threat potential of the left irresistibly continued to decline—not least because the Soviet Union was increasingly difficult to take seriously as a threat to the West. The ultimate phase of the Brezhnev era was the latest that the preconditions for some kind of successful missionary and expansionist activity from Moscow existed. Maoism outside of China never meant more than a straw fire of peasant romanticism in the Third World (think of Che Guevara's confused excursions to Africa and Bolivia) and the waywardness of wealth in Western universities. It was already evident that the East—because of its dogmatic ignorance of the question of property—could not possibly win the confrontation between competing systems. Furthermore, the Russian army provided the proof during its futile ten-year campaign against the Afghan *franc-tireurs*, who were supported by the United States (1979–1989), how little it was able to live up to its former reputation.

Under these circumstances, the organs of the workers of the West lost their privilege of profiting from the fear of communism from the perspective of capital without any effort. The liberal-conservative camp was able to understand: during the wage-negotiation talks it sat next to a debilitated, if not degenerated, counterpart. On the one hand, the latter was out of shape because of its relative level of saturation; on the other hand, it succumbed to a creeping paralysis that resulted from the ideological deflation of the left.

Since the early 1980s, this sense of exhaustion has determined the psychopolitical atmosphere of the West—its results multiply with the climate-changing fallout of September 11. It appears that a neo-authoritarian turn of capitalism with a liberal-bellicist background is more and more likely. The year 1979 needs to be seen from today's perspective as the key time of the twentieth century. The entry into the postcommunist situation begins then in a threefold sense: the beginning of the end of the Soviet Union after the invasion of its armies into Afghanistan, the accession to power of Margaret Thatcher, and the consolidation of the Islamic Revolution in Iran under Ayatollah Khomeini.

What is called neoliberalism was in fact nothing but a recalculation of the costs of inner peace in the countries of European capitalist and social-democratic "mixed economy" or of American-style "regulatory capital-ism."[26] This necessarily led to the result that Western entrepreneurialism had paid too high a price to attain social peace under passing political and ideological pressure from the East. The time for cost-reducing measures had come, measures that aimed to switch priorities from the primacy of full employment to that of corporate dynamics. In fact, a downright reversal of the zeitgeist was brought about: it moved ever quicker away from the revolting and control-centered ethics of comfort during the decades after the war (which survived only in France) in order to give preference to a neo-entrepreneurial risk ethic.

The "market revolution" in Great Britain, which was designed by Joseph Keith and, starting in 1979, realized by Margaret Thatcher (a revolution that would soon spread to the Continent and large parts of the Western world, especially Reagan's and Clinton's America), makes clear how precisely the above diagnosis captures the situation and how radical were the conse-quences that are to be drawn from it. This shows itself most strikingly in the permanent trend of neoliberalism—the long march to mass unemployment that has set the tone from a social-political perspective. The new circum-stances brought with it what could have hardly been imagined until then: unemployment rates of 10 percent and more are accepted more or less with-out a fight by the populations of European nations—even the increasingly visible decrease of welfare benefits has so far not provokes a flaring-up of the fire of class struggle. The relationships of sovereignty have been reversed overnight: organizations of employees have little power to threaten, because the privilege to threaten has, rather one-sidedly, passed onto the business side. The latter can now plausibly claim that everything will become much worse if the other side refuses to understand and abide by the new rules of the game.

The Third Collection: Can Political Islam Set Up a New World Bank of Dissidence?

IT IS NECESSARY TO KEEP THIS SCENARIO IN MIND IN ORDER TO understand the conditions under which Islamic terrorism could celebrate its rise to become a power with the capacity to exert threats. Initially, the Islamists did not seem to be more than parasites of the postcommunist constellation. No one would have thought at the time of Islamism's first appearance that one was witnessing something like a third Catholicism or an Eastern alternative to communism. Nevertheless, day by day the Islamist activists successfully imposed themselves as the new enemy of the West, initially the United States, and then helpless Europe. In this role they have been interpreted ambivalently from the beginning. For tragic-minded political scientists, who are convinced of the need to always have an enemy, the anger of Islamism seemed like a present from heaven. Although Islamism was initially not especially dangerous in a material sense (as long as its agents did not gain access to nuclear, biological, or chemical weapons and the control of migration remained sufficiently strict), it keeps the psychopolitical tone of irritated collectives in the West at the desired level. For the adherents of the liberal idyll, on the other hand, Islamist terror remains an unwelcome guest—a crazy graffiti sprayer who disfigures the façades of enemy-free societies with obscene messages.

However one may evaluate the ambivalent reception of the new terror by its Western addressees, it would never have advanced beyond the level of an irritating marginal phenomenon if it had not become an interesting asset in the recalculation of the costs for social peace in Western societies. While the communist threat led to a significant increase in the social costs of peace, the threat of Islamist terror brings with it, at the bottom line, effects that help lower the costs. By exciting imaginary stressful pressure on the attacked collective, it contributes to a feeling of belonging to a real community, a belonging based on solidarity, a survival unit wrestling for its own future in spite of recently severely deepened social differences. Additionally, the new terror creates, because of its undifferentiated hostility against Western forms of life, a climate of diffuse intimidation in which questions of political and existential security enjoy high priority over those of social justice—*quod erat operandum*.

With the exaggeration of the securitarian imperative to the level of being the omnipotent theme of contemporary media democracies, the zeitgeist readjusted itself after September 11, 2001, to a new ecosystem of threats and defense mechanisms—while, this time, as frivolously as it might sound, the threat tendencies of Islamist terror in general point "in the right direction" when seen from the perspective of radicalized capitalism. To feel threatened by the Middle Eastern sources now means to see reasons why one could perhaps be ready to make peace with the drifting away of Western political culture into postdemocratic conditions. The "war on terror" possesses the ideal quality of not being able to be won—and thus never having to be ended. These prospects suggest that the postdemocratic trends will enjoy a long life. They create the preconditions with which democratically elected leaders can get away with presenting themselves as commanders in chief. If political thinking limits itself to advising the commander in chief, concepts such as democracy and independent judiciary cultures are only chips in a strategic game.[27]

The psychopolitical fate of the United States during the Bush administration illustrates these relations with an abundance of unmistakable examples. Within a few years the world became witness to how a democracy that is proud of its culture of dissent experienced a sudden extinction of political diversity of opinion because it was exposed to the knowingly and willingly induced fiction of a struggle for survival, which needed to be waged by the entire nation. The political field of the nation was influenced by homogenizing forces. Reminiscent of real wars, in this *drôle de guerre* there was a paralyzing of inner opposition through the patriotic imperative. This development to a large extent results from the work of the neoconservatives in the United States, who do not hesitate to proudly conjure up the specter of "World War IV,"[28] to suffocate, wherever possible, every sign of a new opposition in light of growing social inequalities.

An investigation of the redistribution of threat potentials on the geopolitical maps of the present raises the question of how the much-discussed Islamic danger is to be understood. By which media does it affect the psychopolitical system of the West and the Islamic countries? Does it really have the potential to "replace communism as the world dogma," as one can hear it in radical Islamic circles between Khartoum and Karachi for the last decade, and not only from behind closed doors?[29] The new specter, which is haunting Europe, the United States, and other parts of the world—from where does it take its power to threaten the leaders of the established powers? Can political Islam—whether appearing with a terroristic component or without—unfold itself to become an alternative world bank of rage? Will it become a globally attractive collection point of antisystemic or postcapital-ist energies? Can Islamism be used for the continuation of the weary West-ern grand narratives concerning the uprising of the debased and humili-ated against their masters, old and new? Does it suffice to meditate on the concept of jihad as long as it turns into a pseudonym for class struggle? Or do the fronts, which emerge from the eruptions of the Islamic world, not possess a sense of obstinacy that can only be reconciled with Western forms of the narrative of continuing revolution, universalizing emancipation, and progressive realization of human rights at the price of misunderstandings and distortions.

What qualifies political Islam as a potential successor to communism are three advantages, which can be analogously identified with historical com-munism. The first is the fact that an inspiring mission dynamic is inherent to Islamism, a dynamic that predisposes it to become a quickly swelling col-lective of new converts, that is, a "movement" in the narrow sense of the term. It is not only the case that it quasi-universally addresses "all" without discriminating on the basis of nations and social classes. It attracts especially the disadvantaged, undecided, and outraged (insofar as they are not female, and sometimes even those). It does so by presenting itself as the advocate of the spiritually and materially neglected poor and by gaining sympathies as the heart in a heartless world. The low preconditions of admission play an impor-tant part here. As soon as a person has been admitted to the ranks of believ-ers, he is immediately usable for the purpose of the fighting community—in some cases to be immediately used as a martyr. By plunging into a vibrant community, newcomers are often given for the first time the feeling of hav-ing found a home and of not playing an equal and detached spectator but a particular role in the dramas of the world.

The second attraction of political Islam emanates from the fact that it—in a way only preceded by communism—is capable of offering its followers a clear, aggressive, and grandiosely theatrical "worldview" that rests on a clear differentiation of friend and enemy, an unmistakable mission to win, and an exhilaratingly utopian final vision: the reconstitution of the global emirate, which is supposed to provide a shelter for the Islamic millennium, stretched out from Andalusia to the far East. With it the figure of the class enemy is replaced with that of the enemy of the faith, and class struggle is replaced by holy war—while keeping the dualistic schema of a war of prin-ciples, it demands a necessarily long war rich in casualties. As usual, in its last battle the party of the good is destined to win.

It can easily be seen that when it is used for political purposes, so-called fundamentalism is less of a matter of faith than an appeal to act or, more specifically, a matter of providing roles through which great numbers of potential actors are put into a position in which they can move from theory to praxis—or rather from frustration to praxis. In general it is true what demographic research has brought to light: "religion provides . . . additional oil for a fire whose original fuel does not come from it."[30] As a matrix of radical activations, Islam is on a par with historical communism; perhaps it is even superior because it can present itself with regard to its culture of origin not as a movement of radical rupture but as one of a revolutionary reestablishment.

The third and politically most important reason for the inevitably growing dramatics of political Islam (even if at this hour, after a series of defeats, it seems to have lost quite a bit of its initial attraction) results from the demographic dynamic of its field of recruitment. Just like the totalitarian movements of the twentieth century, it is essentially a youth movement or, more specifically, a movement of young men. Its verve to a large degree results from the excess of vitality of an unstoppable giant wave of unemployed and, socially speaking, hopeless male adolescents between the ages of fifteen and thirty—in their majority second, third, and fourth sons, who can enact their futile rage only by participating in the next best aggression programs. By creating in their base countries counter-worlds to the existing one, Islamic organizations create a grid of alternative positions in which angry, ambitious young men can feel important—including the impulse to attack both close and faraway enemies today rather than tomorrow.

These numerically enormous groups constitute the natural allegiance of agitators from the elder generation, whose sermons derive their content almost automatically from the willingness among the members of their congregation to be outraged—whereas the Islamic tradition only provides the semantic forms to add captions to real anger and violence tensions. As in a laboratory experiment, it was possible to observe these conditions during a scheme to create "spontaneous riots" because of the Danish caricatures of Mohammed in February 2006. While politically correct Europeans agonized over how to apologize to allegedly or actually offended Muslims, anonymous activists in Iraq continued to turn the wheel of provocation or, even better, the wheel of combative self-stimulation a bit further by way of destroying the Golden Mosque in Samarra, one of the most important Shiite sacred buildings in the north of Baghdad. They destroyed it with a

bomb attack, which led to dozens of Sunni houses of worship being devastated during counterattacks. These events speak a clear language. They
reveal more about the hunger for a triggering event among the groups who
are ready to attack than about an allegedly inevitable clash of civilizations.
The agitators would feel sorry if they had to realize that the external cata-
lysts were in fact sorry.

From this perspective it is legitimate to claim that Islam, in its Islamist
variation, could transform itself to become a religious readymade excellent for mobilizing purposes.[31] Its suitability comes from characteristics of
Muslim dogmatic theology that from the start were publicly committed to
the war against "infidels." The unprepared reader of the Koran has to be
amazed about how it is possible that a sacred book is not afraid to repudiate
itself when almost on every page it threatens the enemies of the prophet and
of the faith with suffering in the eternal flames. The explanations of scholars hardly help to get over this estrangement, even if they try to trace the
polemical passages of the Koran back to their historical context: the prophet
engages in these passages in a form of early-socialist criticism against the
wealthy of his time, the arrogant and ruthless merchants from Mecca who
did not want to hear anything anymore about the egalitarian and generous values of the old Arab tribal culture. Mohammed's teachings, scholars
argue, ties in with these values as it commits his followers to caring for the
weak. The initially plausible reference to the monotheistic privilege of zealousness both for God and against the infidels fails to provide a sufficient
explanation. It is just as evident to claim that no human being would want
to concern himself with the opaque passages in the Koran if it were not for
the fact that millions of aggressive gangs of searchers for God choose their
words so to fit their coming deeds (while the comparably heated passages
of the psalms of rage in the Old Testament have left the small audience of
churches and synagogues cold for a long time).

The new mobilization movements—whether legitimate or not from the
standpoint of Koran theology—could, assuming that birth rates remain
high, influence a reservoir of several million young men in the Arabic hemisphere by the middle of the twenty-first century, men who probably only
find an existentially attractive horizon of meaning in departing to politically
and religiously concealed projects of self-destruction. In thousands of Koran
schools, which recently sprang up like mushrooms everywhere that has
boiling excesses of adolescent men, the anxious cohorts are indoctrinated
with the concepts of holy war. Only a small portion of them will be able to

manifest themselves in external terrorism. The more significant portion will probably be invested in life-consuming civil wars on Arab soil—wars for which the Iran-Iraq massacre between 1980 and 1988 has provided a hint. In the case of the new wars, however, the quantitative proportions will, it can be predicted, skyrocket to a monstrous level. Giant battles of exterminations between Shiite and Sunni war parties are not unthinkable—the destruction of the mosques and sacred sites of the other side provide the preamble for that. That Israel is anticipating further trials by fire cannot be missed. Without a far-sighted politics of sealing itself off, the Jewish enclave cannot survive the next decades. The truth is: even people who know the situation today do not have the slightest idea of how the approaching Muslim "youth bulge," the most extensive wave of genocidal excesses of adolescent men in the history of mankind, could be contained by peaceful means.[32]

These references to the actual mass-basis of radical Islamic movements mark at the same time the limit at which their commensurability with historical communism ends. The coming adherents of the Islamic goal of expansion do not at all resemble a class of workers and employees who unite to seize governmental power in order to put an end to their misery. Rather, they embody an agitated subproletariat or, even worse, a desperate movement of economically superfluous and socially useless people for whom there are too few acceptable positions available in their own system, even if they should get to power through coups d'état or elections. Because of demographic circumstances, concepts of the enemy in such movements cannot be sociologically defined, as was still possible within a Marxist conception of a "class of exploiters." One can only define them by way of religion, political orientation, and culture—internally they are directed against the, in the eyes of the activists, despicable elites who make too many political concessions to the West. Externally they turn against the West as such, insofar as the latter is portrayed as the manifestation of humiliating, corrosive, and obscene cultural imports. Naturally, Islamist leaders will sooner or later attempt to gain power over the reserve countries of the East in order to occupy positions of command over the redistribution of massive fortunes coming out of the oil business. Thus they could for some time appease their patronage by letting them participate in the oil manna. Since increasing energy prices during the coming decades will support a provocative laziness in bringing about reforms of the existing oil theocracies, riots in these countries are very likely. The case of Iran has shown what can happen next.

However much it might be the case that Islamist theocracy insists on the formally and materially totalitarian demand to regulate all aspects of living in a virtually Islamized global society according to the law of the Koran, it is less capable of confronting the economical, political, technical, and artistic facts of the contemporary age. While communism presented an authentic expression of Western modernization tendencies and, in some respects, though not in terms of economy, was the avant-garde of these tendencies, political Islamism bears the obvious mark of an antimodern disposition and dissynchronicity with the modern world. Part of this is its problematic relationship to the global culture of knowledge, as well as its thoroughly parasitic relationship to the weapons technology of the West. This situation is, for the time being, not changed by the extreme demographic dynamic of the Islamic world, whose population increased between 1900 and 2000 from 150 million to 1.2 billion—eight times its original size. Although the "population weapon" is, as Gunnar Heinsohn has shown, of modern origin,[33] it turns against its owners in the case of a lack of opportunities to expand and emigrate. If one of the leaders of Hamas, the Palestinian physician Abdel Aziz Rantisi, most recently announced that the forthcoming century would be that of Islam, he commits a fallacy common today of confusing culture and biomass. He would be right only in the unlikely case that the Islamic world as a whole is soon successful in escaping from its self-incurred backwardness. Even the most sympathetic interpreters currently have only illusory ideas about how this is supposed to happen.

In considering the hijacking of the airplanes that were flown into the two towers of the World Trade Center in New York on the morning of September 11, 2001, within the context of our observations, it becomes clear that it was not a demonstration of Islamic strength but a symbol of a sardonic lack of means, the compensation for which could only have been the sacrifice of human lives masked as being sacred. No Marx of political Islam will ever be able to argue that although modern technology emerged out of the lap of Western civilization, it will only reach its complete determination in the hands of Islamic operators. The lesson of September 11 is that the enemies of the West expect success exclusively from the vengeful reversal of Western tools against their creators. The Islamophile Friedrich Nietzsche would have to modify his judgments today. The accusations that he leveled in his curse against Christianity have, behind his back, arrived at a different address. Radical Islamism provides the first example of a purely vengeful ideology that only knows how to punish not how to create something new.[34]

The weakness of Islam as a political religion, be it in its modest or radical variations, rests on its backward-looking orientation. So far its leaders have not been capable of formulating nontechnical, romantic, angry concepts for the world of tomorrow. Without a doubt it is possible to set the rising protest masses of the Near and Middle East on their feet by using a rhetoric that is angry and terrific during the forthcoming half century. As a mobilizer of thymotic reserves on a large scale, Islamism has in fact not at all reached its climax. The dream of the activists for a neo-medieval Great Islamic Empire will continue to inspire numerous dreamers, even if the political conditions for its realization are missing in every respect. On the other hand, it is possible that conventional central powers could emerge out of the likely regional formations of empires of Islamic countries. That they would be able to create cultural artifacts, which would awaken a libido of imitation in other places, is unlikely. What remains decisive for the course of events is the fact that the heads of Islamism are, in their current condition, completely incapable of contributing to the writing of the next chapters of cultural evolution, not to mention dictating them, even if their countries of origin carry the "victory banner of procreation"[35] as proudly as possible in front of them.

So far Islamism has little to show that would enable it to creatively continue the technological, economic, and scientific conditions of existence for humankind during the twenty-first century. It would already be a titanic achievement if it were able to realize in due time the modernization of its own inventory. What is certain is that Islam has awakened from its dogmatic slumber. After centuries of stagnation, it returns to the world stage—in order to discover with embarrassment that it is incapable of adding to the major achievements in the area of culture that the cosmopolitan, moderate, and inventive Islam was responsible for up until the thirteenth century. It could take another hundred years until its masterminds will be talked about not because of their threats but because of their achievements.

It will not be an empty time of waiting for the West. Because in the Islamic world there are several demographically explosive countries with plans to implement aggressive empire politics—particularly Iran and Pakistan, to a lesser degree Egypt and Morocco—we will be confronted in future decades with a number of incoherent but spontaneously allied offensives, reminiscent of the semimodern departure movements of angry losers from Italy and Germany during the most unpleasant of times.

Under these circumstances, the expectations of Islamism as a potential successor of communism and its role as a global opposition movement should be set low. In reality they are absolutely illusory. It is not at all possible to see how it would be capable of organizing a new universal collective of dissidence potentials in the countries of globalized capitalism. However, a number of regional major banks of rage will accumulate huge thymotic potentials over longer periods of time. But these will, most likely, waste their capital by spilling blood instead of investing it in promising culture and business companies. For the first half of the twenty-first century, the Islamist youth movements in dozens of countries in the Near and Middle East will be the radiating trouble spots on the crisis maps of strategic analysts. However, whatever the Islamic advances will add to a politics of rage during the next decades—and the next twenty or thirty years could become one of the most fatal periods of all times if worst-case scenarios should materialize—their projects will hardly go beyond the level of a politically black romanticism based on immanent reasons. Thus the mobilization of those who choose a detour through God-given battles aims for a dark goal: the self-destruction of the superfluous.

Anyone holding onto the demand that world history has to proceed as the world's court of judgment is looking forward to disappointing times. In any case, one would have to look out for other judges. Because there is not much good one can hope for from criminal courts, the future will at most hold arbitration courts. Under these circumstances, only global capitalism qualifies for the role. It alone could grow to become its own enemy during the next round of the game, an enemy that excites itself to the point where it has to take itself as seriously as a contender who is deciding who is to be and who is not to be.

CONCLUSION

BEYOND RESENTMENT

AFTER EVERYTHING THAT HAS BEEN SAID DURING THE COURSE of this investigation, it would be absurd to claim that rage's best days are behind it. On the contrary, rage (together with its thymotic siblings, pride, the need for recognition, and resentment) is a basic force in the ecosystem of affects, whether interpersonal, political, or cultural. This thesis remains valid, even if rage cannot concentrate itself in the future in the form of universal collectives of a communist type, but rather only in regional collections. If regression from a certain achieved state of political psychology is not possible, the thymotic energies I have discussed here should be officially accredited as an adequate image of the real, inasmuch as they have fallen victim to an organized misinterpretation.

What has truly reached an end is the psychohistorical constellation of religiously and politically inflated retributive thinking that was characteristic of the Christian, socialist, and Communist courtrooms. Nietzsche found the right concept to characterize its essence when—with an eye to Paul and his invention of "Christianity"—he diagnosed that resentment could become a mark of genius. As long as the liaison of spirit and resentment was stable, the desire for justice in the world—beyond earthly life or within actual history—could find shelter in fictitious beliefs: the theology of the wrath of God and the thymotic global economy of communism. In both systems, nothing less was at stake than the correction of accounts of suffering and injustice in a world that is morally out of balance. Both sought to turn resentment into a positive emotion in order to keep awake the sense of the unacceptability of an unjust world. It is because of their efforts that the highly unlikely phenomenon of "criticism" came into existence in Western civilization—insofar as we understand "criticism" to mean the spirit that has been fueled by ingenious resentment of submission to mere facts, in particular facts of injustice. "Criticism" in this sense is not an absolute privilege of the West, however much it unfolded paradigmatically in the West; it is present in every culture that was successful in withdrawing from domination by servile, holistic, monological, and masochistic motives. Anyone insisting that democratic politics and forms of life could be universal should consider the cultures of counseling, the practices of discussion, and the traditions of criticism of "the others" as regional sources of democracy.[1]

The following insight needs to be asserted like an axiom: under conditions of globalization no politics of balancing suffering on the large scale is possible that is built on holding past injustices against someone, no matter if it is codified by redemptive, social-messianic, or democratic-messianic ideologies. This insight sets narrow limits to the moral productivity of movements of accusation even if they—as in the case of socialism, feminism, and postcolonialism—advocate a cause that is, in itself, respectable. It is much more important to delegitimize the inherited fatal alliance of intelligence and resentment to create a space for future paradigms of detoxified worldly wisdom. The criteria are not all that new—John Locke, the mastermind of the liberal English bourgeoisie, expressed them in a simple language in 1690: the basic rights to life, freedom, and property.[2] With regard to the historical success of this triad, the evidence is clear: only in those areas of the world where these norms are respected do we have true forms of Enlightenment. Two centuries after Locke, Friedrich Nietzsche—although in a form that is, while fully justified from the standpoint of therapy, without doubt too pathetic—complemented these premises of successful civilizations with a hygienic program that puts the liberation from the spirit of resentment on the agenda. Nietzsche was concerned about the replacement of the toxic figure of "vengeful humility" with a form of intelligence that assures itself anew about its thymotic motives. It is obvious that without an open culture of ambition, this cannot be done. Such a culture would have to be post-monotheistic in the sense that it breaks open retributive metaphysics and its political reflexes with an appropriate level of thoroughness. The goal is a meritocracy, which balances, in an intercultural and transcultural way, an antiauthoritarian relaxed morality, on the one hand, and a distinctive normative consciousness and respect for inalienable personal rights, on the other. The adventure of morality takes place through the parallel program of elitist and egalitarian forces. Only within these parameters can a change of accent away from acquisition drives and toward giving virtues be conceived.

The investment costs for this education program are high. What is at stake in it is the creation of a code of conduct for multicivilizational complexes. Such a schema needs to be strong enough to cope with the fact that the condensed or globalized world remains, for the time being at least, structured in a multi-megalomaniac and inter-paranoid way. It is not possible to integrate a universe out of energetic, thymotic, irritable actors through ideal syntheses from the top. It is only possible to keep it at a balance through power relationships. Great politics proceeds only by balancing acts. To stay in balance means not evading any necessary fights and not provoking unnecessary ones. It also means not giving up on the course of the world with its entropic processes, primarily the destruction of the environment and the demoralization of human relationships. Part of this means learning to see oneself always through the eyes of others. What in former times was to be achieved by an overstrained religious humility will have to be accomplished by a culture of rationally built second-order observations. This alone could stop the malignant naïveté by connecting the desire to be respected with the ability to see oneself in relative terms. Time is required to solve these tasks—but not the historical time of the epic and tragedy. Essential time needs to be determined as the time of civilizational learning. Those who only want to make "history" remain below this definition.

The term "transition" should not mislead us into ignoring the fact that one always exercises under conditions of emergency in order to prevent emergency from happening wherever possible. Mistakes are not permitted and yet are likely. If the exercises go well, it might be the case that a set of interculturally binding disciplines emerge that could, for the first time, rightly be referred to with an expression that, until now, has been used prematurely: world culture.

NOTES

INTRODUCTION

1. Cf. Ralf Miggelbrink, *Der zornige Gott. Die Bedeutung einer anstößigen biblischen Tradition* (The wrathful god: The significance of a scandalous biblical tradition) (Darmstadt: Wissenschaftliche Buchgesellschaft, 2002), 13.

2. I thus disagree with the legend, which is popular among theologians, that myth always implies the transfiguration of the existing world. According to this legend myth only comes to being with prophetic speech because of myth's distance from the world and its critical dimension. In reality myth is already as prophetic as prophecy is still mythic.

3. Cf. Raymond Aron, *Clausewitz. Den Krieg denken* (Clausewitz: Thinking war) (Frankfurt: Propyläen, 1980), as well as Robert Kaplan, *Warrior Politics: Why Leadership Demands a Pagan Ethos* (New York: Random House, 2002).

4. Concerning the unconscious nexus of humanism and bellicosity, see Bazon Brock and Gerlinde Koschick, eds., *Krieg und Kunst* (War and art) (Munich: Wilhelm Fink, 2002).

5. Cf. *Iliad* 9.328 f.

6. See Peter Sloterdijk, "Bilder der Gewalt—Gewalt der Bilder: Von der antiken Mythologie zur postmodernen Bilderindustrie," in *Iconic Turn: Die neue Macht der Bilder* (The new power of images), ed. Christa Maar and Hubert Burda (Cologne: Dumont, 2004), 333–34, for a reference to the continuous existence of irruptive ancient rage in the "natural theology of explosion" of modern mass culture.

7. The later stoic phenomenology of rage states that rage does not allow for any past. One can hide all other vices, but "anger parades itself; it shows on the face [*se profert et in faciem exit*]; the greater it is, the more obviously it seethes out. . . . The other affections make themselves seen [*apparent*]. Anger sticks right out [*eminet*]" (Seneca, "On Anger," in *Moral and Political Essays*, ed. John M. Cooper and J. F. Procopé [Cambridge: Cambridge University Press, 1995], 18). During the twentieth century, academic psychology sometimes speaks of "explosive reactions"; cf. Ernst Kretschmer, *Medizinische Psychologie* (Medical psychology) (Leipzig: Thieme 1930), 183–84.

8. Robert Musil, *Der Mann ohne Eigenschaften* (*The Man Without Qualities*) (Hamburg: Rowohlt 1952), 1239–43.

9. The expression is borrowed from Heinrich Mann, who reports in his Napoleon essay from 1925 about the fatal Corsican, "He enters the world like a bullet enters the battle. This is how the revolution sent him." Later I will show that the concept of revolution rests not least in a modernization of ancient *menis*. Its psychological kernel is the transformation of the subject into an active gathering place of world rage.

10. Bruno Snell, "Die Auffassung des Menschen bei Homer," in *Die Entdeckung des Geistes. Studien zur Entstehung des europäischen Denkens bei den Griechen* (The discovery of spirit: Studies of the emergence of European thinking in ancient Greece) (Hamburg: Claassen & Goverts, 1946), 15–37.

11. Cf., for reasons of curiosity, Jürgen Manthey, *Die Unsterblichkeit Achills. Vom Ursprung des Erzählens* (The immortality of Achilles: On the origin of narrating) (Munich: Hanser, 1997), 31–32.

12. Concerning the ancient conception of genius, see the work of the Roman rhetorician Censorinus, *De die natali*, as well as Peter Sloterdijk, *Sphären I, Blasen* (Spheres I: Bubbles) (Frankfurt: Suhrkamp Verlag, 1998), chap. 6, "Divider of Soul Space," 421–85.

13. Seneca *De ira* 1.6: "Non est ergo natura hominis poenae appetens; ideo ne ira quidem secundum naturam hominis, quia poenae appetens èst [therefore punishment does not go with being a good man. Nor, for that reason, does anger, since punishment does go with anger]." One can establish a distant analogy between the philosophical domestication of anger in the Greeks and the civilization of the

rage of God in the theology of "the priestly writings" of post-Babylonian Judaism. The change of emphasis toward individualized repentance withdraws the conditions of the prophetic speeches of threat from the divine penalization and destructive rage. See Miggelbrink, *Der zornige Gott*, 48–49.

14. Gilles Deleuze and Félix Guattari, *What Is Philosophy?* trans. Hugh Tomlinson and Graham Burchell (New York: Columbia University Press, 1994), 146–50.

15. The classic catalogue of cardinal sins still provides an image that balances between erotic and thymotic vices. This is based on the assumption that one rightly can assign *avaritia* (avarice), *luxuria* (voluptuousness), and *gula* (intemperance) to the erotic pole, while *superbia* (arrogance, pride), *ira* (rage), and *invidia* (jealousy, enviousness) belong to the thymotic pole. Only *acedia* (melancholia) does not fit into this categorization because it expresses a sadness without subject and object.

16. The classic expression of this idea is the slogan that was common among bourgeois of the eighteenth century: "*Felix meritis*": happy because of one's owns achievements. This expression decorates the façade of one of the most beautiful classicist buildings in Amsterdam for a good reason. This temple of enlightenment, located at the street Kaisergracht, the canal of the king, was built in 1787 and after 1945 was temporarily the headquarters of the Dutch Communist Party. Today it is the location of one of the most lively cultural centers of the Netherlands.

17. Cf. Robert Shaeffer, *The Resentment Against Achievement: Understanding the Assault Upon Ability* (Buffalo, N.Y.: Prometheus Books, 1988).

18. Cf. Heiner Mühlmann, *Die Natur der Kulturen. Entwurf einer kulturdynamischen Theorie* (The Nature of civilizations: An attempt of a culture-dynamic theory) (Vienna: Springer, 1996).

19. We also owe one of the best summaries of the ancient and more recent discourses about *thymos* to a student of Strauss, Francis Fukuyama. See the rich passages of the unread best-seller *The End of History and the Last Man* (1992; New York: Penguin, 2006). Also see the final section of the introduction, "The Postcommunist Situation," this volume.

20. Aristotle, *Nicomachean Ethics*, 7.7.

21. Seneca, who cites this passage from Aristotle's treatise *On the Soul* (*De anima*) in his work *De ira* (1.9), objects to the Greek thinker with the argument that affects are just as bad as helpers as they are as leaders.

22. Cf. Fukuyama, *The End of History*, 165–66.

23. Jacques Lacan, *Écrits: The First Complete Edition in English*, trans. Bruce Fink (New York: Norton, 2006); Alexander Kojève, *Introduction to the Reading of*

Hegel: Lectures on the Phenomenology of Spirit, ed. Allan Bloom, trans. James H. Nichols (Ithaca, N.Y.: Cornell University Press, 1980).

24. Friedrich Nietzsche, *The Anti-Christ, Ecce Homo, Twilight of the Idols, and Other Writings,* ed. Aaron Ridley, trans. Judith Norman (Cambridge: Cambridge University Press, 2005), 145.

25. Ibid., 144.

26. Concerning the invention of the "symbolic" as the domain of the (holy) father in a situation of an actual weakening of the paternal function, see Michel Tort, *Fin du dogme paternal* (The End of the paternal dogma) (Paris: Aubier, 2005), 123–24.

27. Eric Hobsbawm, *The Age of Extremes: The Short Twentieth Century, 1914–1991* (New York: Penguin, 1994).

28. Cf. the deduction of modern entrepreneurial psychology from the innovation that arises from the pressure of paying off one's debts in Gunnar Heinsohn and Otto Steiger's essential work, *Eigentum, Zins und Geld: Ungelöste Rätsel der Wirschaftswissenschaft* (Property, interest, and money: unsolved riddles of economics) (Reinbek: Rowohlt, 1996).

29. See Walter Burkert, *"Vergeltung" zwischen Ethologie und Ethik. Reflexe und Reflexionen in Texten und Mythologien des Altertums* ("Retaliation" between ethnology and ethics: reflexes and reflections in texts and mythologies of antiquity) (Munich: Siemens Stiftung 1992), 21–22.

30. Friedrich Nietzsche, "On Old and New Tablets," in *Thus Spoke Zarathustra: A Book for All and None,* trans. Adrian Del Caro (Cambridge: Cambridge University Press, 2006), 159.

31. Immanuel Kant, *Groundwork of the Metaphysics of Morals,* trans. Mary Gregor (Cambridge: Cambridge University Press 1997), 42.

32. Boris Groys, *Das kommunistische Postskriptum* (The communist postscript) (Frankfurt: Suhrkamp, 2006).

33. See the discursive justification of this metaphor in Gunnar Heinsohn and Otto Steiger, *Eigentumsökonomik* (Property economics) (Marburg: Metropolis, 2006).

34. Nietzsche, *The Anti-Christ,* 157.

35. Boris Groys, Anne von der Heyden, and Peter Weibel, eds., *Zurueck aus der Zukunft. Osteuropaeische Kulturen im Zeitalter des Postkommunismus* (Back from the future: Eastern European cultures during the age of postcommunism) (Frankfurt: Suhrkamp Verlag, 2005).

36. Jacques Derrida, *Specters of Marx: The State of the Debt, the Work of Mourning, and the New International,* trans. Peggy Kamuf (New York: Routledge, 1994), 61–95.

37. Ibid., 73.

38. Fukuyama, *The End of History*, 284.

39. Cf. Gunnar Heinsohn, *Söhne und Weltmacht. Terror im Aufstieg und Fall der Nationen* (Sons and Global power: terror within the rise and fall of nations) (Zurich: Orell Füssli, 2003), and his *Finis Germaniae*, Kursbuch 162 (Hamburg: Zeit, 2005), 18–29.

40. The proposition concerning the end of history exists in at least four different versions: two are from Kojève: the end of history in Stalinism and the end of history in the American way of life and in Japanese snobbism; one is in Dostoevsky: the end of history in the "Crystal Palace"; and one in Heidegger: the end of history in boredom. Concerning the last two versions, see Peter Sloterdijk, "Heideggers Politik: Das Ende der Geschichte vertagen" (Heidegger's politics: coping with the end of history), closing statement at the conference Heidegger. Le danger et la promesse, Strasbourg, December 5, 2004; as well as Peter Sloterdijk, *Im Weltinnenraum des Kapitals. Für eine philosophische Theorie der Globalisierung* (In the world interior of capital: for a philosophical theory of globalization) (Frankfurt: Suhrkamp Verlag, 2005), 258–348. There you also find the technical definition of "world history" as the successful phase of unilateralism and the constituting phase of the world system (1492–1944).

41. Cf. Bruno Latour, *Politics of Nature: How to Bring the Sciences into Democracy*, trans. Catherine Porter (Cambridge, Mass.: Harvard University Press, 2004); Bruno Latour and Peter Weibel, eds., *Making Things Public: Atmospheres of Democracy* (Cambridge, Mass.: MIT Press, 2005).

1. RAGE TRANSACTIONS

1. Thomas Mann, *Joseph and his Brothers*, trans. John E. Woods (New York: Everyman's Library, 2005), 538.

2. Robert A. F. Thurman, *Anger: The Seven Deadly Sins* (Oxford: Oxford University Press, 2005).

3. Cf. Juliane Vogel, *Die Furie und das Gesetz. Zur Dramaturgie der "grossen Szene" in der Tragoedie des 19. Jahrhunderts* (Fury and law: On the dramaturgy of the "great scene" in the tragedy of the nineteenth century) (Freiburg: Rombach, 2002).

4. Walter Benjamin, "On the Concept of History," in *Selected Writings*, vol. 4, trans. Harry Zorn, (Cambridge, Mass.: Harvard University Press, 2003), 392; Michael Hardt and Antonio Negri, *Empire* (Cambridge, Mass.: Harvard University Press, 2001).

5. Concerning the source of the formula "x as such—x pure and simple," see Karl Marx, *Grundrisse: Foundations of the Critique of Political Economy*, trans. Martin Nicolaus (London: Penguin, 1993), 105.

6. Mann, *Joseph and his Brothers*, 537.

7. Quoted according to Robert Conquest, *The Great Terror: A Reassessment* (Oxford: Oxford University Press, 1990), 56; Conquest is doubtful about the authenticity of this statement.

8. See the doubts concerning the authenticity of the classic quotation in Christopher Read, *Lenin: A Revolutionary Life* (London: Routledge, 2005), 11.

2. THE WRATHFUL GOD

1. Cf. Régis Debray, *God: An Itinerary*, trans. Jeffrey Mehlman (London: Verso, 2004).

2. James Joyce, *A Portrait of the Artist as a Young Man* (1916; New York: Penguin, 2003).

3. Jean Delumeau, *Sin and Fear: The Emergence of a Western Guilt Culture, Thirteenth–Eighteenth Centuries*, trans. Eric Nicholson (New York: St Martin's Press 1990).

4. Gustave Flaubert, *Dictionary of Received Ideas*, trans. Jacques Barzun (New York: New Directions, 1968).

5. Boris Groys, "Readymade," in *Über das Neue. Versuch einer Kulturkommune* (On the new: a study of cultural economics) (Munich: Fischer, 1992), 73–74; "Simulierte Ready-mades von Fischli und Weiss," in *Kunst-Kommentare* (Vienna: Passagen, 1977), 131–32; "Fundamentalismus als Mittelweg zwischen Hoch-und Massenkulture," in *Logik der Sammlung. Am Ende des musealen Zeitalters* (Logic of collection: at the end of the age of the museum) (Munich: Hanser, 1997), 63–64; "On the New," *Research Journal of Anthology and Aesthetics* 38 (2000): 5–17.

6. Cf. Raffaele Pettazzonni, *The All-Knowing God: Researches Into the Early Religion and Culture*, trans. H. J. Rose (London: Methuen, 1956).

7. Cf. Jan Assmann, *Politische Theologie zwischen Ägypten und Israel* (Political theology between Egypt and Israel) (Munich: Carl-Friedrich-von-Siemens-Stiftung, 1992), 85.

8. Ruediger Safranski, *Das Böse oder das Drama der Freihei*t (Evil; or, the drama of freedom) (Munich: Hanser, 1997), 32.

9. The concept of the "archive" is further explained through the cultural philosophical works of Boris Groys in chapter 3.

10. See, especially, Erich Zenger, *A God of Vengeance?* trans. Linda M. Maloney (Louisville, Ky.: Westminster John Knox Press, 1996). Zenger vehemently and for good hermeneutic reasons turns against the elimination of Jewish prayers of hatred from the Christian canon as well as from the hourly prayer of the Church. The theological arguments of the author are not as convincing as his hermeneutic ones. It is not clear what it is supposed to mean when he writes that the

"shrill tones of the psalms of enmity can serve to shock Christianity out of the well-regulated slumber of its structural amnesia about God" (74).

11. Ralf Miggelbrink, *Der zornige Gott. Die Bedeutung einer anstößigen biblischen Tradition* (The wrathful god: The significance of a scandalous biblical tradition) (Darmstadt: Wissenschaftliche Buchgesellschaft, 2002), 450.

12. Isaiah's argument that God only keeps a remainder is taken up again at a decisive passage of Augustine in his merciless teaching of mercy in the year 397: "To Simplician: On Various Questions. Book I (De Diversis Quaestionibus)," in *Augustine: Earlier Writings*, ed. and trans. John H. S. Burleigh (Philadelphia: The Westminster Press, 1953) 370–406, 1.2.

13. Gerd Theißen and Annette Merz, *Der historische Jesus. Ein Lehrbuch* (The historical Jesus: a textbook) (Göttingen: Vandenhoeck and Ruprecht, 1996), 249.

14. Concerning the metaphysical implications of the figure of speech "this world" (or "this life"), see Peter Sloterdijk, "Ist die Welt verneinbar? Über den Geist Indiens und die abendländische Gnosis" (Can the world be unified? on the spirit of India and occidental gnosis), in *Weltfremdheit* (Unworldliness) (Frankfurt: Suhrkamp, 1993), 220–33, especially section 1, "Fingerspitzengedanen" (Fingertip thoughts).

15. Oswald Spengler, *The Decline of the West*, trans. Charles Francis Atkinson, ed. Helmut Werner (Oxford: Oxford University Press, 1991), 287.

16 In this context the works of Jacques Le Goff are most impotant. See his *The Birth of Purgatory*, trans. Arthur Goldhammer (Chicago: University of Chicago Press, 1986).

17. Tertullian, *Apology, De spectaculis*; Minucius Felix, *Octavius*, trans. T. R. Glover (Cambridge Mass.: Harvard University Press, 2003), 297–301.

18. Cf. Nicholas Kwame Apetorgbor, *Tertullian: Die Rache Gottes und die Verpflichtung des Menschen zum Verzicht auf Rache. Die Bedeutung der Theologie Tertullians für das heutige afrikanische Christentum* (Tertullian: The wrath of god and the human duty to renounce revenge. The significance of Tertullian's theology for contemporary African Christianity), (Hamburg: Dr. Kovac, 2004).

19. "Thence we came forth to rebehold the start": Dante, *The Divine Comedy*, *Inferno*, trans. Henry W. Longfellow (New York: Chartwell, 2009), 34.139, 161.

3. The Rage Revolution:
On the Communist World Bank of Rage

1. Tertullian, *Apology, De spectaculis*; Minucius Felix, *Octavius*, trans. T. R. Glover (Cambridge, Mass.: Harvard University Press, 2003), 297–99.

2. Ibid., 295.

3. Restif de la Bretonne, *Revolutionäre Nächte in Paris*, ed. Ernst Gerhards (Bremen: Manholt, 1989). During the turmoil of 1848 similar slogans were used. Alexis de Tocqueville tells the story of a poor young country farmer who found work as servant for a family from Paris. "On the evening of the day when the insurrection started, he heard this child say as he was clearing away after the family dinner: 'Next Sunday (it was on a Thursday) it is we who will be eating the chicken's wings.' To which a little girl who was working in the house answered: 'And it is we who will wear lovely silk dresses'" (Alexis de Tocqueville, *Recollections: The French Revolution of 1848*, ed. and trans. J.-P. Mayer and A. P. Kerr [New Brunswick, N.J.: Transaction, 1987], 143).

4. Antonio Negri, "The Specter's Smile," in *Ghostly Demarcations: A Symposium on Jacques Derrida's Specters of Marx*, ed. Michael Sprinker (New York: Verso, 1999), 15.

5. Christopher Read, *Lenin: A Revolutionary Life* (London: Routledge, 2005), 103.

6. Karl Marx and Frederick Engels, *Correspondence, 1844–1851*, in *Collected Works* (New York: International Publishers, 1982), 38:289.

7. Ibid., 38:289.

8. Rosa Luxemburg, *The Letters of Rosa Luxemburg*, ed. Stephen Eric Bronner, (Boulder, Colo.: Westview Press, 1978), 172.

9. Fritz J. Raddatz, ed., *Mohr an General: Marx und Engels in ihren Briefen* (Vienna: Molden 1980), 203.

10. Michael Hardt and Antonio Negri, *Empire* (Cambridge, Mass.: Harvard University Press, 2001), 159.

11. Albert Camus, *The Rebel: An Essay on Man in Revolt*, trans. Anthony Bower (New York: Vintage, 1984), 165 and 171.

12. Ibid., 22.

13. Heiner Müller, *Der Auftrag* (The mission), in *Werke* (Works) (Frankfurt: Suhrkamp, 2002), 5:40.

14. Mikhail Bakunin, "Die Prinzipien der Revolution" (Principles of revolution), in *Staatlichkeit und Anarchie* (*Statism and Anarchy*; note that this pamphlet is not included in English-language translations of *Statism and Anarchy*) ed. Horst Stuke (Frankfurt: Ullstein, 1983), 103.

15. Concerning the significance of Methodism for democratic history, see Gertrud Himmelfarb, *Roads to Modernity: The British, French, and American Enlightenments* (New York: Knopf, 2004), 116–30.

16. Heinrich Heine, letter dated June 15, 1843, in *Säkularausgabe: Werke, Briefwechsel, Lebenszeugnisse* (Berlin: Akademie, 1970), 202.

17. Bakunin, "Die Prinzipien der Revolution" (Principles of revolution), 101–2.

18. Ibid., 95–99.

19. G. W. F. Hegel, *Aesthetics: Lectures on Fine Art*, vol. 1, trans. T. M. Knox (Oxford: Oxford University Press, 1998), 195.

20. Bakunin, "Die Prinzipien der Revolution" (Principles of revolution), 101.

21. Ibid.

22. Ibid.

23. Ibid.

24. Mikhail Bakunin, *Bakunin on Anarchism*, ed. Sam Dolgoff (Montreal: Black Rose Books, 1996), 354–55.

25. Concerning the early phase of the British workers' movement, which used religious justifications as well as those pertaining to human rights, see Edward P. Thompson, *The Making of the English Working Class* (London: Victor Gollancz, 1980), 19–203.

26. This expression occurs, among other places, in Thomas Mann's diagnostic commentaries during the 1930s and 1940s. Concerning the continuing development of the concept of a worldwide civil war, see Nikolaus Sombart, *Rendezvous mit dem Weltgeist. Heidelberger Reminiszenzen 1945–1951* (Rendezvous with the world spirit: reminiscences from Heidelberg, 1945–1951) (Frankfurt: Fischer, 2000), 268–76.

27. Concerning Lenin's intensification of the concept of class and the resulting compromise, see this chapter, pages 162–63.

28. Cf. Karl Marx, *Critique of Hegel's "Philosophy of Right,"* ed. Joseph O'Malley (Cambridge: Cambridge University Press, 1977), 137.

29. Georg Lukács, *History and Class Consciousness*, trans. Rodney Livingstone (Cambridge, Mass.: MIT Press, 1971), 51.

30. One year after Stalin's death, Lukács published his book *Die Zerstörung der Vernung* (*The Destruction of Reason*, 1954), which shows how a form of thinking, compromised by Leninist and Stalinist convictions, absolves itself. Concerning the ideological show trial as trial of absolution, see this volume, page 167.

31. Lukács, *History and Class Consciousness*, 75–76.

32. Ibid.

33. Ibid., 41.

34. Karlheinz Weißmann, *Schwarze Fahnen, Runenzeichen: Die Entwicklng der politischen Symbolik der deutschen Rechten zwischen 1890 und 1945* (Black flags, rune symbols: the development of political symbolism of the German right between 1890 and 1945) (Dusseldorf: Droste, 1991).

35. Cf. Dirk Baecker, *Womit handeln Banken? Eine Untersuchung zur Risikoverarbeiung in der Wirtschaft* (What is it that banks trade? an investigation into the

processing of risk in the economy), intro. Niklas Luhmann (Frankfurt: Suhrkamp, 1991).

36. See Boris Groys, "Readymade," in *Über das Neue. Versuch einer Kulturkommune* (On the new: a study of cultural economics) (Munich: Fischer Verlag, 1992); "Fundamentalismus als Mittelweg zwischen Hoch-und Massenkulture," in *Logik der Sammlung. Am Ende des musealen Zeitalters* (Logic of collection: at the end of the age of the museum) (Munich: Hanser, 1997); and *Politik der Unsterblichkeit. Vier Gespräche mit Thomas Knoefel* (Politics of immortality: four conversations with Thomas Knoefel) (Munich: Hanser, 2002).

37. See the section "The new as the valuable other," in Groys, *Über das Neue*, 42–43.

38. For a systematic examination of the art world, see Beat Wyss, *Vom Bild zum Kunstsystem* (From image to the system of art) (Cologne: Walther Koenig, 2006), 1:117–284.

39. Heiner Mühlmann, *Die Natur der Kulturen. Entwurf einer kulturgenetischen Theorie* (The Nature of civilizations: An attempt of a culture-dynamic theory) (Vienna: Springer, 1996).

40. Quoted by Ernst Nolte, *Der europaeische Buergerkrieg 1917–1945. Nationalsozialismus und Bolschewismus* (The European civil war, 1917–1945: National Socialism and Bolshevism), 6th ed. (Munich: Herbig, 2000), 339.

41. Quoted in Read, *Lenin*, 178.

42. See Norbert Bolz, *Auszug aus der entzauberten Welt. Philosophischer Extremismus zwischen den Weltkriegen* (Exit from the disenchanted world: philosophical extremism between the world wars) (Munich: Fink, 1989), 13–20.

43. According to Stalin, the Communist Party had three to four thousand highest leaders ("the generals of our party"). Additionally, there were thirty to forty thousand middle leaders ("our party officers") and a hundred to a hundred and fifty thousand lower command personnel ("the sergeants of our party").

44. According to a consulted source, this hunnish thesis is attributed to Grigorij Sinowjew, one of Lenin's closest confidants. At a party meeting in Petrograd on September 17, he declared, "We have to win over ninety of the one hundred million citizens of Soviet Russia. We should not speak to the others; we exterminate them." According to a newspaper article, Sinowjew's speech was very well received. Quoted in Nolte, *Der europaeische Buergerkrieg*, 89, 513–14.

45. Cf. Alexander Jakowlew, *Die Abgründe meines Jahrhunderts. Eine Autobiographie* (The abysses of my century: an autobiography) (Leipzig: Faber und Faber, 2003), 154–55.

46. This is still depicted in the postcommunist literature, e.g., in the satirical novel about the Putin era by Victor Pelewin, *Die Dialektik der Übergangsperiode von*

Nirgendwoher nach Nirgendwohin (The dialectics of the transitional period from nowhere to nowhere) (Munich: Luchterhand, 2004).

47. The thesis that Lenin inaugurated fascism was developed during the 1950s by such Soviet scholars as the Nobel laureate in physics Lew Davidowitsch Landau. After his mysterious encounter with Stalin in July 1935, Romain Rolland was the figurehead of Western pro-Sovietism. At the end of the 1920s he noted that communism had created fascism insofar as fascism was nothing but a "reverse Bolshevism" (*un bolchévisme au rebours*). See Francois Furet, *Le passé d'une illusion. Essai sur l'idée Communiste au XXe siècle* (Paris: Laffont 1995), 321. Antonio Negri admits that even today certain varieties of populism and fascism are deformed descendents of socialism; see Michael Hardt and Antonio Negri, *Multitude: War and Democracy in the Age of Empire* (New York: Penguin 2004), 255. Landau's thesis is more radical and fitting than that of Rolland and Negri, because it identifies Leninism not only "dialectically," as a provocation of fascism, but as its prototype.

48. Camus, *The Rebel*, 142.

49. Bukharin emphatically praised the affiliates of the Cheka, which returned from their "horrible work" as "ruins of themselves." Brecht's didactic play *Die Massnahme* (*The Measures Taken*) from 1930 reveals how important the mobilization of the willingness to kill was for communism. It rehearses the freedom of being allowed to kill and the embarrassment of having to kill in the service of revolutionary necessity. In a related sense, André Malraux shows in the opening scene of *La condition humaine* (1933) that the hero reaches a state of intoxication with revolutionary activism through engaging in murder. Concerning Brecht, see Slavoj Žižek, *The Parallax View* (Cambridge Mass.: MIT Press, 2006), 260–61. During his notorious speech from October 4, 1943, which was presented in the golden hall of the palace in Posen, Heinrich Himmler attempted to inculcate upon ninety-two SS officers that the German elite troops still had to catch up to the level of Soviet commissionaires when it came to an appropriate ability to kill. He believed that the Soviet functionaries assigned with the task of killing massively were twenty years ahead. In 2001 Robert Kaplan, who is a Leninist without knowing so, recommended in his book *Warrior Politics: Why Leadership Demands a Pagan Ethos* (New York: Vintage, 2003) that the American government do away with the Judeo-Christian morality of an unconditional protection of life. In light of coming tasks it should rather adopt a lethal "pagan" mentality. Charles Krauthammer and other neoconservative ideologists describe the unilateralism of the United States, which is ready to kill, a little more discreetly as "democratic realism."

50. Cf. Zeev Sternhell, *Neither Right nor Left: Fascist Ideology in France*, trans. David Maisel (Princeton, N.J.: Princeton University Press, 1996), 187–212.

51. On the readjustment of cultural norms after phases marked by excessive stress, see Mühlmann, *Die Natur der Kulturen*, 50–97.

52. The Comintern did not shy away from any form of exaggeration in the ideological competition against the moderate rage-collecting systems on the left: up until the late 1920s their supporters still thought that it was morally correct and politically useful to denounce the parliamentary socialists of Western countries as "social fascists." The fatalism behind this manner of speaking has perhaps never been explicitly uncovered. After 1945 there were huge efforts to make everyone forget that the antifascist confession, which has been constitutive for the New Left during the second half of the twentieth century, started out as a movement against social democracy during the first half. In fact, Moscow attributed primary importance to the "struggle against the socialist center" after 1919. This directive emphasized the anti-Menshevik line just like a compulsive neurosis of Bolshevism for purposes of foreign politics.

53. Quoted in Alexander Jakowlew, *Die Abgründe meines Jahrhunderts*, 155.

54. Alexander Wat, *My Century*, trans. Richard Lourie (New York: New York Review of Books, 2003), 22.

55. Nadezhda Mandelstam, *Hope Against Hope: A Memoir* (New York: Atheneum, 1970), 257.

56. This is the expression from the *Manifesto of the Communist International Addressed to the Global Proletariat*, written in March 1919.

57. Kautsky's reply did not lack in resolution. See Karl Kautsky, *Terrorismus und Kommunismus. Ein Beitrag zur Naturgeschichte der Revolution* (Terrorism and communism: a contribution to the natural history of the revolution) (Berlin: Neues Vaterland, 1919). In this book he condemns Bolshevism as a "Tartar Socialism" and as an antisocialist regression to a state of barbarism.

58. Walter Benjamin, "On the Concept of History," in *Selected Writings* (Cambridge, Mass.: Harvard University Press, 2003), 4:394. "Hatred as well as the willingness to sacrifice both are nourished by the image of enslaved ancestors rather than that of liberated grandchildren."

59. Eugen Rosenstock-Huessy, *Die europäischen Revolutionen und der Charakter der Nationen* (European revolutions and the character of nations) (Stuttgart: Kohlhammer, 1951), 527.

60. Some time before his epochal speech at the twentieth Party convention of the KPdSU on Stalin's crimes and the devastations of his personal cult, Nikita Khrushchev made the astounding remark: "We have wasted the collected capi-

tal of trust, which the people bring to the party. We cannot exploit the trust of the people indefinitely" (quoted in Jakowlew, *Ein Jahrhundert der Gewalt in Rußland*, 31). In this book I try to explain what capital was in fact at stake.

61. See Robert Conquest, *The Great Terror: A Reassessment* (Oxford: Oxford University Press, 2008), 12–14.

62. Ilya Kabakov and Boris Groys, *Die Kunst des Fliehens. Dialoge über die Angst, das heilige Weiß und den sowjetischen Müll* (The art of escaping: dialogues on anxiety, sacred whiteness, and Soviet garbage) (Munich: Hanser, 1991), 61.

63. See Boris Groys, *Die Erfindung Rußlands* (The invention of Russia) (Munich: Carl Hanser, 1995), 14–15.

64. Karl Marx, *Civil War in France* (1871; Chicago: Charles H. Kerr, 1998), 47. This remark did not stop Marx from soon claiming the opposite in order to excessively praise the actors of the failed Paris Commune.

65. Concerning the figure "terror in one country," see Arno Mayer, *The Furies: Violence and Terror in the French and Russian Revolutions* (Princeton, N.J.: Princeton University Press, 2000), 13 and 607–701.

66. Cf. Heiner Mühlmann, *MSC. Maximal Stress Cooperation. The Driving Force of Cultures* (Vienna: Springer, 2005).

67. It is thus not completely harmless when Antonio Negri reaches the conclusion in *Multitude* that apart from the primary front of worker and capitalist there is "a potentially infinite amount of classes." The simplified translation of fronts into an opposition of poor and rich as "classes" would not be without risks. In light of the background of communist terror the question needs to be raised whether it is not also the case in contemporary discourses that new combative collectives are assigned with an occult mandate to engage in bloody activities.

68. Cf. Boris Groys, *Das kommunistische Postskriptum* (The communist postscript) (Frankfurt: Suhrkamp, 2006).

69. Cf. Simon Leys, *The Chairman's New Clothes: Mao and the Cultural Revolution* (London: Allison Busby, 1981), 20.

70. Sebastian Haffner, *Der neue Krieg* (The new war) (Berlin: Alexander, 2000), 60.

71. See Mao Zedong's key text, "On Protracted War," in *The Art of War* (El Paso: El Paso Norte Press, 2005), 165-288.

72. Cf. Boris Groys, *Gesamtkunstwerk Stalin. Die gespaltene Kultur in der Sowjiet Union* (Holistic work of art Stalin: divided culture in the Soviet Union) (Munich: Hanser, 1988).

73. Both reasons can be identified in the reactions of the Chinese to the disastrous insights of the great biography of Mao by Jung Chang and Jon Halliday: *Mao: The Unknown Story* (London: Jonathan Cape, 2005). The government prohibited

the publication of the book in China; patriotic Chinese intellectuals also reject it, judging from first impressions, as an external interference in intra-Chinese matters. The civilizational implications of this reaction go deep. They are ultimately directed against the import of a victim-centric ethics; that is, if the Chinese do not ask about the victims of Mao's politics inside of the country, emigrants are not supposed to have the right to force such questions on them, particularly not intrusive historians and Western observers. The official terminology since 1981 in China is that the heritage of Mao is 70 percent good and 30 percent bad; this elides the 60 to 70 million lost human lives for which Maoism has been responsible since 1949. These lives are seen as a burden that can be surmounted only through the autochthonous art of taking stock.

74. Xuewu Gu, "List und Politik" (Cunningness and politics), in *Die List* (Cunningness), ed. Harro von Senger (Frankfurt: Suhrkamp, 1999), 428–29.

75. André Glucksmann explicitly regretted his participation in the delusional Mao cult in France between 1968 and 1972 in his memoir *Une rage d'enfant* (Paris: Plon, 2006), 114–15.

76. A defense of "authentic Maoism," which is at the same time an impressive example of sovereign anachronism, is presented by Alain Badiou in his book *Le siècle* (Paris: Seuil, 2005), 89–90.

77. Alexandre Dumas, *The Count of Monte Cristo* (London: Penguin Classics, 2003), 1203.

78. Dumas, *The Count of Monte Cristo*, 187.

79. Søren Kierkegaard, *On the Difference Between a Genius and an Apostle* (1848).

80. Cf. Marx, *Civil War in France*, 98: "They have no ideals to realize, but to set free the elements of the new society with which old collapsing bourgeois society itself is pregnant."

4. The Dispersion of Rage in the Era of the Center

1. Manfred Haettich, *Zornige Bürger. Vom Sinn und Ursinn des Protestierens* (Angry citizens: on sense and senselesness of protest) (Munich: Olzog, 1984).

2. Thomas Hobbes, *Leviathan*, ed. Richard Tuck (Cambridge: Cambridge University Press, 1996), 88.

3. Cf. Henk Oosterlink, *Radicale Middelmatigheid* (Radical mediocracy) (Amsterdam: Boom, 2002).

4. Additionally there was a second form of "theory": the official state philosophy of Marxism and Leninism that was taught in all the countries of the Eastern bloc, a unity of dialectical materialism, historical materialism, and scientific

communism, an amalgam that was so boring that its pupils only remember it as frightening.

5. Cf. Michael Hardt and Antonio Negri, *Empire* (Cambridge, Mass.: Harvard University Press, 2001). Negri's betrayal of the totem of the classical left extends to a point where he delegates it to the other political camp: "The old mole of reactionary thought resurfaces again," he states in a polemic against Huntington (Michael Hardt and Antonio Negri, *Multitude: War and Democracy in the Age of Empire* [New York: Penguin 2004], 34).

6. Cf. Peter Sloterdijk, *Derrida, un égyptien. Le problème de la pyramide juive* (Derrida, an Egyptian: the problem of the Jewish pyramid) (Paris: Editions Maren Sell, 2006). In German: "Derrida, ein Ägypter. Über das Problem der jüdischen Pyramide," lecture for the memorial conference Un jour Derrida, Centre Pompidou, Paris, November 21, 2005.

7. Cf. Boris Groys, *Privatizations; or, The Artificial Paradise of Post-Communism*, catalogue for the exhibition Privatizations: Contemporary Art from Eastern Europe, May–June 2004, ed. Revolver (Frankfurt: Archive for Contemporary Art, 2005), 7–15.

8. Cf. Boris Groys, *Das kommunistische Postskriptum* (The communist postscript) (Frankfurt: Suhrkamp, 2006).

9. See Peter Sloterdijk, "Goodbye Fortschritt: Das heilige Feuer der Unzufriedenheit" ("Good-bye progress: the holy flame of dissatisfaction"), in *Das neue Denken, das Neue denken. Ethik, Energie, Ästhetik* (The new thinking, thinking the new: ethics, energy, aesthetics), ed. Utz Claasen and Jürgen Hogrefe (Gottingen: Steidl, 2005), 69–70.

10. See Hans-Joachim Stadermann, *Die Fesselung des Midax. Eine Untersuching ueber den Aufstieg und Verfall der Zentralbankkunst* (The captivation of Midax: an investigation on the rise and fall of the art of central banking) (Tubingen: Mohr, 1993).

11. The synergy between the deceleration of collapse and the mobilization of compensatory efforts is, to be sure, today suspended in a sensitive subsystem of capitalist nation-states: more and more citizens of European countries are beginning to understand that the welfare state resembles a pyramid scheme, especially with regard to its central construction of retirement systems. In this system, senior citizens, the original investors, take their heavy returns, while the players of the third round are eaten by the dogs. Furthermore, the national budgets of most countries to a large extent resemble Ponzi schemes whose stability rests on the quasi-religious incapacity of the creditors to imagine a state that is unable to pay

(even though the insolvency crises of Russia and Argentina have confirmed that even the unthinkable happens).

12. Andrew Carnegie, *Autobiography of Andrew Carnegie* (1920; New York: Cosimo Classics, 2005), 280.

13. Siegfried Kracauer, *Jacques Offenbach und das Paris seiner Zeit* (Jacques Offenbach and the Paris of his time) (Frankfurt: Suhrkamp, 1994).

14. Quoted in Eric Hobsbawm, *Interesting Times: A Twentieth-Century Life* (London: Pantheon, 2003), 112.

15. See Hobsbawm, *Interesting Times*, 227.

16. Cf. Peter Sloterdijk, "Erwachen im Reich der Eifersucht. Notiz zu René Girards anthropologischer Sendung" (Awakening in the realm of envy: a note on René Girard's anthropological mission), afterword to *Ich sah den Satan fallen wie einen Blitz. Eine kritische Apologie des Christentums* (*I See Satan Falling Like Lightning*), by René Girard (Munich: Carl Hanser, 2002), 241–54. Slavoj Žižek also addresses the perverse structure of the new enjoyment imperative in many parts of his work.

17. In Immanuel Wallerstein, *Utopistik. Historische Alternativen des 21. Jahrhunderts* (Utopistics: historical choices of the twenty-first century) (Vienna: Promedia, 2002), postulates the emergence of a postcapitalist order because of abstract systemic considerations. However, all concrete references to the modus operandi are missing. Concerning the solar-political turn, see Herman Scheer, *Solare Weltwirtschaft. Strategie für die ökologische Moderne* (Solar world economy: strategy for the ecological modernity), 5th ed. (Munich: Antje Kunstmann, 2002); and Scheer, *Energieautonomie. Eine neue Politik für erneuerbare Energien* (Energy autonomy: a new politics of renewable energies) (Munich: Antje Kunstmann, 2005).

18. See Peter Sloterdijk, "Was geschah im 20. Jahrhundert? Unterwegs zu einer Kritik der extremistischen Vernunft" (What happened in the twentieth century? on the way to a critique of extremist reason), inaugural lecture for the Emmanuel Levinas Chair, Strasbourg, March 4, 2005; and Peter Sloterdijk and Hans-Jürgen Heinrichs, *Die Sonne und der Tod. Dialogische Untersuchungen* (Sun and death: dialogical investigations) (Frankfurt: Suhrkamp, 2001), 304–20.

19. Oskar Lafontaine, who published a book called *Die Wut wächst* (Anger grows) (Munich: Econ, 2002), a few years ago, achieves success in the elections in the fall of 2005 for the German leftwing party. This success foreshadows how the chronically weak articulations of complaints of the unemployed, badly paid, and marginalized could again provide for a nucleus of self-affirmations.

20. Jean Baudrillard, "Nique ta mère! Voitures brulées et non au referendum sont les phases d'une meme révolte encore inachavée," *Libération*, November 18, 2005.

21. Concerning the motif of "immigrants in their own country" or postmodern nations as asylums for natives, see Sloterdijk and Heinrichs, *Die Sonne*, 188–89.

22. Hans Magnus Enzensberger *Ausichten auf den Bürgerkrieg* (Expectations of civil war) (Frankfurt: Suhrkamp, 1993), 32.

23. Ibid., 48–49.

24. Ibid., 52.

25. Some psychotherapeutics explain that even strongly destructive tendencies are reversible in the case of bearers of fanatic feelings of hatred if those who are affected with these feelings are given ample opportunities to make compensatory positive experiences; see Carl Goldberg, "Terrorism from a Psychoanalytic Perspective," in *Terrorism, Jihad, and Sacred Vengeance*, ed. Jerry Piven, Chris Boyd, and Henry Lawton (Giessen: Psychosozial, 2004), 212–13. It is uncertain whether this is also the case for the phenomena of amorphous negativism alluded to here. For the countless recruits of militant Islam the information provided by therapeutics does not apply. On the one hand, this much-cited hatred practically does not play a role for them; it is only a code and an infectious habitus, not a personal feeling. More recent social-psychological surveys in the United States have even reached the conclusion that terrorists are less neurotic than the average population. On the other hand, these large groups do not constitute potential patients but political challengers who have to be answered with exclusively political means.

26. See Daniel Yergin and Joseph Stanislaw, *The Commanding Heights: The Battle for the World Economy* (New York: Free Press, 2002), 1–48.

27. See Eliot A. Cohen, *Supreme Command: Soldiers, Statesmen, and Leadership in Wartime* (New York: Free Press, 2002).

28. See Thomas Pany, "Die Fürsten des IV. Weltkriegs. US-Think-Tanks und das Netzwerk der Neokonservativen" (The lords of World War IV: U.S. think tanks and the network of neoconservatives), part 1, *Telepolis*, April 28, 2003. In Western camps the talk of a Fourth World War has been conceived by neoconservative authors such as Eliot Cohen, Irving Kristol, and Norman Podhoretz as a catch phrase for the necessity of an encompassing war plan against political Islam. It should be remembered that the term "World War IV" has been used before by Subcommander Marcos from Chiapas in Mexico to refer to "globalization" as a major offensive of capital against the global poor.

29. Avi Primor, *Terror als Vorwand* (Terror as a pretense) (Dusseldorf: Droste, 2004), 29.

30. Gunnar Heinsohn, *Söhne und Weltmacht. Terror im Aufstieg und Fall der Nationen* (Sons and global power: terror within the rise and fall of nations) (Zurich: Orell Füssli, 2003), 31.

31. On the logic of readymades outside and inside of the art world, see Boris Groys, "Readymade," in *Über das Neue. Versuch einer Kulturkommune* (On the new: a study of cultural economics) (Munich: Fischer, 1992).

32. Concerning the genocidal potentials of the twenty-first century, especially in the Near East, see Gunnar Heinsohn, *Söhne und Weltmacht*. The same author dryly remarks: "let's give the next twenty Nobel Peace Prizes to those people who come up with an idea of dissolving the tensions without using violence!"

33. Gunnar Heinsohn, *Söhne und Weltmach*, 72–112.

34. Concerning the political and cultural creativity of modern Christianity, see Eugen Rosenstock-Huessy, *Die europäischen Revolutionen und der Charakter der Nationen* (European revolutions and the character of nations), (Stuttgart: Kohlhammer, 1951).

35. Gunnar Heinsohn, *Söhne und Weltmacht*, 24–25.

Conclusion: Beyond Resentment

1. Cf. Amartya Sen, *La démocratie des autres: Pourquoi la liberté n'est pas une invention de l'Occident* (Paris: Payot and Rivages).

2. John Locke, *Two Treatises on Government* (1690; Cambridge: Cambridge University Press 1988).

DATE DUE